THIS BOOK BELONGS TO

_____

name

_____

cell

_____

email

TABLE

OF

CONTENTS

—

TABLE OF CONTENTS

(continued)

INTRODUCTION
& HOW TO USE

We are so glad you've decided to join us on this FLOURISH mentorship journey! This project was birthed out of our monthly Grove gatherings, knowing that God didn't simply want us to meet in crowds but also in smaller one-on-one relationships as we grow in our walks with Him. There is power when we stop recycling our own opinions and instead open the pages of Scripture to let it inform our living. God wants to change us through His Word and through the godly relationships with which He's gifted us.

We all desire to belong to a group of people, a family in which we can make a difference. A family where we can know others and be known, loved, and valued. But, if we're honest, it can often feel tough to share life with one another. Vulnerable can feel scary, and it's sometimes even daunting to know how to make connections. We want to know and learn from women who are just a bit ahead of us in life, but we may feel at a loss as to how to even begin.

That's why we created FLOURISH.

The heart of FLOURISH is to see woman be firmly rooted in Jesus and the living Word of God. We believe a mentoring relationship between an older and younger woman can be rich soil for such growth. FLOURISH is a one-year commitment that connects older women with younger women in a curriculum-based mentoring relationship to encourage and challenge one another in their walks with Jesus.

We want to encourage you to make the commitment to follow through. Stay the course, show up, and do the work—we are confident that this journey will be a blessing and a gift to you! We are praying for you as you take your first steps and open your life up to mentoring—for His name and His glory.

we love you!

THE GROVE+FLOURISH TEAM
PASSION CITY CHURCH

1.0

FLOURISH

—

our prayer

[16]That according to the riches of his glory he may grant you to be strengthened with power through his Spirit in your inner being, [17]so that Christ may dwell in your hearts through faith—that you, being rooted and grounded in love, [18]may have strength to comprehend with all the saints what is the breadth and length and height and depth, [19]and to know the love of Christ that surpasses knowledge, that you may be filled with all the fullness of God. [20]Now to him who is able to do far more abundantly than all that we ask or think, according to the power at work within us, [21]to him be glory in the church and in Christ Jesus throughout all generations, forever and ever. Amen.

EPHESIANS 3:16-21, ESV

THIS IS THE BEGINNING
OF SOMETHING

beautiful.

—

Welcome to a fresh start—welcome to FLOURISH. We believe this is the beginning of something beautiful! May this journey be marked with both giant leaps and simple steps in your walk and relationship with Jesus.

What is the heart of FLOURISH?
FLOURISH calls women to a higher standard of living. One where we wholeheartedly love and follow Jesus and aim to view our lives and circumstances through the lens of Scripture.

With much joy, we open our FLOURISH journey with this goal in mind: to position ourselves at the feet of Jesus and place Him at the center of our lives. As we commit ourselves to being *rooted* in His Word and walking daily in His truth, we will be transformed. Chains will be broken. We will experience freedom; and we will *flourish*!

In this journey, you will dive into God's Word and discover for yourself what Scripture says about prayer, identity, calling, kinship, and gratitude. This year you will build special relationships as mentors and mentees and together dig into understanding God's truth and love through His Word. As we begin this journey together, we must first lay aside any routine, norm, obstacle, fear, or excuse we may be gripping tightly and with open hands ask the Spirit to lead us. Will you do that? Even now, with open hands, invite God to lead you, to give you the discipline and hunger to daily seek Him, and to open your heart to receive all He has planned for you over these next twelve months. We agree with Hebrews 12:1-2, "Let us throw off everything that hinders and the sin that so easily entangles. And let us run with perseverance the race marked out for us, fixing our eyes on Jesus, the pioneer and perfecter of faith." Amen!

VISION
& GOAL

FLOURISH calls women to a higher standard of living following the commands in Titus 2:3-5 —a God-filled life for the sake of the gospel! One where we wholeheartedly love and follow Jesus and aim to view our lives and circumstances through the lens of Scripture: the big story of God. To become women who flourish, we benefit from the wisdom and encouragement of those who have gone before us and reflect Jesus. We believe a mentoring relationship between women can be rich soil for such growth.

WHY MENTORING?

IT'S GOD'S IDEA +
IT GOES BEYOND US.

"But as for you [Titus], teach what accords with sound doctrine. … Older women likewise are to be reverent in behavior, not slanderers or slaves to much wine. They are to teach what is good, and so train the young women to love their husbands and children, to be self-controlled, pure, working at home, kind, and submissive to their own husbands, that the word of God may not be reviled" (Titus 2:1,3-5, ESV).

Or how The Message version translates it: "Guide older women into lives of reverence so they end up as neither gossips nor drunks, but models of goodness. By looking at them, the younger women will know how to love their husbands and children, be virtuous and pure, keep a good house, be good wives. We don't want anyone looking down on God's Message because of their behavior."

WE MENTOR BECAUSE …

- We mentor because there is unmistakable evidence in Scripture of the call to mentor the next generation. (See Titus 2; Mal. 4:6; the stories of Elisha and Elijah in 1 and 2 Kings; Isa. 8:18; etc.)
- We mentor because the way we live matters, and we are called to influence the way others live as well. We are called to mentor not only because of the quality and the look of our lives, but because of the way we demonstrate God in our lives. We are also called to advance the gospel as Titus 2 describes!

- We mentor because these intentional relationships create a safe place for us to listen, ask hard questions, unearth potential, diligently pray for, and unconditionally love the young mentees in our care in all areas of their lives. The goal of this relationship is to point the mentees to Jesus, and He will work out their purposes and places in this world. Mentors serve as a compass always pointing to True North—Jesus.
- FLOURISH is a call for women to embrace a higher standard of living by learning how to see every aspect of their lives through Jesus' eyes. We believe mentoring propels us to reach that goal of God-centered living.
- The mentoring model described in Titus 2 is one way we obey Christ's Great Commission. It is one way we give the legacy of biblical womanhood to the next generation.

"So I exhort the elders among you, as a fellow elder and a witness of the sufferings of Christ, as well as a partaker in the glory that is going to be revealed: shepherd the flock of God that is among you, exercising oversight, not under compulsion, but willingly, as God would have you; not for shameful gain, but eagerly; not domineering over those in your charge, but being examples to the flock. And when the chief Shepherd appears, you will receive the unfading crown of glory. Likewise, you who are younger, be subject to the elders. Clothe yourselves, all of you, with humility toward one another, for 'God opposes the proud but gives grace to the humble'" (1 Peter 5:1-5, ESV).

WE'RE WALKING ALONGSIDE

you.

———

We have some special training and additional resources for you in your journey as a mentor.

As a team, we want to walk alongside you in this mentoring journey, giving you training, resources, and tips. Don't be intimidated. Nobody is completely equipped to be a mentor, but we are called to mentor the younger women in our churches.

Visit **FlourishMentor.com** for extra equipping and support.

DEFINITION
OF MENTORING

- Mentors ask questions, help mentees envision goals, and help them achieve goals according to their faith and trust in Jesus.

- Mentors provides guidance, not answers.

- Guides are people who've traveled a path before, learned along the way, and are willing to assist another traveler. When mentors serve as guides, they show younger travelers the way, offer helpful information, warn of dangers, share their own experiences on the road, and provide first aid if necessary.

- Mentoring relationships help push us forward in our faith and challenge us to a higher standard of living in every area of our lives and pursuit of Jesus.

- Although mentors don't need to be experts of Scripture, the FLOURISH goal is growth, a higher standard of living encouraged by women who have grown—women who actively produce fruit because of their knowledge of, closeness to, and journey with Jesus.

- FLOURISHING happens when women confidently guide women in the path of processing their lives through the lens of Scripture, while loving and pursuing Jesus more.

- Mentoring points to Jesus, not to the mentor.

- Jesus is the ultimate model. Christ told us that some of what He taught might not be understood until much later, but He continuously taught with sensitivity and patience (see John 13:7). Jesus took time to answer the disciples' questions (see John 13:6) and used day-to-day dilemmas to illustrate gospel-centered truths.

SOME OF THE FRUIT OF MENTORING:

Our purpose as mentors will be accomplished as we:

- Value and practice time with Jesus.
- Learn to think scripturally about all of life.
- Seek to bring our lives under the authority of God's Word.
- Apply scriptural principles to relationships and circumstances.
- Establish positive relationships.
- Desire to mentor other women and pour out what you've received.
- Grow in our love for and service to the Church.
- Cultivate a life-giving culture in the Church where women share the gospel and share their lives with one another.
- Set and achieve specific life goals.

HOW DO WE MENTOR?

▲ FLOURISH is a "show me" journey. The Greek word translated "train" in Titus 2:4 is *sophrŏnizo*. It carries the idea of helping women cultivate sound judgment by demonstrating or modeling wisdom and discernment for them. It happens when one woman shows another woman the shape of a life with Jesus. Mentoring is relational ministry. Paul captures the essence of mentoring in 1 Thessalonians 2:7-8, "We were gentle among you, like a nursing mother taking care of her own children. So, being affectionately desirous of you, we were ready to share with you not only the gospel of God but also our own selves, because you had become very dear to us" (ESV).[1]

▲ Our main job as mentors is to model a life that glorifies God while praying for and loving our mentees. With the FLOURISH journal, we've provided a devotional foundation for the relationship, but mentoring goes beyond studying Scripture—it's about doing life together and letting the mentees see the fruit you have reaped in your life by following Jesus.

▲ Ideally, the focus of your time with your mentees will be on the practical applications of the themes for each session and not solely the devotional content.

AS MENTORS:

▲ We meet in groups, individually, or both.

▲ We invite mentees into our lives.

▲ We ask a lot of questions and let mentees process their answers.

▲ We keep mentees accountable to their commitment in FLOURISH.

▲ We maintain a delicate balance between accountability and grace.

▲ We confront when necessary.

▲ We are transparent with our own stories and lives, building trust with one another as early as possible in the journey.

---

1. We owe a debt of gratitude to our friend, Susan Hunt, whose insight inspired much of the wisdom in this paragraph.

YOUR WALK

DAILY WALK:

Your own personal walk with Jesus will be reflected in all you do. As you seek Jesus in your own life, you will inspire young women to set intimacy with Christ as a high priority in their own lives. Time with God was a priority for Jesus no matter how busy He was. Your own daily walk needs to be strong so you can point others to Jesus and not to yourself. Your goal is to encourage other women to be followers of Christ, not followers of you.

Oswald Chambers said, "The lasting value of our public service for God is measured by the depth of the intimacy of our private times of fellowship and oneness with Him."[2] You can only influence others to spend time with Jesus as they see the results of your time spent with God.

DAILY DEPENDENCY:

Recognize that your ability to mentor is not based on your talents, your gifts, or even your experiences and success, but on your dependency on living in Christ and dwelling in the Word. He will equip you to do what He's called you to do. It is often in our weakness that God's greatest work is done (see 2 Cor. 12:10). Remember, without Him we can do nothing (see John 15:5); but with Him, we can do all things (see Phil. 4:13).

2. Oswald Chambers, "Worship," *My Utmost for His Highest*, January 6, https://utmost.org/worship/.

YOUR ROLE

SOME OF THE DO'S:

- Great mentors listen often— and speak when needed.

- Great mentors facilitate by asking open-ended questions and encouraging dialogue.

- Great mentors encourage by offering whatever God has given them.

- Great mentors advise by coaching others as to how to get answers—rather than by giving answers.

  Try to only share from your experiences, what you've done or observed others do firsthand, or from Scripture. You'll never go wrong if you stay within those two guardrails.

- Great mentors are present— which is a huge gift!

- Great mentors initiate relationship.

- Great mentors become loving friends.

SOME OF THE DON'TS:

- You're NOT going to be her mom.

- You're NOT going to be her babysitter.

- You're NOT going to be her professional counselor.

- You're NOT going to tell her what to do.

- You're NOT going to project your life on her.

- You're NOT going to fill a void in your life with her.

In summary, your role is to do life with this girl or these girls for a season of time. Be who you are, share what you know, let her see how you think, act, live, pray, and serve. Don't take responsibility for "changing" her. Leave that to Jesus. Just show up and be you.

ATTRIBUTES OF A MENTOR

- A personal walk with Jesus is foundational!

- As you are pouring into other women, it will be important that you're allowing Jesus and His Word to pour into you.

- You'll need God to give you wisdom and discernment as you mentor.

- You'll be modeling a personal walk with Jesus.

- Be open and transparent about your life experiences.

- Be available for coffee—and for godly advice.

- Demonstrate godly character in all things.

- Share wisdom gained through your personal life experiences.

- Recognize that out of your life experiences, not knowledge, you'll have the greatest impact on others.

- Be humble and dependent on Jesus, recognizing this is His ministry.

- Be confident that God will equip you.

- Persevere. There'll be times when you feel like quitting, but know God has called you to this mentorship. You want to be faithful.

"Such is the confidence that we have through Christ toward God. Not that we are sufficient in ourselves to claim anything as coming from us, but our sufficiency is from God. … But we have this treasure in jars of clay, to show that the surpassing power belongs to God and not to us" (2 Cor. 3:4-5; 4:7, ESV).

This is not about us and our abilities. It's about making our lives and all that we've learned through the years available to those who are a season or more behind us, so they might benefit.

YOUR EXPERIENCE

Setting appropriate expectations early in the process is key to a successful experience.

01 Learn what expectations your mentee has, if any. You may ask these three questions to help identify her expectations:

▲ Why do you desire to be in a mentoring relationship?

▲ What do you hope to gain from being mentored?

▲ What are your expectations of me as your mentor?

02 Take time to express your expectations for your mentee.

▲ Commitment: what she'll be asked to do.

▲ Time requirements: how often you will meet and for how long.

CONTENT WILL GUIDE THE CONVERSATION.

1. Focus on relevant topics, based on the mentee's needs.

2. Have a plan—prioritize the curriculum.

3. Meet regularly.

YOUR ENCOURAGEMENT

▲ Rely on God.

▲ Have a big picture perspective.

▲ Celebrate her unique story.

FLOURISH EXPECTATIONS FOR MENTORS

AS A MENTOR, I WILL AIM TO:

- Mentor each woman in Jesus' name.
- Guide my mentee according to my experiences—share what I have learned.
- Consistently pray for my mentee.
- Love her, inspired by 1 Thessalonians 2:9 and 1 Corinthians 13.
- Believe in my mentee, and believe God for her.
- Live out what I am teaching.
- Be humble.
- Be transparent.
- Never give up on her.
- Be available.
- Maintain trust in the relationship.
- Hold her life and conversations with the highest confidentiality.
- Keep the end goal in focus.
- Make time and keep time set aside for my mentee.
- Create a safe space for my mentee to process, speak, and share.
- Respond with the love, grace, and truth of Jesus.
- Admit when I don't know the answers.
- Creatively find ways to encourage my mentee in her walk with Jesus and pursuit of Jesus.
- Sit under the authority of the Church's leadership team and trust their direction for the year. Forsake *they* in favor of *we*.
- Hold commitment over compatibility.
- Initiate, lead, and steward the relationship.
- Point my mentee to Jesus, not to myself.
- Be patient and walk at her pace, not my own.
- Hold the relationship with purpose and intentionality, without allowing it to become solely social.
- Have the courage to confront.
- Refuse to focus on my mentee's problems, remembering I am a guide, not someone who fixes.
- Pray she will apply wisdom and work out her own struggles with her eyes on Jesus.
- Display my own submission to Jesus.

There is great potential for meaningful and fruitful relationship between mentor and mentee. We believe these relationships can be rich soil for incredible growth. Reach out to your Church leadership and ask them to help encourage and protect your mentorship relationship. If a match is not experiencing a healthy connection beyond what is normal, consider consulting your Church leadership to help assess and consider whether or not you and your mentee(s) should continue meeting together. Work together to make a decision in the best interest of both mentor and mentee. Feel free to communicate the following expectations to your mentee(s).

FLOURISH EXPECTATIONS FOR MENTEES

WE ARE ASKING MENTEES TO:

- Have focused time with Jesus five days a week.

- Complete assignments for each FLOURISH session throughout the year.

- Set goals and work diligently to reach them.

- Commit to predetermined meeting dates with mentor throughout the year, and make them a priority.

- Be punctual for meetings and respectful of their mentor's time.

- Be real and intentional in each meeting, making the most of the opportunity.

- Be accountable for assigned work. Be accountable in areas where it's been agreed that growth is needed.

We are beyond excited for all God has for you and your mentees in FLOURISH this year! We are praying for you and believing that FLOURISH's best days are before us and trusting that God is already at work paving the way for you and your mentees.

We've put together some thoughts and guidelines that you may find helpful in your monthly and group meetings.

Walk confidently in knowing that Jesus is your greatest champion, helper, guide, and resource for all you need as a mentor!

GROUP AND INDIVIDUAL MEETING OBJECTIVES

BUILD OR INVEST: To meet regularly to build relationship and create consistent, ongoing opportunities to move into life with your mentees.

SAFETY: To create a safe place for your mentees to process life, share their struggles, heartaches, concerns, joys, accomplishments, and prayer needs. Meeting with your mentees in your home is the best scenario for this.

TRUE NORTH: To point them to Jesus and the Word, reminding them that He is all-sufficient, caring, confident, strong, bold, and poised to move on their behalf in every situation. Your goal as a mentor is to help them find answers in Scripture for their life questions.

ACCOUNTABILITY: To be willing to ask hard questions, encourage them to keep their commitments, move into the mess, and bring accountability for worship, time in the Word, and prayer.

LISTEN: To listen well to their hearts and the deep dreams that are stirring in them. Cheer them on. Challenge them to live boldly for Jesus and to make Him their greatest pursuit.

LOOK BACK TO LOOK FORWARD: To revisit goals you've set and/or previous prayer requests to see how they are doing in those areas.

PRAY: To take seriously the powerful privilege of prayer and what it means to your mentees that you are someone who is truly invested in their lives and wants to go before the throne of God on their behalf.

The best way for you to be prepared to lead well in relationship with your mentees is to personally be committed to time with Jesus—in worship, the Word, and prayer. We're trusting that you're asking your mentees to go where you've already been walking!

We all know that if we're spending time in the same material our mentees are, we'll have so much more to offer and contribute to the conversation. So, even if the FLOURISH curriculum is not your main source of study, take time each week to learn what your mentees will be learning and spend some time in the books of the Bible they will be going through.

IN YOUR HOME:

During your meeting time, we strongly encourage you to invite your mentees into your home. This is a better environment for conversation and prayer—providing freedom and quiet to be able to truly "go there" together.

Keep a journal handy to write down specific things your mentees share for prayer. You may use this as a way to reconnect with them throughout the weeks beyond your meeting.

If it's entirely impossible to meet in your home, choose wisely when meeting in a public place. Look for a place where you'll be able to have privacy in conversation and room for prayer.

GROUP MEETING FORMAT:

OBJECTIVES:

- To bring all your girls together to allow for more connection and community.

- To create space for your girls to open up, share, talk life.

- To allow the girls to speak into one another's lives and encourage each other.

- To speak into their lives through the FLOURISH curriculum and through your own life experiences.

- To point them to Jesus and the Word.

EXAMPLE LAYOUT FOR A TWO-HOUR MEETING:

Remember to text or email your girls a few days ahead to connect and let them know you're looking forward to being with them all.

- Share dinner, dessert, snacks, drinks, etc., at the beginning of the night.

- Allow time for everyone to mingle and talk.

- Find a natural place in the conversation to transition to talking about what God has been revealing to them about Himself, focusing on the topic of the session (e.g. prayer, identity, etc.). These topics may come from the FLOURISH curriculum, Sunday's message, a book they are reading, a Scripture they are memorizing, a conversation they had with someone, or other sources. Just invite them to share.

- Speak into the moment as the Holy Spirit leads.

- Allow space for mentees to speak into each other's lives.

- Encourage your girls to share goals and prayer requests so they can come around and encourage each other in those.

- Close out the night by praying over your girls, and if they are comfortable, allowing them to pray for each other.

Encourage your mentees to get involved by taking turns bringing a dessert or hosting in their homes if they're comfortable.

ONE-ON-ONE FORMAT:

OBJECTIVES:

- To meet with your mentee individually as needed.

- To create the opportunity for her to share life.

- To listen and move into areas of life where she needs guidance and prayer.

- To point her to Jesus and the Word for answers.

EXAMPLE LAYOUT FOR AN HOUR AND A HALF TO TWO-HOUR MEETING:

Text or email your mentee a day or two ahead of your meeting to let her know you're looking forward to time with her.

- Take time to talk and reconnect.

- Find out what's going on in life. Ask about her job, boyfriend, vacation, school, family, husband, kids, etc.

- Ask about her time with Jesus! How's that going?

- Discuss what God has been revealing to you both as you've spent time in the Word and prayer.

- Share Scripture and your own life experiences, as the Holy Spirit leads, to continue to further point her to Jesus.

- Write down specific prayer requests and take time to pray over her as you close out your time together.

let's get started.

FIRST, WE BEGIN WITH THE STORY.

The first session of FLOURISH is an opportunity for us to look at the big story of God, as seen in His Word, and begin to see how each of our smaller stories fits into the greatest story of all. Many of us try to squeeze God into what we are doing or experiencing. Instead, the correct approach is to see where we fit in His story that has been in motion for all of eternity. Through that lens, we can more clearly see the real story God is writing—one that is always for our good and for His glory.

This is where we will begin.

TO BECOME WOMEN WHO *flourish*

We benefit from the wisdom and encouragement of those who have gone before us. We believe a mentoring relationship between women can be rich soil for such spiritual growth.

God created us to be in community with other believers because He knew we couldn't do this life alone. Mentoring is God's idea! There are many examples of mentoring relationships in Scripture, and it has been the pattern of teaching and training since the early Church was founded. While the word *mentor* is not used in Scripture, the Greek term *meno* (enduring relationship, to remain) occurs in the New Testament 118 times, and 33 times in the Gospel of John alone. We trust that God will use your mentor as a stewarding force in your life as you embark on this journey!

SESSION STEPS

01   Commit to meet with Jesus five times per week for the next twelve months. You determine when, where, and for how long.

02   Focus on the passages of Scripture and the one daily assignment. Follow the readings for each day. Always end your time with God in prayer.

03   Incorporate weekly additional Scripture reading to see your story in God's story

04   Meet with your mentor at the times you have agreed upon.

THE WORD

SESSION ONE

It is our heart that over the next twelve months, we will fall more in love with the Word of God. We hope that you will be able to say, from personal experience, that you know its power to revive the soul, break the chains of lies, and provide a firm foundation for all of life. What a privilege to daily dive into the Word of God. We are bravely and humbly laying our lives before Scripture because it is "God-breathed [given by divine inspiration] and is profitable for instruction, for conviction [of sin], for correction [of error and restoration to obedience], for training in righteousness [learning to live in conformity to God's will, both publicly and privately—behaving honorably with personal integrity and moral courage]" (2 Tim. 3:16, AMP). Instruction, conviction, correction, and training take backbone and humility, both to receive and to act upon. How amazing that the Father loves us *so* much He wants us to rise up to our fullest potential and the most radiant representation of His nature! Our time in the Word *will* change us when we unclench our fists and ask His Spirit to reveal His truth to our hearts.

------------------ PSALM 119 ------------------

Psalm 119 is both the longest psalm and the longest chapter in the Bible. It may have been written by Ezra after the temple was rebuilt (see Ezra 6:14-15) as a repetitive meditation on the beauty of God's Word and how it helps us stay pure as we grow in faith. This psalm has twenty-two carefully constructed sections, each corresponding to a different letter in the Hebrew alphabet (in order) and each verse beginning with the letter of its section (an acrostic poem). Almost every line mentions God's Word. Such repetition was common in the Hebrew culture since people did not have personal copies of the Scripture to read as we do. Instead, God's people memorized His Word, and passed it along orally. The structure of this Psalm allowed for easy memorization.

We pray this psalm will move you to wonder at the vastness of God's Word. We pray it will help you see the constancy of its theme and show you the unity of Scripture. It is one big story from beginning to end!

PSALM 119

VV. 1 - 32

¹ Blessed are those whose ways are blameless, who walk according to the law of the Lord. ² Blessed are those who keep his statutes and seek him with all their heart—³ they do no wrong but follow his ways. ⁴ You have laid down precepts that are to be fully obeyed. ⁵ Oh, that my ways were steadfast in obeying your decrees! ⁶ Then I would not be put to shame when I consider all your commands. ⁷ I will praise you with an upright heart as I learn your righteous laws. ⁸ I will obey your decrees; do not utterly forsake me.

⁹ How can a young person stay on the path of purity? By living according to your word. ¹⁰ I seek you with all my heart; do not let me stray from your commands. ¹¹ I have hidden your word in my heart that I might not sin against you. ¹² Praise be to you, Lord; teach me your decrees. ¹³ With my lips I recount all the laws that come from your mouth. ¹⁴ I rejoice in following your statutes as one rejoices in great riches. ¹⁵ I meditate on your precepts and consider your ways. ¹⁶ I delight in your decrees; I will not neglect your word.

¹⁷ Be good to your servant while I live, that I may obey your word. ¹⁸ Open my eyes that I may see wonderful things in your law. ¹⁹ I am a stranger on earth; do not hide your commands from me. ²⁰ My soul is consumed with longing for your laws at all times. ²¹ You rebuke the arrogant, who are accursed, those who stray from your commands. ²² Remove from me their scorn and contempt, for I keep your statutes. ²³ Though rulers sit together and slander me, your servant will meditate on your decrees. ²⁴ Your statutes are my delight; they are my counselors.

²⁵ I am laid low in the dust; preserve my life according to your word. ²⁶ I gave an account of my ways and you answered me; teach me your decrees. ²⁷ Cause me to understand the way of your precepts, that I may meditate on your wonderful deeds. ²⁸ My soul is weary with sorrow; strengthen me according to your word. ²⁹ Keep me from deceitful ways; be gracious to me and teach me your law. ³⁰ I have chosen the way of faithfulness; I have set my heart on your laws. ³¹ I hold fast to your statutes, Lord; do not let me be put to shame. ³² I run in the path of your commands, for you have broadened my understanding.

SESSION QUESTIONS

—

WEEK ONE

DAY 01 Read Psalm 119:1-32. Underline any phrases or words that stand out to you. Reflect on your highlights, noting what they reveal about God's Word. Make one of these highlights a personal prayer for your day, and write it down.

DAY 02 Read verse 1. Look up 1 Corinthians 1:4-9. How do Paul's words add depth to what the psalmist said about being "blameless"? Go back to your prayer from yesterday and copy it somewhere, adding to it a prayer from your reading today. Post it somewhere you will see it every day this week.

DAY 03 Review verse 18, then turn to Ephesians 1:18-21 where Paul also prays for eyes to be opened. Look for the three things he asks for us to be able to see. Which one do you need a new vision for the most?

DAY 04 Read Psalm 119:1-32 in your copy of Scripture. Compare the differences in word choice between the two versions. (If you have the same version, find a new one online at BibleGateway.com.) What new insights do you gain from the different translations?

DAY 05 Read through the entire section again, concentrating on verses 30-32. Look up Hebrews 4:12-13. What do you learn from both passages about the truth and power of God's Word? Make notes in your journal. Your mentee will be reaching out to discuss insights she gained from this week's personal study, feel free to share what God is teaching you as well.

▶ **ENGAGE WITH THE WORD: SEE YOUR STORY IN HIS STORY**

As you read chapter 1 of Genesis, consider: God created the first man and woman in His own image. (See Gen. 1:27.) As one of their descendants, how should realizing that you are an "image-bearer" of God change the way you view yourself? Consider this in your journal today, ending with a prayer asking God to show you how He sees you.

PSALM 119

VV. 33-72

33 Teach me, LORD, the way of your decrees, that I may follow it to the end. 34 Give me understanding, so that I may keep your law and obey it with all my heart. 35 Direct me in the path of your commands, for there I find delight. 36 Turn my heart toward your statutes and not toward selfish gain. 37 Turn my eyes away from worthless things; preserve my life according to your word. 38 Fulfill your promise to your servant, so that you may be feared. 39 Take away the disgrace I dread, for your laws are good. 40 How I long for your precepts! In your righteousness preserve my life.

41 May your unfailing love come to me, LORD, your salvation, according to your promise; 42 then I can answer anyone who taunts me, for I trust in your word. 43 Never take your word of truth from my mouth, for I have put my hope in your laws.

[44] I will always obey your law, for ever and ever. [45] I will walk about in freedom, for I have sought out your precepts. [46] I will speak of your statutes before kings and will not be put to shame, [47] for I delight in your commands because I love them. [48] I reach out for your commands, which I love, that I may meditate on your decrees.

[49] Remember your word to your servant, for you have given me hope. [50] My comfort in my suffering is this: Your promise preserves my life. [51] The arrogant mock me unmercifully, but I do not turn from your law. [52] I remember, LORD, your ancient laws, and I find comfort in them. [53] Indignation grips me because of the wicked, who have forsaken your law. [54] Your decrees are the theme of my song wherever I lodge. [55] In the night, LORD, I remember your name, that I may keep your law. [56] This has been my practice: I obey your precepts.

[57] You are my portion, LORD; I have promised to obey your words. [58] I have sought your face with all my heart; be gracious to me according to your promise. [59] I have considered my ways and have turned my steps to your statutes. [60] I will hasten and not delay to obey your commands. [61] Though the wicked bind me with ropes, I will not forget your law. [62] At midnight I rise to give you thanks for your righteous laws. [63] I am a friend to all who fear you, to all who follow your precepts. [64] The earth is filled with your love, LORD; teach me your decrees.

[65] Do good to your servant according to your word, LORD. [66] Teach me knowledge and good judgment, for I trust your commands. [67] Before I was afflicted I went astray, but now I obey your word. [68] You are good, and what you do is good; teach me your decrees. [69] Though the arrogant have smeared me with lies, I keep your precepts with all my heart. [70] Their hearts are callous and unfeeling, but I delight in your law. [71] It was good for me to be afflicted so that I might learn your decrees. [72] The law from your mouth is more precious to me than thousands of pieces of silver and gold.

SESSION QUESTIONS

—

WEEK TWO

DAY 01   Read this week's Scripture passage. Pick out one verse that especially impacts you, and copy it to your journal. Write it on an index card or sticky note, and put it in a place you will see every day, so you can think about it all week.

DAY 02   Meditate on verse 33. Then cross-reference (compare it with a related Scripture) it with what Jesus said in John 14:1-10. Jot down any new insights you gain about "the way" of God.

DAY 03   Reread verses 49-64. How does the psalmist get through his times of darkness and "night"? Think about how you might apply his words to your journeys through dark times. If you are in a time of darkness now, which verse has been most powerful for you? If you're not, think of a friend who is going through a hard time and pray this verse over him or her today.

DAY 04   Reread the last section of this passage, especially taking note of what you learn about God's character from verse 68. What else do you learn about Him from Psalm 86:5-12? How might these insights shift your willingness to follow God's commands?

DAY 05   Go back to the verse you picked out on Day One of this week. In your journal, write any personal understanding or application of the passage you've gained from thinking about it all week. Your mentee will be reaching out to share some of the insights she gained this week via text, email, or phone.

▶ **ENGAGE WITH THE WORD: SEE YOUR STORY IN HIS STORY**

As you read Genesis 12:1-9, consider: Abraham left his homeland and family to follow God. What might God be asking you to "leave" to follow Him?

PSALM 119

VV. 73-96

⁷³ Your hands made me and formed me; give me understanding to learn your commands. ⁷⁴ May those who fear you rejoice when they see me, for I have put my hope in your word. ⁷⁵ I know, LORD, that your laws are righteous, and that in faithfulness you have afflicted me. ⁷⁶ May your unfailing love be my comfort, according to your promise to your servant. ⁷⁷ Let your compassion come to me that I may live, for your law is my delight. ⁷⁸ May the arrogant be put to shame for wronging me without cause; but I will meditate on your precepts. ⁷⁹ May those who fear you turn to me, those who understand your statutes. ⁸⁰ May I wholeheartedly follow your decrees, that I may not be put to shame.

⁸¹ My soul faints with longing for your salvation, but I have put my hope in your word. ⁸² My eyes fail, looking for your promise; I say, "When will you comfort me?" ⁸³ Though I am like a wineskin in the smoke, I do not forget your decrees. ⁸⁴ How long must your servant wait? When will you punish my persecutors? ⁸⁵ The arrogant dig pits to trap me, contrary to your law. ⁸⁶ All your commands are trustworthy; help me, for I am being persecuted without cause. ⁸⁷ They almost wiped me from the earth, but I have not forsaken your precepts. ⁸⁸ In your unfailing love preserve my life, that I may obey the statutes of your mouth.

⁸⁹ Your word, LORD, is eternal; it stands firm in the heavens. ⁹⁰ Your faithfulness continues through all generations; you established the earth, and it endures. ⁹¹ Your laws endure to this day, for all things serve you. ⁹² If your law had not been my delight, I would have perished in my affliction. ⁹³ I will never forget your precepts, for by them you have preserved my life. ⁹⁴ Save me, for I am yours; I have sought out your precepts. ⁹⁵ The wicked are waiting to destroy me, but I will ponder your statutes. ⁹⁶ To all perfection I see a limit, but your commands are boundless.

SESSION QUESTIONS

—

WEEK THREE

DAY 01 Begin your reading of the Scripture with prayer. Read the entire passage without stopping. What one big idea do you take away from it? Write this big idea in the margin of your Bible or in your journal. Also, pick out one verse that speaks to you, and copy it in your journal.

DAY 02 Focus on the first section of the passage (vv. 73-80) and notice how the psalmist highlights God's personal involvement in his life. Apply this to your situation. Read Psalm 139 to further explore an understanding of God's knowledge of the intricacies of your life. End your time with a favorite worship song, or respond with a time of prayer.

DAY 03 Read through the second section (vv. 81-88). Here the psalmist recounts a time of great distress in his life. Answer the following questions in your journal: What did the psalmist do during these times? Can you relate?

Cultural Connection: (v. 83) In this time period, skins were used to contain liquids. When hung in the smoke, skins would quickly become black, cracked, and shriveled. The psalmist used this everyday idea to illustrate his distressed mental and physical condition.

DAY 04 Review the last section of the passage in which the writer exalts the faithfulness of God (vv. 89-96). Now read Psalm 100, and note the necessary response of those who understand and embrace these truths. How can you incorporate similar responses in your own times of worship?

DAY 05 Go through Psalm 119:73-96 in your own copy of Scripture. Note any changes or additions that a different version brings to the big idea you wrote down on Day One. Be intentional to share your thoughts with your mentee.

▶ ## ENGAGE WITH THE WORD: SEE YOUR STORY IN HIS STORY

Read all or part of Genesis 37:17b-28; 39; 40 and consider: Joseph was the recipient of all kinds of injustice, but it was clear, even to him, God had a plan. Looking over your life experiences, how have you seen God work through bleak and hopeless situations to bring about good? How can these examples help you face your situation now or any future difficulties?

PSALM 119

—

VV. 97-120

⁹⁷ Oh, how I love your law! I meditate on it all day long. ⁹⁸ Your commands are always with me and make me wiser than my enemies. ⁹⁹ I have more insight than all my teachers, for I meditate on your statutes. ¹⁰⁰ I have more understanding than the elders, for I obey your precepts. ¹⁰¹ I have kept my feet from every evil path so that I might obey your word. ¹⁰² I have not departed from your laws, for you yourself have taught me.

¹⁰³ How sweet are your words to my taste, sweeter than honey to my mouth! ¹⁰⁴ I gain understanding from your precepts; therefore I hate every wrong path.

¹⁰⁵ Your word is a lamp for my feet, a light on my path. ¹⁰⁶ I have taken an oath and confirmed it, that I will follow your righteous laws. ¹⁰⁷ I have suffered much; preserve my life, LORD, according to your word.

[108] Accept, LORD, the willing praise of my mouth
and teach me your laws. [109] Though I constantly
take my life in my hands, I will not forget your law.
[110] The wicked have set a snare for me, but I have
not strayed from your precepts. [111] Your statutes
are my heritage forever; they are the joy of my
heart. [112] My heart is set on keeping your decrees
to the very end.

[113] I hate double-minded people, but I love
your law. [114] You are my refuge and my shield;
I have put my hope in your word. [115] Away from
me, you evildoers, that I may keep the commands
of my God! [116] Sustain me, my God, according
to your promise, and I will live; do not let my
hopes be dashed. [117] Uphold me, and I will be
delivered; I will always have regard for your
decrees. [118] You reject all who stray from your
decrees, for their delusions come to nothing.
[119] All the wicked of the earth you discard
like dross; therefore I love your statutes.
[120] My flesh trembles in fear of you;
I stand in awe of your laws.

SESSION QUESTIONS

—

DAY 01 Read through the entire passage of Scripture for this week. Pick one verse that stands out to you above all the others. Spend some time thinking about why that verse is significant to you as you copy it in your journal.

DAY 02 After reading through the verses again, make a list of the benefits of loving God's Word and keeping His commands. Keep this list on hand as you think about the passage for the rest of the week.

DAY 03 Review the passage again, focusing specifically on verse 105. Look up John 1:1-14; 3:18-21; 8:12 to gain more understanding about the source of light. Note a few insights in your journal.

DAY 04 Meditate on God as "my refuge and my shield" (v. 114) and how you can put your hope in His Word. Study Psalm 18 for more evidence of how God provides protection and security for His children. Summarize the verses, and make that summary your personal prayer today.

DAY 05 Go through the passage again. Stop on your verse from Day One, and spend a moment pondering the verse. Write down any other insight God has given you about why that verse is significant.

▶ **ENGAGE WITH THE WORD:** SEE YOUR STORY IN HIS STORY

As you read Exodus 1:6-14; 2:23-25; 3:1-10, consider: How did God display His concern and love for His people after hearing their cries for deliverance? What assurance does this give you when you feel like God has not heard your prayers?

PSALM 119

—

VV.121-144

[121] I have done what is righteous and just; do not leave me to my oppressors. [122] Ensure your servant's well-being; do not let the arrogant oppress me. [123] My eyes fail, looking for your salvation, looking for your righteous promise. [124] Deal with your servant according to your love and teach me your decrees. [125] I am your servant; give me discernment that I may understand your statutes. [126] It is time for you to act, LORD; your law is being broken. [127] Because I love your commands more than gold, more than pure gold, [128] and because I consider all your precepts right, I hate every wrong path.

[129] Your statutes are wonderful; therefore I obey them. [130] The unfolding of your words gives light; it gives understanding to the simple. [131] I open my mouth and pant, longing for your commands. [132] Turn to me and have mercy on me, as you always do to those who love your name. [133] Direct my footsteps according to your word; let no sin rule over me. [134] Redeem me from human oppression, that I may obey your precepts.

[135] Make your face shine on your servant
and teach me your decrees. [136] Streams
of tears flow from my eyes, for your law
is not obeyed.

[137] You are righteous, LORD, and your
laws are right. [138] The statutes you have
laid down are righteous; they are fully
trustworthy. [139] My zeal wears me out,
for my enemies ignore your words.
[140] Your promises have been thoroughly
tested, and your servant loves them.

[141] Though I am lowly and despised,
I do not forget your precepts.
[142] Your righteousness is everlasting
and your law is true. [143] Trouble and
distress have come upon me, but your
commands give me delight.
[144] Your statutes are always righteous;
give me understanding that I may live.

SESSION QUESTIONS

—

WEEK FIVE

DAY 01 Ask God to teach you His truth as you read the passage today and throughout this week. Did a specific verse grab your attention? Why was it meaningful? Write the verse in your journal and think upon it this week.

DAY 02 Focus your attention on the first section of the passage. Think about what the writer might want when he asks for discernment (see v. 125). Look up Proverbs 2 for more on the benefits of wisdom. In which areas of your life do you desire more wisdom or discernment? Write down a few.

DAY 03 Read through section two of this passage (vv. 129-136). Consider what it means for God's Word to "unfold" (v. 130). What a beautiful word picture. What might this idea of God's Word unfolding mean for your ability to grasp, apply, and share the truth with the people in your path?

DAY 04 Look through the last section of this week's passage and find the common word in the first and last verses. Cross-reference with Romans 8:10-26.

DAY 05 Review the entire passage, focusing again on the verse you chose on Day One. Make any notes about its impact on you, and share them with your mentee.

▶ **ENGAGE WITH THE WORD:** SEE YOUR STORY IN HIS STORY

While you read Exodus 33:7-23, think about the fact that the Lord spoke to Moses "as one speaks to a friend" (Ex. 33:11). What needs to be added, removed, or shifted in your life to encourage a similar relationship with God?

PSALM 119

—

VV.145-176

¹⁴⁵ I call with all my heart; answer me, LORD, and I will obey your decrees. ¹⁴⁶ I call out to you; save me and I will keep your statutes. ¹⁴⁷ I rise before dawn and cry for help; I have put my hope in your word. ¹⁴⁸ My eyes stay open through the watches of the night, that I may meditate on your promises. ¹⁴⁹ Hear my voice in accordance with your love; preserve my life, LORD, according to your laws. ¹⁵⁰ Those who devise wicked schemes are near, but they are far from your law. ¹⁵¹ Yet you are near, LORD, and all your commands are true. ¹⁵² Long ago I learned from your statutes that you established them to last forever.

¹⁵³ Look on my suffering and deliver me, for I have not forgotten your law. ¹⁵⁴ Defend my cause and redeem me; preserve my life according to your promise. ¹⁵⁵ Salvation is far from the wicked, for they do not seek out your decrees. ¹⁵⁶ Your compassion, LORD, is great; preserve my life according to your laws. ¹⁵⁷ Many are the foes who persecute me, but I have not turned from your statutes. ¹⁵⁸ I look on the faithless with loathing, for they do not obey your word. ¹⁵⁹ See how I love your precepts; preserve my life, LORD, in accordance with your love. ¹⁶⁰ All your words are true; all your righteous laws are eternal.

¹⁶¹ Rulers persecute me without cause, but my heart trembles at your word. ¹⁶² I rejoice in your promise like one who finds great spoil. ¹⁶³ I hate and detest falsehood but I love your law. ¹⁶⁴ Seven times a day I praise you for your righteous laws. ¹⁶⁵ Great peace have those who love your law, and nothing can make them stumble. ¹⁶⁶ I wait for your salvation, LORD, and I follow your commands. ¹⁶⁷ I obey your statutes, for I love them greatly. ¹⁶⁸ I obey your precepts and your statutes, for all my ways are known to you.

¹⁶⁹ May my cry come before you, LORD; give me understanding according to your word. ¹⁷⁰ May my supplication come before you; deliver me according to your promise. ¹⁷¹ May my lips overflow with praise, for you teach me your decrees. ¹⁷² May my tongue sing of your word, for all your commands are righteous. ¹⁷³ May your hand be ready to help me, for I have chosen your precepts. ¹⁷⁴ I long for your salvation, LORD, and your law gives me delight. ¹⁷⁵ Let me live that I may praise you, and may your laws sustain me. ¹⁷⁶ I have strayed like a lost sheep. Seek your servant, for I have not forgotten your commands.

SESSION QUESTIONS

—

WEEK SIX

DAY 01   Open this week's reading with prayer, and then go through the passage, finding one significant verse to add to your journal.

DAY 02   Read verses 145-160. Underline all the activities or actions in which the psalmist engages. Note also the writer's attitude toward God's Word during difficult times. How could you shift your thinking in seasons of adversity?

DAY 03   Look through verses 161-176, focusing on what the psalmist wrote about praise. Cross-reference Psalm 68:4-5; 73:25-26; Isaiah 25:1; Romans 8:31-39; 2 Corinthians 1:3-4 for other truths that relate to worship. Choose a worship song, and listen to it every day for the next seven days.

DAY 04   Read back through the verses you chose during each week of this session. Were there any common themes among them? Which one seems most significant to where you are in life right now? Write it on a note card or sticky note so you can memorize it.

DAY 05   Look back over the Scripture and/or your notes from this session. Take a moment to journal your reflections about this study, including anything powerful you learned and how the Word of God has impacted you.

▶ **ENGAGE WITH THE WORD:** SEE YOUR STORY IN HIS STORY

As you read Exodus 16:1-16, consider times when you have felt like you were wandering in the desert. How can having faith in what God has already promised help you keep moving forward?

THE WORD

—

GOALS

▲ To help us grasp the significance of having a consistent quiet time with Jesus and being rooted in the Word.

▲ To help us see the beautiful promises connected to being in the Word and hiding it in our hearts.

▲ To offer tools we can use to create the habit of spending time in the Word.

▲ To establish how to bring accountability to each mentee and provide suggestions for how to pursue a daily habit of being in the Word.

SESSION QUESTIONS

---

1. How do you think your life would practically change with a commitment to being in the Word daily?

2. What Scripture has stood out the most to you this session and influenced your desire to daily spend time with Him?

3. If you're not in a habit of daily spending time with Jesus in the Word, what needs to change in order for this to become a habit?

PRAYER

Pray to the Father through the Son by the Holy Spirit.

Throughout this session we are focusing on the beautiful opportunity we have called *prayer*. What does prayer mean to you? Be intensely honest with yourself. When you pray, do you feel like you're talking to the ceiling? Do you actually believe God not only hears all your prayers, but can and will respond? Prayer can be misunderstood, and it is often overlooked. But it is central in our journey with Jesus. Prayer isn't an itemized list or simply a task to check off our busy schedules. God doesn't want proper words or mindless, rote recitations; He wants our hearts. While talking with Jesus can take many forms, it is always about relationship. It's about spending time together, talking and listening, becoming familiar with God's heart and character. It's about being authentic and truthful, exposing your deepest pain, most secret hopes, and wildest dreams for your life. We were made to have that kind of relationship with our Father, and it is profoundly reciprocal. Prayer strengthens our roots, fastened to the Rock—Jesus—and built upon the foundation of His Word. We begin to hear the Holy Spirit speaking to our hearts through the Scripture and our lives become linked to what God is already doing in the world, for our good and His glory!

Jesus put a high priority on prayer and often retreated to quiet places to pray. When His disciples asked Him to teach them how to pray, He could have directed them to the Psalms, the Old Testament model of prayer. Instead, He gave them a new pattern that we now call, "The Lord's Prayer." (See Matt. 6 and Luke 11.) This model, coupled with Jesus' instruction in Matthew 6:6-8, gives us beautiful insight into the prayer life of Jesus, a prayer life available to all believers. In Mark 14:36, Jesus calls God, "*Abba*, Father." *Abba* was the Aramaic word for father. Before Jesus said it, the word was not used for God. This is a picture of the relationship God desires with His people through Christ. Incredibly, this is the invitation we are given as followers of Jesus! We have received the Spirit of adoption into the family of God; we are daughters of God, and we too can cry, "*Abba*, Father!" (Rom. 8:15). The Lord's Prayer gives us a framework around which to build a thriving prayer life—a crucial step in growing in Christ, dispelling lies of the enemy, and searing the truth into our hearts every day. We will explore a different element of the Lord's Prayer each week, engaging our hearts with this timeless prayer.

PSALMS

We will intertwine our journey through the Lord's Prayer with the Book of Psalms. Psalms is both beautifully poetic and very pragmatic, revealing who God is and who we are in relation to Him. It gives us a picture of how great and vast God is, while also showing us how He is completely involved in the details of our lives. Written over the span of around one thousand years, this worshipful book is woven together by multiple authors under the inspiration of the Spirit of God. Many psalms are attributed to King David (this is the same shepherd-boy David who took down Goliath and grew to be Israel's greatest king). Although he experienced hardship and possessed tragic character flaws, he is described as "a man after [God's] own heart" in 1 Samuel 13:14 and Acts 13:22. Written in Hebrew poetic form, Psalms is filled with "wisdom literature," or principles that show God's people how to live. It is also a book full of the prayers and praises of God's people to the one, true, Living God of Israel. As Christ followers, we have the incredible privilege of joining in these prayers—these worship songs— as those who have been made a part of God's people through faith in Jesus. We are invited to read, experience, and pray these words knowing that we are in Christ and that God hears every single word. Many Psalms can become tools to kick-start a conversation with God that powerfully changes our hearts and moves His. The Book of Psalms stands as an immovable and abiding source of comfort, encouragement, and insight into God, one that has sustained countless generations of God's people through the highs, lows, and in-betweens of life.

Over the next few weeks, ask God to awaken your awareness of His presence everywhere and His involvement in everything. Sitting at your desk. Running errands. Driving your car. Chasing the kids. He is there, and He cares. As we read and journey into the topic of prayer this session, we hope it will press a reset button on our view of God so we will see Him as He is—high and lifted up. It's there, in humble surrender, that we will become more like Jesus and find peace, joy, and hope.

"Our Father in heaven ..."

With these words, Jesus tenderly reminds us to begin our approach to the throne as a daughter would approach her perfect Father: with confidence, peace, and intimacy.

PSALM 24

—

VV. 1-10

[1] The earth is the LORD's, and everything in it, the world, and all who live in it; [2] for he founded it on the seas and established it on the waters. [3] Who may ascend the mountain of the LORD? Who may stand in his holy place? [4] The one who has clean hands and a pure heart, who does not trust in an idol or swear by a false god. [5] They will receive blessing from the LORD and vindication from God their Savior. [6] Such is the generation of those who seek him, who seek your face, God of Jacob. [7] Lift up your heads, you gates; be lifted up, you ancient doors, that the King of glory may come in. [8] Who is this King of glory? The LORD strong and mighty, the LORD mighty in battle. [9] Lift up your heads, you gates; lift them up, you ancient doors, that the King of glory may come in. [10] Who is he, this King of glory? The LORD Almighty— he is the King of glory.

SESSION QUESTIONS

—

WEEK ONE

DAY 01 Before you begin the session, take time to think about how you pray. What routines are helpful to you? What is lacking? List some realistic goals that you'd like to achieve in this session. Pray over these today, and ask God to guide you as you seek Him. (Add to or adjust this list of goals throughout the session.)

DAY 02 Read Psalm 24. Meditate on God as the "King of glory." What might that mean? How does it impact you? Write your thoughts down in your journal. Do some extra investigation, and define "glory."

DAY 03 Read the passage again, focusing on verses 3-6. What kind of person can "stand in his holy place" (v. 3)? How are those requirements fulfilled for us through Christ? Read Matthew 5:8; Hebrews 10:19-22; and 1 John 1:7.

DAY 04 Turn to the Gospel of John. In chapter 14, Jesus gives us a look into His tender relationship with the Father. Write down what you learn about the Father, the Son, and yourself from verses 1-14.

DAY 05 Go back through Psalm 24 again. Think about this psalm in light of the Lord's Prayer and how it might give a deeper understanding of God as "Our Father in heaven." Pray with those truths in mind today.

▶ **ENGAGE WITH THE WORD:** SEE YOUR STORY IN HIS STORY

As you read Joshua 1:1-9, reflect on God's command to Joshua. How could these instructions help you face any intimidating situations you encounter?

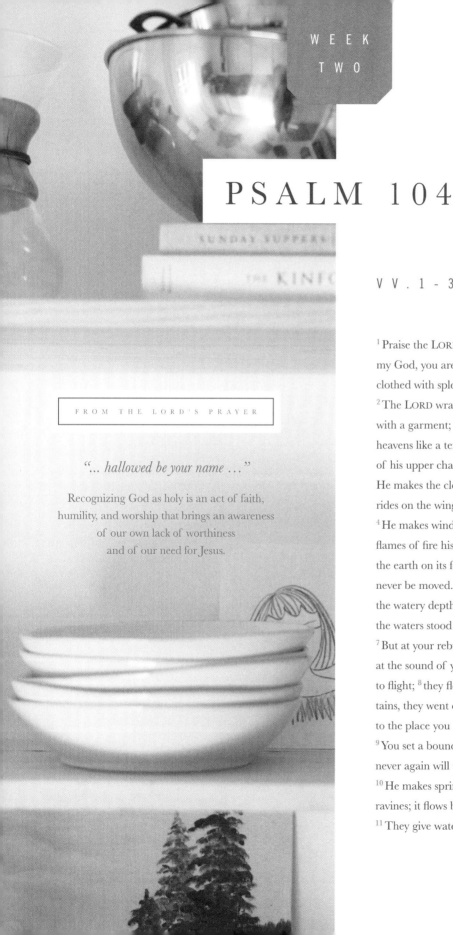

PSALM 104

V V . 1 - 3 5

FROM THE LORD'S PRAYER

"... hallowed be your name ..."

Recognizing God as holy is an act of faith,
humility, and worship that brings an awareness
of our own lack of worthiness
and of our need for Jesus.

[1] Praise the LORD, my soul. LORD
my God, you are very great; You are
clothed with splendor and majesty.
[2] The LORD wraps himself in light as
with a garment; he stretches out the
heavens like a tent [3] and lays the beams
of his upper chambers on their waters.
He makes the clouds his chariot and
rides on the wings of the wind.
[4] He makes winds his messengers,
flames of fire his servants. [5] He set
the earth on its foundations; it can
never be moved. [6] You covered it with
the watery depths as with a garment;
the waters stood above the mountains.
[7] But at your rebuke the waters fled,
at the sound of your thunder they took
to flight; [8] they flowed over the mountains, they went down into the valleys,
to the place you assigned for them.
[9] You set a boundary they cannot cross;
never again will they cover the earth.
[10] He makes springs pour water into the
ravines; it flows between the mountains.
[11] They give water to all the beasts

of the field; the wild donkeys quench their thirst. ¹²The birds of the sky nest by the waters; they sing among the branches. ¹³He waters the mountains from his upper chambers; the land is satisfied by the fruit of his work. ¹⁴He makes grass grow for the cattle, and plants for people to cultivate— bringing forth food from the earth: ¹⁵wine that gladdens human hearts, oil to make their faces shine, and bread that sustains their hearts. ¹⁶The trees of the LORD are well watered, the cedars of Lebanon that he planted.¹⁷There the birds make their nests; the stork has its home in the junipers. ¹⁸The high mountains belong to the wild goats; the crags are a refuge for the hyrax. ¹⁹He made the moon to mark the seasons, and the sun knows when to go down. ²⁰You bring darkness, it becomes night, and all the beasts of the forest prowl. ²¹The lions roar for their prey and seek their food from God. ²²The sun rises, and they steal away; they return and lie down in their dens. ²³Then people go out to their work, to their labor until evening. ²⁴How many are your works, LORD! In wisdom you made them all;

the earth is full of your creatures. ²⁵There is the sea, vast and spacious, teeming with creatures beyond number—living things both large and small. ²⁶There the ships go to and fro, and Leviathan, which you formed to frolic there. ²⁷All creatures look to you to give them their food at the proper time. ²⁸When you give it to them, they gather it up; when you open your hand, they are satisfied with good things. ²⁹When you hide your face, they are terrified; when you take away their breath, they die and return to the dust. ³⁰When you send your Spirit, they are created, and you renew the face of the ground.³¹May the glory of the LORD endure forever; may the LORD rejoice in his works— ³²He who looks at the earth, and it trembles, who touches the mountains, and they smoke. ³³I will sing to the LORD all my life; I will sing praise to my God as long as I live. ³⁴May my meditation be pleasing to him, as I rejoice in the LORD. ³⁵But may sinners vanish from the earth and the wicked be no more. Praise the LORD, my soul. Praise the LORD.

2

SESSION QUESTIONS

—

WEEK TWO

DAY 01 Webster's dictionary defines "hallowed" as sacred, respected, and honored as holy.[1] Read Psalm 104. What did you learn about God that would help you "hallow" His name? Write out last week's and this week's portion of the Lord's Prayer in your own words. Begin to make it your personal prayer.

DAY 02 Part of honoring God as holy involves worship. Read the passage again. What insights do you discover that might motivate you to worship Him? Begin your prayers today with some of those truths.

DAY 03 God is our intimate Father, but He is also to be revered as the almighty Creator. Go over the Scripture again to see how the psalmist responded to his understanding of God. Pray today with the same attitude, writing down your prayer in your journal.

DAY 04 Read through the passage again. What words or phrases stand out as relating specifically to God's holiness? What do they teach you about Him? How can you incorporate these truths into your prayers?

DAY 05 Listen to a worship song that centers on the character of God. Mix it into your prayer time today as you intentionally choose to "hallow" the Lord's name.

▶ **ENGAGE WITH THE WORD:** SEE YOUR STORY IN HIS STORY

Read Joshua 24:14-15, and reflect on Joshua's final words to the people. If you considered his statement as a personal challenge, what might need to change in your life?

1. "Definition of Hallowed." *Merriam-Webster's Dictionary*, https://www.merriam-webster.com/dictionary/hallowed.

2

SESSION TWO / WEEK THREE

FROM THE LORD'S PRAYER

"... your kingdom come ..."

Unlike the broken kingdoms of this world, Jesus' perfect kingdom of grace
and righteousness has the power to bring harmony between all created things
and God's will. For this reason, we pray for His kingdom to come quickly!

PSALM 61

—

VV. 1-8

¹ Hear my cry, O God; listen to my prayer. ² From the ends of the earth I call to you, I call as my heart grows faint; lead me to the rock that is higher than I. ³ For you have been my refuge, a strong tower against the foe. ⁴ I long to dwell in your tent forever and take refuge in the shelter of your wings. ⁵ For you, God, have heard my vows; you have given me the heritage of those who fear your name. ⁶ Increase the days of the king's life, his years for many generations. ⁷ May he be enthroned in God's presence forever; appoint your love and faithfulness to protect him. ⁸ Then I will ever sing in praise of your name and fulfill my vows day after day.

SESSION QUESTIONS

—

WEEK THREE

DAY 01   Read Psalm 61. Look for evidence of the psalmist's attitude of surrender. When we ask for God's kingdom to "come," we're praying for Him to rule over the world, both now and forever. Our two-fold prayer is that we would live in the fullness of God's will for our lives in the present, while also eagerly looking forward to the day when Jesus will come again.

DAY 02   Choose a couple of verses from Psalm 61 that draw your attention. Write them on a card or sticky note. Work on memorizing them for the rest of the week.

DAY 03   Sometimes our prayers may be solely filled with specific requests, detailing what we want God to do for us. Read this psalm again. What kinds of things does the writer ask for? How would implementing the psalmist's pattern affect the way you pray today?

DAY 04   Read this week's passage again, focusing on verses 3-4. Think about how living in God's presence could be like a literal "shelter" or "strong tower." Be as specific as possible, and jot your thoughts in your journal.

DAY 05   Review the passage and any notes you made this week. Add any new insights or reflections to your journal. Include specifics about how you can pray for God's kingdom to come in your life.

▶ **ENGAGE WITH THE WORD: SEE YOUR STORY IN HIS STORY**

As you read Judges 6:7-24, notice how Gideon thought of himself. How can God's choice of Gideon as a leader be an encouragement to you when you feel uncertain about your gifts and abilities?

"... your will be done, on earth as it is in heaven."

In this humble request, we declare and accept God's will as the best plan for our lives. We surrender our agendas and submit to Him, because we believe His plan is perfectly loving and righteous. We pray His glory and restoration would come powerfully through the Church, and that His perfect love and peace would prevail on earth, just as it already does in heaven.

PSALM 19

—

¹ The heavens declare the glory of God; the skies proclaim the work of his hands. ² Day after day they pour forth speech; night after night they reveal knowledge. ³ They have no speech, they use no words; no sound is heard from them. ⁴ Yet their voice goes out into all the earth, their words to the ends of the world. In the heavens God has pitched a tent for the sun. ⁵ It is like a bridegroom coming out of his chamber, like a champion rejoicing to run his course. ⁶ It rises at one end of the heavens and makes its circuit to the other; nothing is deprived of its warmth. ⁷ The law of the LORD is perfect, refreshing the soul. The statutes of the LORD are trustworthy, making wise the simple. ⁸ The precepts of the LORD are right, giving joy to the heart. The commands of the LORD are radiant, giving light to the eyes. ⁹ The fear of the LORD is pure, enduring forever. The decrees of the LORD are firm, and all of them are righteous. ¹⁰ They are more precious than gold, than much pure gold; they are sweeter than honey, than honey from the honeycomb. ¹¹ By them your servant is warned; in keeping them there is great reward. ¹² But who can discern their own errors? Forgive my hidden faults. ¹³ Keep your servant also from willful sins; may they not rule over me. Then I will be blameless, innocent of great transgression. ¹⁴ May these words of my mouth and this meditation of my heart be pleasing in your sight, LORD, my Rock and my Redeemer.

SESSION QUESTIONS

—

WEEK FOUR

DAY 01   Read Psalm 19. Think about what it means that God's "will be done." How do you see His will being manifested in these verses? Refer also to the following verses about the will of God: Ephesians 5:15-20; 1 Thessalonians 4:3-7; 5:16-19; 1 Timothy 2:3-4; 1 Peter 2:13-16; 3:17. Write down any common themes you find in these passages, and pray over how you can live out God's will for your life.

DAY 02   Read the psalm again. Meditate on verse 14 specifically. How can the psalmist's words become a practical way to say, "Your will be done"? Note any changes in your attitude as you learn to posture your heart this way throughout the week. Work on memorizing this beautiful declaration this week.

DAY 03   Think about the first six verses of Psalm 19. As you go about your day, make a conscious effort to notice how the natural world, in both big and small ways, "declare[s] the glory of God" (v. 1). Write down some of the things you have observed in your journal. End by praising the Lord for who He is and what He's done, joining your voice to their declaration of God's majesty and glory.

DAY 04   By the power of the Holy Spirit, our prayers can impact individuals, communities, and even nations. Read the passage again, this time paying close attention to what it says about God's involvement in groups of people. Then, look at a map of your city, state, country, or the world. As you are drawn to a specific area, pray that God's "will be done" in that place "as it is in heaven" (Matt. 6:10).

DAY 05   Look up Micah 6:8, and note the three things the prophet says are pleasing to the Lord. Consider them in the context of the study you have done this week and how your reading has changed your understanding of God's kingdom and how His will should be done.

▶   **ENGAGE WITH THE WORD:** SEE YOUR STORY IN HIS STORY

Read through Ruth 1–4. In what way do Ruth's actions and responses challenge and/or encourage you?

"Give us today our daily bread."

In this petition, we humbly ask God to meet our daily needs,
rest in His promise to provide, and accept what He gives as good.

PSALM 20

—

VV. 1-9

¹ May the LORD answer you when you are in distress; may the name of the God of Jacob protect you. ² May he send you help from the sanctuary and grant you support from Zion. ³ May he remember all your sacrifices and accept your burnt offerings. ⁴ May he give you the desire of your heart and make all your plans succeed. ⁵ May we shout for joy over your victory and lift up our banners in the name of our God. May the LORD grant all your requests.

⁶ Now this I know: The LORD gives victory to his anointed. He answers him from his heavenly sanctuary with the victorious power of his right hand. ⁷ Some trust in chariots and some in horses, but we trust in the name of the LORD our God. ⁸ They are brought to their knees and fall, but we rise up and stand firm. ⁹ LORD, give victory to the king! Answer us when we call!

SESSION QUESTIONS

—

DAY 01 Read Psalm 20, and circle the different things the psalmist trusts God to provide. What are you trusting God to provide? Begin to memorize a verse from this psalm that you find significant. Text it to a friend today as an encouragement.

DAY 02 As you review this passage, note the response of the psalmist to God's provision. Think about how God has provided and what God has given you. Take time in your prayers today to reflect on God's faithfulness in the past and present. How could this change your attitude toward anything that "seems" to be missing for the future?

DAY 03 Go back through Psalm 20. If you are praying for something specific, how do these verses encourage you to press on? (Also reference Isa. 40:28-31 and Phil. 4:6-7.)

DAY 04 Some of the statements in Psalm 20 are prayers of the psalmist to God and others are firm promises. Journal your thoughts about the difference between the two. Incorporate some promises from Scripture into your prayers today.

DAY 05 Read 2 Peter 1:3-9. What has God provided? What attitudes and actions should be evident in your life as a result? Write down anything you have learned about God's promise to provide this week. Include insights about this psalm or prayer in general.

▶ ## ENGAGE WITH THE WORD: SEE YOUR STORY IN HIS STORY

Read 1 Samuel 8:1-22, considering why it was wrong for Israel to ask for a king. How can you keep from making the same fundamental error in your decision-making?

FROM THE LORD'S PRAYER

"... forgive us our debts, as we also have forgiven our debtors."

In this heart cry, we focus on confession, openly acknowledging our sin for what it is and accepting the forgiveness, grace, and righteousness that is ours through Christ.

PSALM 32

—

VV. 1-11

[1] Blessed is the one whose transgressions are forgiven, whose sins are covered. [2] Blessed is the one whose sin the LORD does not count against them and in whose spirit is no deceit. [3] When I kept silent, my bones wasted away through my groaning all day long. [4] For day and night your hand was heavy on me; my strength was sapped as in the heat of summer. [5] Then I acknowledged my sin to you and did not cover up my iniquity. I said, "I will confess my transgressions to the LORD." And you forgave the guilt of my sin. [6] Therefore let all the faithful pray to you while you may be found; surely the rising of the mighty waters will not reach them. [7] You are my hiding place; You will protect me from trouble and surround me with songs of deliverance. [8] I will instruct you and teach you in the way you should go; I will counsel you with my loving eye on you. [9] Do not be like the horse or the mule, which have no understanding but must be controlled by bit and bridle or they will not come to you. [10] Many are the woes of the wicked, but the LORD's unfailing love surrounds the one who trusts in him. [11] Rejoice in the LORD and be glad, you righteous; sing, all you who are upright in heart!

SESSION QUESTIONS

—

WEEK SIX

DAY 01
Read Psalm 32. What is forgiveness? (See Eph. 1:7 and 1 John 1:9.) Make note of the results of righteousness and the consequences of disobedience. Meet with Jesus in prayer regarding anything that comes to your attention regarding forgiveness.

DAY 02
Confession and repentance are essential in dealing with our sin. Confession is acknowledging that you did something wrong. Repentance is a choice to turn away from it and move forward in righteousness. Read Psalm 32 again. Look for evidence of these two essential elements in the psalm.

DAY 03
Meditate on this week's passage just before you pray. Focus on the promise associated with forgiveness in verse 5. Spend some time being quiet, and ask the Holy Spirit to bring to light anything that needs attention, confession, or repentance.

DAY 04
As you become more aware of the forgiveness that you've received from God, think about how you can reflect that forgiveness to others who have wronged you. (For future study, read Matt. 6:14-15; Eph. 4:32; Col. 3:13; and 1 Pet. 3:9.)

DAY 05
Read Luke 7:36-50. What truth from this story can you incorporate into your actions and attitudes? Reach out to your mentee and offer to cover any needs or requests in prayer with her. Ask if she has any specific concerns she may want to share.

▶ **ENGAGE WITH THE WORD:** SEE YOUR STORY IN HIS STORY

Read 1 Samuel 13:7b-14. Take note of how Saul responded when he was confronted with his sin. How can you avoid his mistake when you are confronted with your own shortcomings?

"And lead us not into temptation, but deliver us from the evil one."

In this petition, we ask God for an awareness of the temptations that surround us
and trust in His protective power to guard and keep us from evil.

PSALM 7

—

VV. 1 - 17

[1] LORD my God, I take refuge in you; save and deliver me from all who pursue me, [2] or they will tear me apart like a lion and rip me to pieces with no one to rescue me. [3] LORD my God, if I have done this and there is guilt on my hands— [4] if I have repaid my ally with evil or without cause have robbed my foe— [5] then let my enemy pursue and overtake me; let him trample my life to the ground and make me sleep in the dust. [6] Arise, LORD, in your anger; rise up against the rage of my enemies. Awake, my God; decree justice. [7] Let the assembled peoples gather around you, while you sit enthroned over them on high. [8] Let the LORD judge the peoples. Vindicate me, LORD, according to my righteousness, according to my integrity, O Most High. [9] Bring to an end the violence of the wicked and make the righteous secure—you, the righteous God who probes minds and hearts. [10] My shield is God Most High, who saves the upright in heart. [11] God is a righteous judge, a God who displays his wrath every day. [12] If he does not relent, he will sharpen his sword; he will bend and string his bow. [13] He has prepared his deadly weapons; he makes ready his flaming arrows. [14] Whoever is pregnant with evil conceives trouble and gives birth to disillusionment. [15] Whoever digs a hole and scoops it out falls into the pit they have made. [16] The trouble they cause recoils on them; their violence comes down on their own heads. [17] I will give thanks to the LORD because of his righteousness; I will sing the praises of the name of the LORD Most High.

SESSION QUESTIONS

—

DAY 01 In the Lord's Prayer, Jesus urges us to ask the Father to lead us away from anything that would be harmful. James 1:13 assures us that God never tempts anyone. Read through Psalm 7, and then pray with this truth in mind.

DAY 02 After reading the psalm again, ask God to help you become aware of your personal areas of weakness and temptation. (See also 1 Cor. 10:12-13.) Think about your responsibility to look for and use the "way of escape" (v. 13, ESV) God provides when temptation comes. Write down an action plan— something tangible and practical you can do when faced with a personal struggle or temptation.

DAY 03 Read the passage again, looking intently at verses 11-17. What is God's attitude and response to the evil around us? Consider how that might meld with His love. Choose a verse from the entire psalm that stands out to you, and memorize it.

DAY 04 Read 2 Corinthians 10:3-6. Reread Psalm 7 in light of what you've learned about your real enemy.

DAY 05 Go through Ephesians 6:10-18. What are God's instructions when it comes to standing up to darkness and the "devil's schemes"? According to verse 18, when are we to pray? Think about what this week's study has taught you regarding temptation and how to pray effectively against it. Check in with your mentee, asking if there's anything she needs you to join her in praying against.

▶ **ENGAGE WITH THE WORD:** SEE YOUR STORY IN HIS STORY

Read 1 Samuel 16:1-13. David was called and anointed to be king long before he actually took the throne. What encouragement can you receive from this account in times when your goals or plans are a long way from coming true?

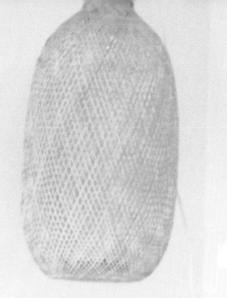

*"For Yours is the kingdom and the power
and the glory forever. Amen" (NASB).*

This addition to the Lord's Prayer expresses our confidence in Christ and in every promise of God. Although the closing words are not a part of the original biblical text, we can use them as an example of how to express our worship, reverence, and confidence in God's promises and authority.

PSALM 9

—

VV. 1-20

¹ I will give thanks to You, LORD, with all my heart; I will tell of all your wonderful deeds. ² I will be glad and rejoice in you; I will sing the praises of your name, O Most High. ³ My enemies turn back; they stumble and perish before you. ⁴ For you have upheld my right and my cause, sitting enthroned as the righteous judge. ⁵ You have rebuked the nations and destroyed the wicked; you have blotted out their name for ever and ever. ⁶ Endless ruin has overtaken my enemies, you have uprooted their cities; even the memory of them has perished. ⁷ The LORD reigns forever; he has established his throne for judgment. ⁸ He rules the world in righteousness and judges the peoples with equity. ⁹ The LORD is a refuge for the oppressed, a stronghold in times of trouble. ¹⁰ Those who know your name trust in you, for you, LORD, have never forsaken those who seek you. ¹¹ Sing the praises of the LORD, enthroned in Zion; proclaim among the nations what he has done. ¹² For he who avenges blood remembers; he does not ignore the cries of the afflicted. ¹³ LORD, see how my enemies persecute me! Have mercy and lift me up from the gates of death, ¹⁴ that I may declare your praises in the gates of Daughter Zion, and there rejoice in your salvation. ¹⁵ The nations have fallen into the pit they have dug; their feet are caught in the net they have hidden. ¹⁶ The LORD is known by his acts of justice; the wicked are ensnared by the work of their hands. ¹⁷ The wicked go down to the realm of the dead, all the nations that forget God. ¹⁸ But God will never forget the needy; the hope of the afflicted will never perish. ¹⁹ Arise, LORD, do not let mortals triumph; let the nations be judged in your presence. ²⁰ Strike them with terror, LORD; let the nations know they are only mortal.

SESSION QUESTIONS

—

WEEK EIGHT

DAY 01 The Lord's Prayer ends with what can be called a "doxology" (a short statement of praise) which can literally be translated to mean "glory words." Read through Psalm 9. Look for any verses or phrases you might identify as "glory words." Make these your personal prayer this week.

DAY 02 Focus on the qualities of God listed in this passage. There is power in affirming who God is and what He has done! Speak some of His qualities back to Him as you pray. Choose a verse or section to memorize. How can meditating on and memorizing these words reflect the truth of Psalm 19:14 (a verse we memorized in Week Four of this session)?

DAY 03 Read Psalm 9 again. Highlight any new words or phrases that catch your attention. What do they tell you about God? About yourself?

DAY 04 Turn to Matthew 6:5-14 in your own copy of Scripture. Pick out the words or phrases in this passage that most impact you. Write the Lord's Prayer in your own personal words, and make it your honest prayer today.

DAY 05 Go back and read through the initial thoughts and goals that you made on Day One of this session. How have you grown in your prayer time with Jesus? In what ways do you still want to grow? Review the verses you chose to memorize during this session. Thank God for His truth that isn't just a routine or rote statement, but is now hidden in and written on your heart! (See Ps. 119:11 and Prov. 7:1-3.)

▶ **ENGAGE WITH THE WORD:** SEE YOUR STORY IN HIS STORY

Read 1 Samuel 24:1-22. Take note of David's singular goal that grew out of his deep love for God: for God to be glorified. What can you do to begin cultivating a heart like David's?

PRAYER

—

▲ To build a consistent habit of meeting in prayer with Jesus.

▲ To see the significance of being a prayer warrior as shown in the Word.

▲ To gain greater understanding of the impact and power of prayer in our own lives and the lives of those we pray for.

SESSION QUESTIONS

1. What is the greatest challenge for you in responding to the call to pray without ceasing?

2. How can you begin to weave a consistency of prayer into your life daily?

3. Do you believe that your prayers can change how things happen? In other words, do you believe prayer makes a difference?

4. What is the greatest prayer request on your heart right now?

III

IDENTITY

As we move into our next session on *identity*, our hope is that we would lean into all we have learned about prayer; namely, that our growth in Christ hinges on the foundation of Scripture and our relationship to God through prayer. How can you or I know who we are if we don't first know what God says about us?

WHO AM I?

So many voices vie for our attention. It can be easy to hear others above the voice of God. For some, it's falling into a social media coma, only to awaken feeling completely inadequate. (*Why can't I prepare organic farm-to-table meals for my perfectly-dressed children, who are doing age-appropriate crafts while lounging on a pristinely white sofa?*) For others, it is the constant barrage of opinions, whether good or bad, from friends and family. It may be negativity from a spouse or a discouraging work environment. We may even think that we define our own identities. Whoever or whatever it may be, many things influence our thinking, beliefs, and actions. At times, it may be tempting to conform our thoughts and views of ourselves to what we see and hear from others—good, bad, or indifferent. In a sea of confusing voices and opinions, there is only one voice that offers the true and right answer to the critical question: Who am I? The Living God has given us His Word and His Spirit. And He has told us who we are in Christ. He has the final word on who we are, not a social media feed, not our latest success or failure, not our moms, our bosses, our kids, our past, our worst enemies, or even

ourselves. We, as followers of Jesus, have to understand God's truth and what He says about who we are. He is our identity-maker and identity-shaper. His Word is the very place we find our identity defined and where we go daily to stay rooted in who He says we are.

What you believe about yourself will determine the direction of your life. If we want to truly live out the life He has purposed for us—godly, righteous, holy, beautiful lives for His glory—we have to know what God says about who we are and believe it. Knowing is one thing, but ultimately, what we believe about ourselves will determine the direction of our lives. This is powerful and true. If we don't believe we have been empowered to overcome sin or equipped to make revolutionary changes in our lives because of what Jesus has done for us, we will struggle to both define and live out our true identities. That's why it's so essential for us to believe the truth as outlined by God alone and believe what He victoriously declares about who we are in Christ. Accepted. Chosen. Loved. Holy. Blameless. Redeemed. Completely made new. Purposed. Free. These are only a few of the wonderful things god says about us!

EPHESIANS

Ephesians is a letter that the apostle Paul wrote from prison around AD 60, about 30 years after Jesus came to earth and died on a cross for the sins of mankind. Once Christ was resurrected and ascended back into heaven, the Holy Spirit descended on the believers who were gathered in Jerusalem, and the Church was born (Acts 1–2). The Church spread like wildfire, and small gatherings of believers popped up all over the known world. One of these Churches took root in the city of Ephesus. Paul wrote the Ephesians to remind the young believers of the glorious truth they possess by believing in Christ: that dead sinners are made alive in Him. He explains in great detail what grace means for both the Church and the individual, and he ends his letter stressing prayer and putting on the "armor of God" to guard against the lies of the enemy. As we spend nine weeks pouring over and absorbing this pivotal book of Scripture, we pray that it will captivate our thoughts and hearts, and that the Spirit will breathe these foundational realities about who we are in Christ into every gap that needs to be filled in our lives.

SESSION THREE / WEEK ONE

EPHESIANS 1

—

V V . 1 - 1 4

[1] Paul, an apostle of Christ Jesus by the will of God, To God's holy people in Ephesus, the faithful in Christ Jesus: [2] Grace and peace to you from God our Father and the Lord Jesus Christ.

PRAISE FOR SPIRITUAL BLESSINGS IN CHRIST

[3] Praise be to the God and Father of our Lord Jesus Christ, who has blessed us in the heavenly realms with every spiritual blessing in Christ. [4] For he chose us in him before the creation of the world to be holy and blameless in his sight. In love [5] he predestined us for adoption to sonship through Jesus Christ, in accordance with his pleasure and will— [6] to the praise of his glorious grace, which he has freely given us in the One he loves. [7] In him we have redemption through his blood, the forgiveness of sins, in accordance with the riches of God's grace

[8] that he lavished on us. With all wisdom and understanding, [9] he made known to us the mystery of his will according to his good pleasure, which he purposed in Christ, [10] to be put into effect when the times reach their fulfillment— to bring unity to all things in heaven and on earth under Christ. [11] In him we were also chosen, having been predestined according to the plan of him who works out everything in conformity with the purpose of his will, [12] in order that we, who were the first to put our hope in Christ, might be for the praise of his glory. [13] And you also were included in Christ when you heard the message of truth, the gospel of your salvation. When you believed, you were marked in him with a seal, the promised Holy Spirit, [14] who is a deposit guaranteeing our inheritance until the redemption of those who are God's possession—to the praise of his glory.

SESSION QUESTIONS

—

Before you begin, take time to clear your mind of distractions and ask for God's Spirit to help you understand and apply His truth today and each day during this entire session.

DAY 01 Read the passage through completely. Then go back and reread just verse 1. What words does Paul use to describe the believers in Ephesus? Cross-reference with Philippians 1:1; 1 Corinthians 1:2; 2 Corinthians 1:1; Romans 1:7; Colossians 1:2; and Jude 1–2. Do you recognize similar language in these passages? What do these opening phrases mean specifically for you as a believer in Jesus?

DAY 02 Go through the Scripture again and draw a circle around "in Christ," "in Him," "in the One," or other similar phrases. Pause and reflect on Paul's emphasis on your position "in Christ." What is your response to this truth? How can this truth erase and replace any wrong views of yourself?

DAY 03 As you reread this section, highlight any words that relate to God's activity on our behalf. Make notes on what these words tell you about His character and attitude toward you. Which one is most meaningful to you in the season of life you're currently in? Why?

DAY 04 Read the Scripture again, this time noting the phrases that talk about who you are or what you have as a believer. If you found connections that overlap from yesterday, consider what that might mean. Make a list of everything these verses tell you that you already possess as a child of God. Leave space to add to this list as you'll revisit it later in Week Four and Six.

DAY 05 Meditate on the last two verses of this passage. Write a short sentence stating what you know to be "the gospel of your salvation." Refer to John 3:13-21,36; Romans 3:23-24; 5:1-11. For example, "I know that I am saved by grace through faith in Christ and that while I was still a sinner, Christ died for me so I could have life forever with him." Write it on your mirror so that every time you look in it you can remember who God says you are.

▶ **ENGAGE WITH THE WORD: SEE YOUR STORY IN HIS STORY**

Both Saul and David sinned against God, but each responded differently. Read 2 Samuel 12:1-13, and think back to the story of Saul that we read in Session Two, Week Six. What you can learn from their examples that will help you avoid making the same mistakes?

EPHESIANS 1

—

V V . 1 5 - 2 3

THANKSGIVING AND PRAYER

¹⁵ For this reason, ever since I heard about your faith in the Lord Jesus and your love for all God's people, ¹⁶ I have not stopped giving thanks for you, remembering you in my prayers. ¹⁷ I keep asking that the God of our Lord Jesus Christ, the glorious Father, may give you the Spirit of wisdom and revelation, so that you may know him better. ¹⁸ I pray that the eyes of your heart may be enlightened in order that you may know the hope to which he has called you, the riches of his glorious inheritance in his holy people, ¹⁹ and his incomparably great power for us who believe. That power is the same as the mighty strength ²⁰ he exerted when he raised Christ from the dead and seated him at his right hand in the heavenly realms, ²¹ far above all rule and authority, power and dominion, and every name that is invoked, not only in the present age but also in the one to come. ²² And God placed all things under his feet and appointed him to be head over everything for the church, ²³ which is his body, the fullness of him who fills everything in every way.

SESSION QUESTIONS

—

WEEK TWO

DAY 01 This section of Ephesians 1 is essentially a prayer by Paul for his readers. Because we are also believers in Christ and a part of His Church, it is for us too. Go through the passage and underline what Paul asked God for on their/your behalf. How are his requests different from most prayers you hear? From the prayers you pray?

DAY 02 Pay attention to verse 17 as you read the passage today. For what purpose does Paul ask for wisdom and revelation? Add this request to your prayers today. Cross-reference 2 Peter 1:3-11 and John 14:20-21 for more on knowing Jesus.

DAY 03 Slow down your reading of the Scripture to reflect on and absorb three things the "eyes of your heart" need to be enlightened to see. Write them in your journal, making extra notes concerning one truth you think you need most right now. Pray for yourself and for someone close to you who may also need the eyes of his or her heart enlightened.

DAY 04 Meditate on verses 19-21, thinking about the great power of God that works on your behalf. Take time to consider the things that trouble you today. Go to the Lord in prayer, and by faith, turn them over to the capable and truly awesome power of Jesus.

DAY 05 Turn to Judges 6 and 7 to read the story of Gideon. Note how Gideon thought about himself compared to how the angel of the Lord addressed him. Relate this story to yourself as you consider how you think about yourself. Begin to replace any wrong assessments with the truths you have read so far in Ephesians 1. Beside each lie write the truth counterpart and Scripture reference, and pray that the truth of who you are in Christ would overcome anything less than God's best for you. Resist the urge to skip this process—identifying lies and replacing them with God's truth is a key element of freedom. (See John 8:32.) It is for freedom that Christ has set you free! (See Gal. 5:1.)

▶ **ENGAGE WITH THE WORD: SEE YOUR STORY IN HIS STORY**

Read 1 Chronicles 22. How do you think David felt when he was allowed to plan, but not build, the temple for God? What can you learn from his response that may help you work through times when things don't turn out the way you may have hoped?

EPHESIANS 2

—

VV. 1-10

MADE ALIVE IN CHRIST

[1] As for you, you were dead in your transgressions and sins, [2] in which you used to live when you followed the ways of this world and of the ruler of the kingdom of the air, the spirit who is now at work in those who are disobedient. [3] All of us also lived among them at one time, gratifying the cravings of our flesh and following its desires and thoughts. Like the rest, we were by nature deserving of wrath. [4] But because of his great love for us, God, who is rich in mercy, [5] made us alive with Christ even when we were dead in transgressions—it is by grace you have been saved. [6] And God raised us up with Christ and seated us with him in the heavenly realms in Christ Jesus, [7] in order that in the coming ages he might show the incomparable riches of his grace, expressed in his kindness to us in Christ Jesus. [8] For it is by grace you have been saved, through faith—and this is not from yourselves, it is the gift of God— [9] not by works, so that no one can boast. [10] For we are God's handiwork, created in Christ Jesus to do good works, which God prepared in advance for us to do.

SESSION QUESTIONS

—

WEEK THREE

DAY 01 Think about this Scripture in light of your own journey of faith. Regardless of what kind of life you've lived, what does the Bible say about your life before you trusted Jesus as Savior? What changed? What is different about the description after you've become a follower of Jesus? Be specific as you write these things in your journal.

DAY 02 Go back through the verses again as you think about what this passage says about God. Take notes on what you learn about His character and heart toward you. How could this change the way you view yourself?

DAY 03 This passage highlights God's amazing grace. Focus on verses 4-9 in this section. Add to it what you find in Romans 1:1-5; 5:1-2,12-21 to answer the questions: What is grace? How do you receive it?

DAY 04 Find the section of this passage that tells about the love of God. Read 1 John 4:9-21. Since God loves you so much, what should your attitude toward yourself be? Reflect also on Matthew 22:37-39 and journal how it might be connected to what you've read so far. Why is it important to love ourselves in light of this passage?

DAY 05 Read back through the passage, resting on verse 10. What do you think an authentic, proper response should be based on what you've read? End your time in the Scriptures with a prayer of thanksgiving and surrender.

▶ **ENGAGE WITH THE WORD: SEE YOUR STORY IN HIS STORY**

Read 2 Chronicles 1:7-12, and think about why Solomon's request for wisdom was so pleasing to the Lord. How can what you read change the way you pray?

EPHESIANS 2

—

VV.11-22

JEW AND GENTILE RECONCILED THROUGH CHRIST

[11] Therefore, remember that formerly you who are Gentiles by birth and called "uncircumcised" by those who call themselves "the circumcision" (which is done in the body by human hands)— [12] remember that at that time you were separate from Christ, excluded from citizenship in Israel and foreigners to the covenants of the promise, without hope and without God in the world. [13] But now in Christ Jesus you who once were far away have been brought near by the blood of Christ. [14] For he himself is our peace, who has made the two groups one and has destroyed the barrier, the dividing wall of hostility, [15] by setting aside in his flesh the law with its commands and regulations. His purpose was to create in himself one new humanity out of the two, thus making peace, [16] and in one body to reconcile both of them to God through the cross, by which he put to death their hostility. [17] He came and preached peace to you who were far away and peace to those who were near. [18] For through him we both have access to the Father by one Spirit.

[19] Consequently, you are no longer foreigners and strangers, but fellow citizens with God's people and also members of his household, [20] built on the foundation of the apostles and prophets, with Christ Jesus himself as the chief cornerstone. [21] In him the whole building is joined together and rises to become a holy temple in the Lord. [22] And in him you too are being built together to become a dwelling in which God lives by his Spirit.

SESSION QUESTIONS

—

WEEK FOUR

Read through the passage slowly. What initial thoughts do you have about it? Before you read any extra commentaries, ask God to give you understanding. Write down any questions or insights you have and share one of them with your mentee via text or email today.

Our ability (good or bad) to handle the inevitable conflict and turmoil of life can unintentionally affect how we view ourselves. Go through the passage again, and then go back to look at Ephesians 1:2 as well. Who is the source of genuine peace? How can this truth give you confidence and stability even in unstable situations?

Pull out the list you started in Week One. Go back through the passage and add to your list all the things that are true about those (*you!*) who are in Christ.

Concentrate on verses 19-22 in your reading today. Cross-reference with Galatians 3:23-29 and 1 Peter 2:9-12. Write what you learn about yourself in your journal.

Look up this passage in another translation of the Bible. Compare it to the NIV passage from this week. What new understanding does this give? Write down anything you learn from these verses that could shift the way you think and change the way you live.

▶ **ENGAGE WITH THE WORD: SEE YOUR STORY IN HIS STORY**

Read 1 Kings 11:1-13. Consider how pride and lust contributed to the downfall of Solomon, and how you can be careful not to make the same mistakes.

SESSION THREE / WEEK FOUR

EPHESIANS 3

VV. 1 - 13

GOD'S MARVELOUS PLAN FOR THE GENTILES

[1] For this reason I, Paul, the prisoner of Christ Jesus for the sake of you Gentiles— [2] Surely you have heard about the administration of God's grace that was given to me for you, [3] that is, the mystery made known to me by revelation, as I have already written briefly. [4] In reading this, then, you will be able to understand my insight into the mystery of Christ, [5] which was not made known to people in other generations as it has now been revealed by the Spirit to God's holy apostles and prophets. [6] This mystery is that through the gospel the Gentiles are heirs together with Israel, members

together of one body, and sharers together in the promise in Christ Jesus. [7] I became a servant of this gospel by the gift of God's grace given me through the working of his power. [8] Although I am less than the least of all the Lord's people, this grace was given me: to preach to the Gentiles the boundless riches of Christ, [9] and to make plain to everyone the administration of this mystery, which for ages past was kept hidden in God, who created all things. [10] His intent was that now, through the church, the manifold wisdom of God should be made known to the rulers and authorities in the heavenly realms, [11] according to his eternal purpose that he accomplished in Christ Jesus our Lord. [12] In him and through faith in him we may approach God with freedom and confidence. [13] I ask you, therefore, not to be discouraged because of my sufferings for you, which are your glory.

SESSION QUESTIONS

—

DAY 01   Read through the entire passage. Then go back to verse 1, noting how Paul describes himself compared to his actual physical location at the time he wrote this letter (refer to the background of Ephesians on p. 97 or an introduction to the letter in a study Bible). How can Paul, seeing himself as a "prisoner of Christ Jesus," help you shift your perspective regarding negative situations you find yourself in?

DAY 02   It's easy to let circumstances define us without realizing the reason God allows them. Go back through this passage again, looking for the bigger "mystery" with which Paul was entrusted, a mystery that dwarfed both prison (see v. 1) and suffering (see v. 13) in his eyes. Cross-reference Romans 8:18-31 for insight into what God says about your difficult circumstances. List the things you can know for certain from these verses.

DAY 03   Focus your attention on verses 10-13. How do you gain access to God? Read more about it in Hebrews 10:11-23.

DAY 04   Turn to 1 Chronicles 13:1-13 to read the story of Uzzah. How is this story different from what you read in Ephesians 3:12? (See also Heb. 4:14-16.)

DAY 05   Isn't it crazy to think that because Christ came, we are all now included in the family of God? How does knowing you are included in His family and invited to approach God at any time change your attitude about Him? About yourself? (See also Gal. 3:28 and Col. 3:11.)

▶ ENGAGE WITH THE WORD: SEE YOUR STORY IN HIS STORY

Read 1 Kings 12:1-20. What caused the kingdom to be divided? List the mistakes that both Rehoboam and Jeroboam made. What practical advice can you glean from these accounts that will help you in your daily decisions?

EPHESIANS 3

—

VV. 14-21

A PRAYER FOR THE EPHESIANS

[14] For this reason I kneel before the Father, [15] from whom every family in heaven and on earth derives its name. [16] I pray that out of his glorious riches he may strengthen you with power through his Spirit in your inner being, [17] so that Christ may dwell in your hearts through faith. And I pray that you, being rooted and established in love, [18] may have power, together with all the Lord's holy people, to grasp how wide and long and high and deep is the love of Christ, [19] and to know this love that surpasses knowledge—that you may be filled to the measure of all the fullness of God. [20] Now to him who is able to do immeasurably more than all we ask or imagine, according to his power that is at work within us, [21] to him be glory in the church and in Christ Jesus throughout all generations, forever and ever! Amen.

SESSION QUESTIONS

—

01 This section of Ephesians is a beautiful prayer from Paul for the Church at Ephesus and for every believer. Meditate on these stunning and wonderful thoughts as you turn them into a personal prayer for yourself.

02 As you read through this passage today, make a list of the truths you learn about God and yourself. Which is most meaningful to you and why?

03 Find the list you started in Week One on which you wrote down all the things you possess as a child of God (see Eph. 1:1-14). Go back through the passage, and add to your list all the things that Paul prayed would be yours through Christ.

04 Often we determine our worth based on how others react to us. Paul's words remind us that, as believers, we always exist in the unalterable, unending, and unconditional love of God. Sit quietly and breathe in the weight of verses 18-19, letting the vastness of God's love wash over you. Before you end your time with Jesus, write down any response, prayer, or worship song you may have in your heart as a result.

05 Begin by reading about the power of God in 1 Chronicles 29:11-12; Psalm 146:5-10; Isaiah 45:5-7; and Revelation 5:1-14. Then turn back to Ephesians 3:20-21. Where is God's power at work? What does it mean that God is the God who is "able to do immeasurably more"? How does it encourage you to think that this God of "immeasurably more" is at work within you?

▶ ENGAGE WITH THE WORD: SEE YOUR STORY IN HIS STORY

Read 1 Kings 16:29-33. Think about the times you've strayed from God and what caused your wandering. In what ways was God kind to you even when you didn't deserve it?

EPHESIANS 4

UNITY AND MATURITY IN THE BODY OF CHRIST

VV. 1-32

[1] As a prisoner for the Lord, then, I urge you to live a life worthy of the calling you have received. [2] Be completely humble and gentle; be patient, bearing with one another in love. [3] Make every effort to keep the unity of the Spirit through the bond of peace. [4] There is one body and one Spirit, just as you were called to one hope when you were called; [5] one Lord, one faith, one baptism; [6] one God and Father of all, who is over all and through all and in all. [7] But to each one of us grace has been given as Christ apportioned it. [8] This is why it says: "When he ascended on high, he took many captives and gave gifts to his people." [9] (What does "he ascended" mean except that he also descended to the lower, earthly regions? [10] He who descended is the very one who ascended higher than all the heavens, in order to fill the whole

universe.) [11] So Christ himself gave the apostles, the prophets, the evangelists, the pastors and teachers, [12] to equip his people for works of service, so that the body of Christ may be built up [13] until we all reach unity in the faith and in the knowledge of the Son of God and become mature, attaining to the whole measure of the fullness of Christ. [14] Then we will no longer be infants, tossed back and forth by the waves, and blown here and there by every wind of teaching and by the cunning and craftiness of people in their deceitful scheming. [15] Instead, speaking the truth in love, we will grow to become in every respect the mature body of him who is the head, that is, Christ. [16] From him the whole body, joined and held together by every supporting ligament, grows and builds itself up in love, as each part does its work.

INSTRUCTIONS *for* CHRISTIAN LIVING

[17] So I tell you this, and insist on it in the Lord, that you must no longer live as the Gentiles do, in the futility of their thinking. [18] They are darkened in their understanding and separated from the life of God because of the ignorance that is in them due to the hardening of their hearts. [19] Having lost all sensitivity, they have given themselves over to sensuality so as to indulge in every kind of impurity, and they are full of greed. [20] That, however, is not the way of life you learned [21] when you heard about Christ and were taught in him in accordance with the truth that is in Jesus. [22] You were taught, with regard to your former way of life, to put off your old self, which is being corrupted by its deceitful desires; [23] to be made new in the attitude of your minds; [24] and to put on the new self, created to be like God in true righteousness and holiness. [25] Therefore each of you must put off falsehood and speak truthfully to your neighbor, for we are all members of one body. [26] "In your anger do not sin": Do not let the sun go down while you are still angry, [27] and do not give the devil a foothold. [28] Anyone who has been stealing must steal no longer, but must work, doing something useful with their own hands, that they may have something to share with those in need. [29] Do not let any unwholesome talk come out of your mouths, but only what is helpful for building others up according to their needs, that it may benefit those who listen. [30] And do not grieve the Holy Spirit of God, with whom you were sealed for the day of redemption. [31] Get rid of all bitterness, rage and anger, brawling and slander, along with every form of malice. [32] Be kind and compassionate to one another, forgiving each other, just as in Christ God forgave you.

SESSION QUESTIONS

—

01   In chapter 4, Paul transitions from his emphasis on who we are in Christ to how we are to live based on and rooted in that understanding. As you read verses 1-16, think about the various relationships in your life at home, work, church, social settings, etc. How do those interactions influence how you think about yourself? Write down anything you discover in these verses that could provide a firm foundation from which to interact with those people.

02   Go back through the first section of the passage again, focusing on verses 14-16. What causes you to feel "tossed back and forth" and in what ways do you need to "grow to become in every respect the mature body of him"? Be as specific as you can when you write in your journal. Pray for wisdom to identify concrete steps you can take to move toward stability and maturity in these areas. Your mentee will reach out to you for accountability and encouragement as she put these steps into practice.

03   Move on to the middle portion of the chapter today, reading verses 17-24. Notice the difference between how the Gentiles live and what Paul says should be evident in a believer's life. Think more about any attitudes, actions, beliefs, and so forth. that are still hanging around from your "former way of life" and need to be "put off." Journal your thoughts.

04   Back up and start your reading today at verse 20, continuing through the end of the passage. Make two columns on a piece of paper. In the left column, list the attitudes and actions that Paul instructs us to "put off." Across from those, list the new thoughts and behaviors that we are told to "put on." Put a star by the one(s) that you struggle with the most. Cross-reference with Colossians 3:5-10; 1 Peter 2:1-3; and 2 Timothy 3:10-17. How can you specifically replace your old life attitudes with the new life you possess in Christ?

05   Read verse 1 carefully, and then go all the way through the entire passage. After your intentional study of this passage all week, underline or highlight anything you've learned about God or yourself that will help you "live a life worthy of the calling you have received."

▶   ENGAGE WITH THE WORD: **SEE YOUR STORY IN HIS STORY**

As you read 1 Kings 18:20–19:8, consider what you can learn about faith from Elijah's ups (victory at Mount Carmel) and downs (depression in the wilderness). What can you draw out of God's interaction with Elijah that will help you through your own ups and downs?

EPHESIANS 5

VV. 1-33

[1] Follow God's example, therefore, as dearly loved children [2] and walk in the way of love, just as Christ loved us and gave himself up for us as a fragrant offering and sacrifice to God. [3] But among you there must not be even a hint of sexual immorality, or of any kind of impurity, or of greed, because these are improper for God's holy people. [4] Nor should there be obscenity, foolish talk or coarse joking, which are out of place, but rather thanksgiving. [5] For of this you can be sure: No immoral, impure or greedy person—such a person is an idolater—has any inheritance in the kingdom of Christ and of God. [6] Let no one deceive you with empty words, for because of such things God's wrath comes on those who are disobedient. [7] Therefore do not be partners with them. [8] For you were once darkness, but now you are light in the Lord. Live as children of light [9] (for the fruit of the light consists in all goodness, righteousness and truth) [10] and find out what pleases the Lord.

¹¹ Have nothing to do with the fruitless deeds of darkness, but rather expose them. ¹² It is shameful even to mention what the disobedient do in secret. ¹³ But everything exposed by the light becomes visible—and everything that is illuminated becomes a light. ¹⁴ This is why it is said: "Wake up, sleeper, rise from the dead, and Christ will shine on you. ¹⁵ Be very careful, then, how you live—not as unwise but as wise, ¹⁶ making the most of every opportunity, because the days are evil. ¹⁷ Therefore do not be foolish, but understand what the Lord's will is. ¹⁸ Do not get drunk on wine, which leads to debauchery. Instead, be filled with the Spirit, ¹⁹ speaking to one another with psalms, hymns, and songs from the Spirit. Sing and make music from your heart to the Lord, ²⁰ always giving thanks to God the Father for everything, in the name of our Lord Jesus Christ.

INSTRUCTIONS FOR CHRISTIAN HOUSEHOLDS

---

²¹ Submit to one another out of reverence for Christ. ²² Wives, submit yourselves to your own husbands as you do to the Lord. ²³ For the husband is the head of the wife as Christ is the head of the church, his body, of which he is the Savior. ²⁴ Now as the church submits to Christ, so also wives should submit to their husbands in everything. ²⁵ Husbands, love your wives, just as Christ loved the church and gave himself up for her ²⁶ to make her holy, cleansing her by the washing with water through the word, ²⁷ and to present her to himself as a radiant church, without stain or wrinkle or any other blemish, but holy and blameless. ²⁸ In this same way, husbands ought to love their wives as their own bodies. He who loves his wife loves himself. ²⁹ After all, no one ever hated their own body, but they feed and care for their body, just as Christ does the church— ³⁰ for we are members of his body. ³¹ "For this reason a man will leave his father and mother and be united to his wife, and the two will become one flesh." ³² This is a profound mystery— but I am talking about Christ and the church. ³³ However, each one of you also must love his wife as he loves himself, and the wife must respect her husband.

SESSION QUESTIONS

—

01 Chapter 5 is a direct continuation of the exhortations Paul gave for living a life worthy of your calling in Christ Jesus in Ephesians 4:1. Read through verses 1-20, then grab your two-columned list that you started last week. In the same way as last week, add what you find in this passage. Again, star any areas that are especially troublesome for you. Be available should your mentee desire your help in praying through these things.

02 Go back through verses 1-20 again, this time looking for the motivation Paul gives for making these changes. Why is it so important to understand all you have been given in Christ and let it affect your thinking before it affects your actions? Pull out your list again and circle the things on the right side that you are most thankful for today. End your time praying and worshiping God, asking Him to help you live a life worthy of His call—not to earn love or favor, but because you've already been given everything in Christ.

03 Start your day with a practical application of verses 19-20. Listen to some worship music, and play it several times throughout the rest of the week. Which lyrics from the songs grabbed your attention and spoke to your heart? Write them down someplace you can see them throughout the week.

04 Move into the second half of Ephesians 5 and read verses 21-33. Consider carefully how verse 21 relates to the rest of the chapter. Make notes on how submission and love go hand in hand.

05 Revisit all of Ephesians 5 to close out this week of study with emphasis on what it says about relationships to others. Cross-reference 1 Corinthians 13; 2 Corinthians 6:14-16; and Titus 2:1-15. Your mentee may share something that comes up in her reading that she does not understand, that she is having trouble with in her life, or that amazes her and is blowing her heart up in the best way. If she does, meet her with love and encouragement.

Continue listening to worship music in your routine for the rest of the session.

▶ ENGAGE WITH THE WORD: **SEE YOUR STORY IN HIS STORY**

Read 2 Kings 6:8-19. Think about the way God was faithful to Elisha and apply that to your own story of faith. Thank God for His faithfulness to you today.

EPHESIANS 6

VV. 1-24

[1] Children, obey your parents in the Lord, for this is right. [2] "Honor your father and mother"—which is the first commandment with a promise— [3] "so that it may go well with you and that you may enjoy long life on the earth." [4] Fathers, do not exasperate your children; instead, bring them up in the training and instruction of the Lord. [5] Slaves, obey your earthly masters with respect and fear, and with sincerity of heart, just as you would obey Christ. [6] Obey them not only to win their favor when their eye is on you, but as slaves of Christ, doing the will of God from your heart. [7] Serve wholeheartedly, as if you were serving the Lord, not people, [8] because you know that the Lord will reward each one for whatever good they do, whether they are slave or free. [9] And masters, treat your slaves in the same way. Do not threaten them, since you know that he who is both their master and yours is in heaven, and there is no favoritism with him.

THE ARMOR OF GOD

[10] Finally, be strong in the Lord and in his mighty power. [11] Put on the full armor of God, so that you can take your stand against the devil's schemes. [12] For our struggle is not against flesh and blood, but against the rulers, against the authorities, against the powers of this dark world and against the spiritual forces of evil in the heavenly realms. [13] Therefore put on the full armor of God, so that when the day of evil comes, you may be able to stand your ground, and after you have done everything, to stand. [14] Stand firm then, with the belt of truth buckled around your waist, with the breastplate of righteousness in place, [15] and with your feet fitted with the readiness that comes from the gospel of peace. [16] In addition to all this, take up the shield of faith, with which you can extinguish all the flaming arrows of the evil one. [17] Take the helmet of salvation and the sword of the Spirit, which is the word of God. [18] And pray in the Spirit on all occasions with all kinds of prayers and requests. With this in mind, be alert and always keep on praying for all the Lord's people. [19] Pray also for me, that whenever I speak, words may be given me so that I will fearlessly make known the mystery of the gospel, [20] for which I am an ambassador in chains. Pray that I may declare it fearlessly, as I should.

FINAL GREETINGS

[21] Tychicus, the dear brother and faithful servant in the Lord, will tell you everything, so that you also may know how I am and what I am doing. [22] I am sending him to you for this very purpose, that you may know how we are, and that he may encourage you. [23] Peace to the brothers and sisters, and love with faith from God the Father and the Lord Jesus Christ. [24] Grace to all who love our Lord Jesus Christ with an undying love.

SESSION QUESTIONS

—

WEEK NINE

01   Before you read the first section of Ephesians 6, go back and reread 5:21 from last week. Write it above Ephesians 6:1. Think about how that verse gives context and motivation for what you read in 6:1-9.

02   Begin by thinking about how your connections to parents, children, friends, employees, employers, and others shape your view of yourself. Reread the section from yesterday again, pausing at verse 7. How could serving others change the dynamics in those relationships and provide lasting stability? What specific relationships come to mind and in what ways could you serve them?

03   Continue reading Ephesians 6, starting at verse 10 and moving through the end of the chapter. Look up Matthew 16:23; John 8:44; John 10:10; 2 Corinthians 11:3,14; and 1 Peter 5:8-11 to learn more about the character and mission of Satan. What do you gather about him from these passages? How does that help your understanding and appreciation of Ephesians 6:10-20?

04   Find and read Job 1:1–2:10. Notice the different strategies Satan used to attack Job and the power he had to manipulate forces and environments. Think about this story in the context of what you learn from Ephesians 6:10-18, and then relate it to your specific situation(s).

05   Go back through Ephesians 6:10-24. Underline every command to "stand" and every reference to "pray" or "prayer." What can you conclude from what you found? What are some people or situations you want to cover in prayer? How can you "put on" the armor of God today? Be specific, going through each piece of armor and thinking about what it means and how it can be personal to you today.

▶   ENGAGE WITH THE WORD: **SEE YOUR STORY IN HIS STORY**

Observe how Isaiah foretold the rise and fall of nations as you read Isaiah 3:1-3,8-14; 14:1-5; 49:8-9,13-18. What can you learn from this that helps you find stability in light of the instability in our world today?

IDENTITY

—

GOALS

▲   To become well-established in the truth of who we are in Christ.

▲   To grasp the importance of knowing what God says about our identities in order to protect ourselves from the lies of the enemy or others' hurtful words.

▲   To understand how an identity rooted in Christ will determine the direction of our days, weeks, and lives.

SESSION QUESTIONS
---

1. What are some lies you've believed about your identity?

2. Which lie do you feel will be the hardest to overcome in regard to who you truly are in Christ?

3. What truth have you found in God's Word to replace that lie?

4. How can you begin to uproot the lies and build on truth? (For example: memorize a verse or passage of Scripture, prayer, accountability.)

IV

CALLING

SESSION FOUR

—

Calling: noun call•ing \ˈkȯ-liŋ\ : "a strong inner impulse toward a particular course of action especially when accompanied by conviction of divine influence."[1] Do you know your calling? Or is it more like a dream right now? Could it be possible that it's not up to us to figure out our grand calling, but we should instead position ourselves in God's hand and wait for Him to reveal it to us and, by faith, lead us there? We believe the answer is *yes*. Thankfully, our first calling is to a Person, to Jesus, not to a role or talent (i.e., career, motherhood, or missions) or to a place (i.e., workplace, inner city, or another nation). Although roles, talents, and locations are great and often God given, what freedom we have knowing that we are called to our Father through Christ and given the power of the Holy Spirit to first and foremost know Him and bring Him glory! Any other calling is secondary, marked by the truth that we all have specific gifts, desires, and unique ways in which our primary calling is lived out.

1. "Definition of Calling." *Merriam-Webster's Dictionary* https://www.merriam-webster.com/dictionary/calling

This means in every season, and wherever we are on the spectrum of knowing this secondary "calling," we are only responsible for our personal answer to God's ultimate call. Of course, we can say we are called to be a teacher, a mama, a doctor, a missionary, an artist, or an entrepreneur. We may sense a pull toward politics or the corporate world, and the list goes on and on. However, these roles always complement, bolster, and point to the One who first called us by name. We have been called "out of darkness into his marvelous light"! (1 Pet. 2:9, ESV). He knows our names, and through Christ He has redeemed and restored us so that we can step into all He dreams for us—for our good and for His glory. When this truth transforms our hearts, it becomes infused into our dreams and desires and helps shape, guide, and even unearth the gifts and talents God has given us.

PHILIPPIANS

Some of the most memorable verses and inspiring teaching in all the Scriptures are found in the Book of Philippians. It is in this letter to the Church at Philippi that the apostle Paul articulates the importance of dying completely to this world in order to know Christ, to have the power of His resurrection at work in our lives, and to take hold of the high calling which God has assigned us to achieve in Jesus Christ. It is in Philippians that some of the most comforting and reassuring words are said about our trials in this life and how we can have peace in our hearts in the midst of the storms. Paul gets personal as he speaks of his deep love for the Church and his desire for unity and humility, urging the Philippians to live lives worthy of the calling they've received. We as followers of Jesus can also look to this Scripture and let it soak straight into our lives, asking for the same humility Jesus has and praying God will give us beautiful dreams and lives that are "worthy of the calling."

PHILIPPIANS 1

—

VV. 1-11

[1] Paul and Timothy, servants of Christ Jesus, To all God's holy people in Christ Jesus at Philippi, together with the overseers and deacons: [2] Grace and peace to you from God our Father and the Lord Jesus Christ.

THANKSGIVING AND PRAYER

[3] I thank my God every time I remember you. [4] In all my prayers for all of you, I always pray with joy [5] because of your partnership in the gospel from the first day until now, [6] being confident of this, that he who began a good work in you will carry it on to completion until the day of Christ Jesus. [7] It is right for me to feel this way about all of you, since I have you in my heart and, whether I am in chains or defending and confirming the gospel, all of you share in God's grace with me. [8] God can testify how I long for all of you with the affection of Christ Jesus. [9] And this is my prayer: that your love may abound more and more in knowledge and depth of insight, [10] so that you may be able to discern what is best and may be pure and blameless for the day of Christ, [11] filled with the fruit of righteousness that comes through Jesus Christ— to the glory and praise of God.

SESSION QUESTIONS

—

WEEK ONE

DAY 01   Grab a study Bible or search BibleGateway.com to read a more in-depth background and overview of the Book of Philippians. With a fresh understanding of the context, read verses 1-11. Make notes about your first impressions. What verse stood out to you?

DAY 02   Go back through the passage again, this time remembering our calling to be like Christ, and underline any specific phrases or words that speak directly to you. How can you apply this uniquely to your own life today?

DAY 03   Focus in on verse 6, and write it in your journal. How might this promise be an encouragement in times when you are unsure about God's will? Offer a prayer to God for something you know He "began … in you," and commit your trust to Him that He will "carry it on to completion."

DAY 04   Often our struggle with calling centers on the need to provide for ourselves and our families. Turn to Matthew 6:25-33 to hear Jesus speak to those issues. How do you feel after reading this Scripture?

DAY 05   Thoughts of food and clothing occupied much of the disciples' lives, and perhaps we can relate. Meditate on the passage from yesterday. What things occupy your thinking and lead to worry? What does Jesus say here to alleviate those anxieties?

▶ **ENGAGE WITH THE WORD:** SEE YOUR STORY IN HIS STORY

As you read Jeremiah 2:4-8,13 and Ezekiel 6:1-10, take note of the main themes of the prophets' messages. How is what they said to Israel relevant to your life today?

SESSION FOUR / WEEK TWO

PHILIPPIANS 1

—

PAUL'S CHAINS ADVANCE THE GOSPEL

[12] Now I want you to know, brothers and sisters, that what has happened to me has actually served to advance the gospel. [13] As a result, it has become clear throughout the whole palace guard and to everyone else that I am in chains for Christ. [14] And because of my chains, most of the brothers and sisters have become confident in the Lord and dare all the more to proclaim the gospel without fear. [15] It is true that some preach Christ out of envy and rivalry, but others out of goodwill. [16] The latter do so out of love, knowing that I am put here for the defense of the gospel. [17] The former preach Christ out of selfish ambition, not sincerely, supposing that they can stir up trouble for me while I am in chains. [18] But what does it matter? The important thing is that in every way, whether from false motives or true, Christ is preached. And because of this I rejoice. Yes, and I will continue to rejoice, [19] for I know that through your prayers and God's provision of the Spirit of Jesus Christ what has happened to me will turn out for my deliverance. [20] I eagerly expect and hope that I will in no way be ashamed, but will have sufficient courage so that now as always Christ will be exalted in my body, whether by life or by death. [21] For to me, to live is Christ and to die is gain. [22] If I am to go on living in the body, this will mean fruitful labor for me. Yet what shall I choose? I do not know! [23] I am torn between the two: I desire to depart and be with Christ, which is better by far; [24] but it is more necessary for you that I remain in the body. [25] Convinced of this, I know that I will remain, and I will continue with all of you for your progress and joy in the faith, [26] so that through my being with you again your boasting in Christ Jesus will abound on account of me.

SESSION QUESTIONS

—

WEEK TWO

DAY 01 Before you read, remind yourself of Paul's physical location and the circumstances that led to the writing of this letter. As you read this week, continually remember the lens of his circumstances through which he wrote.

DAY 02 Turn to Acts 9:1-22. Briefly describe the clear calling on Paul's life. How does reading Paul's story of coming to faith remind you of your own story with Jesus? How did God call you to Himself? How has your primary calling affected your secondary calling? (Or, if you are still in the process of figuring that out, how does your primary calling apply to your current job, title, role, position, or gifting?)

DAY 03 If you were in Paul's situation, what would likely be your normal response? Go back through this week's passage and think about how Paul's godly, heavenward perspective can challenge you when you face things that seem like a setback to your calling.

DAY 04 Read the passage again. Highlight the two benefits of captivity that Paul recognized. (See Phil. 1:12-14.) Pray for courage and for Christ to be exalted as you live your day-to-day life and calling; make the prayer specific to you. Think about different situations or relationships in which you want to infuse the gospel with love and bravery.

DAY 05 Reread the last half of this section of Philippians as you think about the disappointments, interruptions, or complications that have cropped up in the pursuit of your calling. Consider how God could be using what may seem like blockades to actually further, widen, or deepen His call on your life. Journal your thoughts, and share them with your mentee the next time you meet.

▶ **ENGAGE WITH THE WORD:** SEE YOUR STORY IN HIS STORY

Read Ezekiel 37:1-14. How does God's promise of restoration for His people give you hope today?

PHILIPPIANS 1

—

VV. 27-30

LIFE WORTHY OF THE GOSPEL

[27] Whatever happens, conduct yourselves in a manner worthy of the gospel of Christ. Then, whether I come and see you or only hear about you in my absence, I will know that you stand firm in the one Spirit, striving together as one for the faith of the gospel [28] without being frightened in any way by those who oppose you. This is a sign to them that they will be destroyed, but that you will be saved—and that by God. [29] For it has been granted to you on behalf of Christ not only to believe in him, but also to suffer for him, [30] since you are going through the same struggle you saw I had, and now hear that I still have.

SESSION QUESTIONS

—

WEEK THREE

DAY 01   Read the Scripture, and mark any phrases or words that jump out at you. What do you learn about God from this section? About yourself?

DAY 02   Revisit the same passage of Scripture again, and reflect on the portion of verse 27 that begins: "Whatever happens …" Write your thoughts in your journal.

DAY 03   Read the passage again and jot down a few notes about what you think it means to "conduct yourselves in a manner worthy of the gospel of Christ." Also check out Galatians 5:13-26 and 1 Peter 2:11-25. Write down the verse from these three passages that speaks to you most today.

DAY 04   Look at verses 27-28. In what ways can people "who oppose you" (or your attitude toward them) interfere with your calling? Think of practical ways to "stand firm" in these situations. Refer back to yesterday for help on how to "conduct yourselves."

DAY 05   Meditate on verse 29 of the passage and think about what it means "to suffer for him." Flip to Romans 5:1-5 and 1 Peter 4:12-19, and add any insight from those passages to your notes. How does this truth reframe any suffering you may be experiencing?

▶ ENGAGE WITH THE WORD: SEE YOUR STORY IN HIS STORY

Read Daniel 1:8-21. In what ways do you see Daniel exhibit his faith in God? How can truths from Daniel's life be applied to your life when you face difficult circumstances?

PHILIPPIANS 2

—

VV. 1-11

IMITATING CHRIST'S HUMILITY

[1] Therefore if you have any encouragement from being united with Christ, if any comfort from his love, if any common sharing in the Spirit, if any tenderness and compassion, [2] then make my joy complete by being like-minded, having the same love, being one in spirit and of one mind. [3] Do nothing out of selfish ambition or vain conceit. Rather, in humility value others above yourselves, [4] not looking to your own interests but each of you to the interests of the others. [5] In your relationships with one another, have the same mindset as Christ Jesus: [6] Who, being in very nature God, did not consider equality with God something to be used to his own advantage; [7] rather, he made himself nothing by taking the very nature of a servant, being made in human likeness. [8] And being found in appearance as a man, he humbled himself by becoming obedient to death—even death on a cross! [9] Therefore God exalted him to the highest place and gave him the name that is above every name, [10] that at the name of Jesus every knee should bow, in heaven and on earth and under the earth, [11] and every tongue acknowledge that Jesus Christ is Lord, to the glory of God the Father.

SESSION QUESTIONS

—

DAY 01   Read the Scripture, and make a list of everything you learn about God in this passage. What words or phrases stand out?

DAY 02   When thinking about your unique calling, it's easy to have tunnel vision on your personal dreams, desires, ambitions, and goals. What critical shift in focus does this passage give? How does it provide a renewed perspective?

DAY 03   Read the passage again. Explore the concepts of "selfish ambition" and "vain conceit" (v. 3). What practical, others-centered instructions does Paul give believers in Romans 12:3-21? Journal through a couple of the verses that stood out to you. What is one way you can put these verses into practice today?

DAY 04   Read the Scripture again and ponder the place of humility in the pursuit of your calling. Refer to Matthew 23:11-12; Luke 18:9-14; and James 4:7-10. Text your mentee the passage that spoke to you most and why.

DAY 05   Go back and reread your list from Day One of this week. Think of practical ways to apply verse 5 and how you can have "the same mindset" as Jesus in your relationships with others.

▶   **ENGAGE WITH THE WORD:** SEE YOUR STORY IN HIS STORY

    Think about what you learned about prayer from Daniel as you read Daniel 6.

PHILIPPIANS 2

VV. 12 - 30

DO EVERYTHING WITHOUT GRUMBLING

¹² Therefore, my dear friends, as you have always obeyed—not only in my presence, but now much more in my absence—continue to work out your salvation with fear and trembling, ¹³ for it is God who works in you to will and to act in order to fulfill his good purpose. ¹⁴ Do everything without grumbling or arguing, ¹⁵ so that you may become blameless and pure, "children of God without fault in a warped and crooked generation." Then you will shine among them like stars in the sky ¹⁶ as you hold firmly to the word of life. And then I will be able to boast on the day of Christ that I did not run or labor in vain. ¹⁷ But even if I am being poured out like a drink offering on the sacrifice and service coming from your faith, I am glad and rejoice with all of you. ¹⁸ So you too should be glad and rejoice with me.

TIMOTHY & EPAPHRODITUS

[19] I hope in the Lord Jesus to send Timothy to you soon, that I also may be cheered when I receive news about you. [20] I have no one else like him, who will show genuine concern for your welfare. [21] For everyone looks out for their own interests, not those of Jesus Christ. [22] But you know that Timothy has proved himself, because as a son with his father he has served with me in the work of the gospel. [23] I hope, therefore, to send him as soon as I see how things go with me. [24] And I am confident in the Lord that I myself will come soon. [25] But I think it is necessary to send back to you Epaphroditus, my brother, co-worker and fellow soldier, who is also your messenger, whom you sent to take care of my needs. [26] For he longs for all of you and is distressed because you heard he was ill. [27] Indeed he was ill, and almost died. But God had mercy on him, and not on him only but also on me, to spare me sorrow upon sorrow. [28] Therefore I am all the more eager to send him, so that when you see him again you may be glad and I may have less anxiety. [29] So then, welcome him in the Lord with great joy, and honor people like him, [30] because he almost died for the work of Christ. He risked his life to make up for the help you yourselves could not give me.

SESSION QUESTIONS

—

DAY 01 Reread verses 5-11 before moving on to this section. What practical instruction does Paul offer in verses 12-30, and how can it lead to having "the same mindset as Christ Jesus" in your relationships with others?

DAY 02 Read the passage again then return to verse 12. Consider how your attitude, actions, and obedience to God might differ in the "presence" or "absence" of others. How might these differences or discrepancies positively or negatively impact the pursuit of your calling?

DAY 03 Look up verses 12-13 in several versions of the Bible. (Choose at least one modern language paraphrase.) Compare what you read to gain insight into what it means to "work out your salvation with fear and trembling." Connect this phrase with what you read in verse 13. For deeper understanding, consult the notes in a study Bible or commentary on the Book of Philippians. Journal your thoughts, and thank God for His work in you to "fulfill his good purpose."

DAY 04 Move on to verses 14-18. How is verse 14 the key to the rest of what Paul says? Commit to do this truly radical thing for one entire day. Can you make it two days? Three? Write down how this practice might benefit your pursuit of Christ and the realization of your calling.

DAY 05 Go through the last half of the passage, thinking about what you can learn about dedication to your calling from the words Paul used to describe Timothy and Epaphroditus. From yesterday: What has been the most challenging part of not complaining? Journal any patterns you may have noticed and anything that surprised you. Ask God to help you with the things revealed by this exercise and to continue to put "do everything without grumbling" into practice.

▶ **ENGAGE WITH THE WORD: SEE YOUR STORY IN HIS STORY**

Read Zechariah 8:1-8. Parallel God's mercy toward Israel to any experience you have with His rescuing power.

PHILIPPIANS 3

NO CONFIDENCE IN THE FLESH

[1] Further, my brothers and sisters, rejoice in the Lord! It is no trouble for me to write the same things to you again, and it is a safeguard for you. [2] Watch out for those dogs, those evildoers, those mutilators of the flesh. [3] For it is we who are the circumcision, we who serve God by his Spirit, who boast in Christ Jesus, and who put no confidence in the flesh — [4] though I myself have reasons for such confidence. If someone else thinks they have reasons to put confidence in the flesh, I have more: [5] circumcised on the eighth day, of the people of Israel, of the tribe of Benjamin, a Hebrew of Hebrews; in regard to the law, a Pharisee; [6] as for zeal, persecuting the church; as for righteousness based on the law, faultless. [7] But whatever were gains to me I now consider loss for the sake of Christ. [8] What is more, I consider everything a loss because of the surpassing worth of knowing Christ Jesus my Lord, for whose sake I have lost all things. I consider them garbage, that I may gain Christ [9] and be found in him, not having a righteousness of my own that comes from the law, but that which is through faith in Christ—the righteousness that comes from God on the basis of faith. [10] I want to know Christ—yes, to know the power of his resurrection and participation in his sufferings, becoming like him in his death, [11] and so, somehow, attaining to the resurrection from the dead.

[12] Not that I have already obtained all this, or have already arrived at my goal, but I press on to take hold of that for which Christ Jesus took hold of me. [13] Brothers and sisters, I do not consider myself yet to have taken hold of it. But one thing I do: Forgetting what is behind and straining toward what is ahead, [14] I press on toward the goal to win the prize for which God has called me heavenward in Christ Jesus.

SESSION QUESTIONS

—

WEEK SIX

DAY 01 Read through the passage, then return to verse 1. Write down how rejoicing in the Lord is a "safeguard." Worship is simply our response to what God has done. Use Psalm 5 as a guide and, as with all the psalms this week, feel free to journal, sing, pray, draw (or whatever your response of choice may be) as you respond to what these verses elicit in your heart for God.

DAY 02 Compare this passage with a paraphrase version of it. What new understanding does the comparison provide? Rejoice in the Lord using Psalm 11.

DAY 03 Read through Paul's personal résumé in verses 4-6. Write down some things you would include on your own résumé. Name as many accomplishments and achievements as you can. Copy verse 7 at the top of your list. Use Psalm 16 as your worship song to Jesus today. Write down the verse from the Psalms passage that is most meaningful to you today, and share it with your mentee.

DAY 04 Begin at verse 7, reading the rest of the passage. Add notes to the list you began yesterday about how your strengths could actually become a detriment to your calling. Let Psalm 19 become your guide to rejoicing in the Lord today.

DAY 05 Zero in on the last three verses of this passage. What do you need to forget in order to "press on toward the goal" of your calling? Be specific. Use Psalm 33 to rejoice in the Lord.

Continue this habit of rejoicing in the Lord next week and beyond.

▶ **ENGAGE WITH THE WORD: SEE YOUR STORY IN HIS STORY**

Read Ezra 1–2:1. As you consider the Jews returning to their land to rebuild the temple, think about where God dwells today. Refer to 1 Corinthians 6:19; Galatians 2:20; and Hebrews 9:1-26; 10:19-22.

PHILIPPIANS 3

VV. 15-21

FOLLOWING PAUL'S EXAMPLE

[15] All of us, then, who are mature should take such a view of things. And if on some point you think differently, that too God will make clear to you. [16] Only let us live up to what we have already attained. [17] Join together in following my example, brothers and sisters, and just as you have us as a model, keep your eyes on those who live as we do. [18] For, as I have often told you before and now tell you again even with tears, many live as enemies of the cross of Christ. [19] Their destiny is destruction, their god is their stomach, and their glory is in their shame. Their mind is set on earthly things. [20] But our citizenship is in heaven. And we eagerly await a Savior from there, the Lord Jesus Christ, [21] who, by the power that enables him to bring everything under his control, will transform our lowly bodies so that they will be like his glorious body.

SESSION QUESTIONS

—

DAY 01 Read through Philippians 3:15-21. Go back and reread verse 15. What "things" are we to have a correct "view" of? Read the last few verses from last week's study to help you answer this question.

DAY 02 Focus your attention on verses 17-21 as you go through the passage again. Compare what Paul says to what you read in Psalm 1.

DAY 03 Make a list of people you interact with regularly. Which of them exhibit godly characteristics to be emulated (see v. 17), and which could be better described by verses 18-19? How does Paul's posture in verse 18 illustrate the attitude we are to have toward those people?

DAY 04 Think more about how your calling can be encouraged or discouraged by the relationships you listed yesterday. Add insights from Proverbs 13:20; 22:24-25; 27:5-6,17; and Ecclesiastes 4:9-10 to what you've learned in this passage. Identify a mutually beneficial and encouraging relationship in your life that could be described as iron sharpening iron. Today thank someone who is pushing you toward all God has called you to be.

DAY 05 At the end of the passage, Paul shifts focus from this life to the reality of the life to come. Read verses 20-21, thinking about how a heavenly mind-set can be a catalyst to embracing your calling.

▶ **ENGAGE WITH THE WORD: SEE YOUR STORY IN HIS STORY**

As you read Esther 3:1-6; 4:1-17 this week, observe the character qualities in Queen Esther that you can cultivate in your life.

EIGHT

PHILIPPIANS 4

VV. 1-9

CLOSING APPEAL FOR STEADFASTNESS AND UNITY

[1] Therefore, my brothers and sisters, you whom I love and long for, my joy and crown, stand firm in the Lord in this way, dear friends! [2] I plead with Euodia and I plead with Syntyche to be of the same mind in the Lord. [3] Yes, and I ask you, my true companion, help these women since they have contended at my side in the cause of the gospel, along with Clement and the rest of my co-workers, whose names are in the book of life.

FINAL EXHORTATIONS

[4] Rejoice in the Lord always. I will say it again: Rejoice! [5] Let your gentleness be evident to all. The Lord is near. [6] Do not be anxious about anything, but in every situation, by prayer and petition, with thanksgiving, present your requests to God. [7] And the peace of God, which transcends all understanding, will guard your hearts and your minds in Christ Jesus. [8] Finally, brothers and sisters, whatever is true, whatever is noble, whatever is right, whatever is pure, whatever is lovely, whatever is admirable—if anything is excellent or praiseworthy—think about such things. [9] Whatever you have learned or received or heard from me, or seen in me—put it into practice. And the God of peace will be with you.

SESSION QUESTIONS

—

WEEK EIGHT

DAY 01   Read last week's passage again before moving on to this week's reading. How do the passages speak to your ability to "stand firm" (v. 1)?

DAY 02   Verses 2-3 address Euodia and Syntyche, two women in the Church at Philippi whose disagreement was significant enough to be addressed by Paul publicly. What was his instruction to these women and to the Church in general about the situation? Apply this to any disagreements you have with other believers.

DAY 03   Pick up your reading at verse 4. How do your fears and anxieties get in the way of pursuing your calling?

DAY 04   Read through the same section of Scripture you read yesterday. According to these verses, what is the remedy for anxiety? Look up Isaiah 41:8-10, and add any new insights, citing specific verses from either passage that spoke to you. Write them on a card, and place it where you'll see it daily, asking God to remind you of the peace He gives you.

DAY 05   Read through the entire passage again and focus on verse 8. Consider how your thoughts positively or negatively impact your calling. Copy this verse on a sticky note or set a phone reminder with the verse to pop up daily. Use it as a practical challenge to shift your thinking according to its instruction. Memorize it and meditate on it.

▶ **ENGAGE WITH THE WORD:** SEE YOUR STORY IN HIS STORY

Read Nehemiah 4. Think about Nehemiah's difficulties in rebuilding Jerusalem's walls and how you can cultivate a similar dependence on God when you face opposition.

PHILIPPIANS 4

V V . 1 0 - 2 3

THANKS FOR THEIR GIFTS

[10] I rejoiced greatly in the Lord that at last you renewed your concern for me. Indeed, you were concerned, but you had no opportunity to show it. [11] I am not saying this because I am in need, for I have learned to be content whatever the circumstances. [12] I know what it is to be in need, and I know what it is to have plenty. I have learned the secret of being content in any and every situation, whether well fed or hungry, whether living in plenty or in want. [13] I can do all this through him who gives me strength.

[14] Yet it was good of you to share in my troubles. [15] Moreover, as you Philippians know, in the early days of your acquaintance with the gospel, when I set out from Macedonia, not one church shared with me in the matter of giving and receiving, except you only; [16] for even when I was in Thessalonica, you sent me aid more than once when I was in need. [17] Not that I desire your gifts; what I desire is that more be credited to your account. [18] I have received full payment and have more than enough. I am amply supplied, now that I have received from Epaphroditus the gifts you sent. They are a fragrant offering, an acceptable sacrifice, pleasing to God. [19] And my God will meet all your needs according to the riches of his glory in Christ Jesus. [20] To our God and Father be glory for ever and ever. Amen.

FINAL GREETINGS

[21] Greet all God's people in Christ Jesus. The brothers and sisters who are with me send greetings. [22] All God's people here send you greetings, especially those who belong to Caesar's household. [23] The grace of the Lord Jesus Christ be with your spirit. Amen.

SESSION QUESTIONS

—

DAY 01   Read the passage of Scripture completely, then return to verses 11-12. Does your sense of contentment change according to your circumstances? How? What does this tell you about the source of your contentment?

DAY 02   Read the passage again. What was the "secret" of Paul's contentment? Look up Psalm 28 to remind yourself of the strength and trustworthiness of God. Reflect on and memorize Psalm 28:7.

DAY 03   What were the gifts Paul was speaking of in verses 14-18? As you think about the investment that the Philippian Church made in Paul, consider how investing in others (individuals and ministries) might be a part of your calling. Who or what comes to mind?

DAY 04   Verse 19 is an often quoted passage of Scripture. Write how it is connected to what the Philippian Church did for Paul. How might that change your desire to invest in kingdom activities?

DAY 05   Get your Scripture, and read through all four chapters of Philippians. With regard to your calling, write out the biggest lesson, insight, challenge, or encouragement that you learned from the study of this book.

▶   **ENGAGE WITH THE WORD:** SEE YOUR STORY IN HIS STORY

As you read Malachi 3:6-14, think about how the Israelites displeased the Lord. Do you make similar mistakes? What can you do to safeguard yourself from these errors?

CALLING

—

⛰ To align our lives with our true calling—to follow Jesus.

⛰ To be able to come under the love Jesus has for us and trust His perfect plan and timing.

⛰ To see the magnitude of how important it is to first align ourselves with our true calling—to follow Jesus

⛰ To understand how our true calling will ultimately lead us to better live out other expressions of calling in our lives through passions, gifts, skills, work, and life goals.

SESSION QUESTIONS

1. What have you believed about your calling up to this point in your life?

2. How is God changing your perspective on your calling through His Word?

3. Your true calling is to follow Jesus. If that is your first and greatest priority, how do you think that priority will influence all other areas of life you feel called to live out? (For example, through work, passions, gifts, and goals.)

KINSHIP

SESSION FIVE

Parents and children. Friends and coworkers. Siblings and in-laws. Marriage and dating. Our lives are filled with relationships, and we were created to be in close community with others. Relationships are amazing and challenging, inspiring, and at times just plain hard. Isn't it true that in many of the connections with those whom we love the most, we experience communication breakdowns, discouragement, and unmet expectations? As we depend on Christ to do within us that which we cannot do on our own, we (and our relationships) will be strengthened and filled with the fruit of the Spirit.

If we have placed our faith in Jesus, He has brought us to new life and His Spirit lives in us! As we learn to walk with the Spirit, He produces His fruit in our lives: "love, joy, peace, patience, kindness, goodness, faithfulness, gentleness, self-control" (Gal. 5:22-23, ESV). In our own strength, growing in godliness is a daunting and impossible task. But God has given us His Spirit, and as we draw near to Him, we are able to see ourselves and our relationships through the lens of His heart and all He has both for us and for those around us. We may feel like we have relationship struggles that are outside of our control, and we may in part. We cannot control others, but we have full access to the God in heaven who made each person. As we are filled with His love, we can love truly and deeply. When we experience His peace, we rest in confidence and are able to be secure in our relationships with others. When the patience and kindness of God, the goodness and faithfulness and gentleness and self-control of Christ flow into our lives in a steady stream, all of our relationships will be affected by the torrent of grace it produces. This overflow transforms us and touches every single relationship in our lives inasmuch as we will surrender it to Christ. He fills every communication gap and meets all of the expectations people around us just can't meet. As we dive into the Scripture in the weeks to come, we pray we'll see how we are powerful influences to the people closest to us and to an unbelieving world.

RUTH

Set in the dark, immoral time when judges ruled over Israel, the Book of Ruth is the beautiful story of the redemption of a Moabite woman and her family. The fact that a non-Jewish woman made it into the Scriptures, even headlining an entire book, is actually pretty unbelievable. Ruth is set in the original Jewish Scriptures directly after Proverbs, with the same word for "noble woman" used in Proverbs 31 also used to describe Ruth just pages later. Her story opens after a desperate time of famine in Israel and the surrounding land. Naomi, Ruth's mother-in-law, lost her husband and both her sons. Ruth lost her husband. They both lost everything. Ruth was encouraged to return to her family to start over, yet the faith of her husband's family had sparked something in her heart, and she followed their God. With conviction she exclaimed to her mother-in-law Naomi, "Your people will be my people and your God my God" (Ruth 1:16b). What grace this displays, reminding us that no matter the "foreign land" we've come from, we are never excluded from being a part of God's family! All over the pages of this book we find Ruth's beautiful character, her (and our) God, and a hint of His perfect Son to come. We see Jesus foreshadowed especially through the person of Boaz, who shows up at the moment of Ruth's greatest need to extend grace, mercy, generosity, and love by "buying" Ruth into a family and meeting her greatest earthly needs. Boaz was her kinsman redeemer (guardian-redeemer in NIV)—in other words, a next of kin who was able to give Ruth a hope and a future. Through their bloodline would come King David and ultimately, through the line of David would come Jesus Christ, the perfect Kinsman Redeemer, our closest "next of kin" whose perfect blood would buy us into an eternal family and give us a hope and a future now and forever!

"Chrestotes"

(Greek) meaning: Moral goodness, tenderness, integrity, gentleness, forbearance (patient self-control).

RUTH 1

—

VV. 1-10

[1] In the days when the judges ruled, there was a famine in the land. So a man from Bethlehem in Judah, together with his wife and two sons, went to live for a while in the country of Moab. [2] The man's name was Elimelek, his wife's name was Naomi, and the names of his two sons were Mahlon and Kilion. They were Ephrathites from Bethlehem, Judah. And they went to Moab and lived there. [3] Now Elimelek, Naomi's husband, died, and she was left with her two sons. [4] They married Moabite women, one named Orpah and the other Ruth. After they had lived there about ten years, [5] both Mahlon and Kilion also died, and Naomi was left without her two sons and her husband. [6] When Naomi heard in Moab that the LORD had come to the aid of his people by providing food for them, she and her daughters-in-law prepared to return home from there. [7] With her two daughters-in-law she left the place where she had been living and set out on the road that would take them back to the land of Judah. [8] Then Naomi said to her two daughters-in-law, "Go back, each of you, to your mother's home. May the LORD show you kindness, as you have shown kindness to your dead husbands and to me. [9] May the LORD grant that each of you will find rest in the home of another husband." Then she kissed them goodbye and they wept aloud [10] and said to her, "We will go back with you to your people."

SESSION QUESTIONS

—

WEEK ONE

DAY 01 Read and think about the definition of kindness. Go through the passage in Ruth looking for evidence of this definition expressed to and through the different people in the opening section of the story. How can you apply these different definitions to specific relationships in your life?

DAY 02 Read Titus 3:3-8. What benefit did you receive as a result of God's kindness? What did it cost Him?

DAY 03 Go back through the opening section of Ruth. Highlight a verse that stands out to you. Write it in your journal, and add any thoughts as to why it's meaningful to you.

DAY 04 Look up Ephesians 4:22-32. Make a list of the various ways these verses could help you show genuine kindness to the people in your life.

DAY 05 Reread the passage from Ruth. Think about Naomi's instructions to her daughters-in-law. How was this request others centered? Consider how acts of kindness in your relationships could show a similar others-centered attitude. Text your response to this question or anything else you've learned this week to your mentee.

▶ **ENGAGE WITH THE WORD:** SEE YOUR STORY IN HIS STORY

As you read Luke 2:41-52 and John 1:1-5, think about what this section reveals about who Jesus is and jot down a few of your thoughts as it relates to your own walk with Jesus.

RUTH 1

"Agape"

(Greek) meaning: Unconditional, self-sacrificing love resulting in passionate
actions taken for the benefit and well-being of others.

V V . 1 1 - 2 2

[11] But Naomi said, "Return home, my daughters. Why would you come with me? Am I going to have any more sons, who could become your husbands? [12] Return home, my daughters; I am too old to have another husband. Even if I thought there was still hope for me— even if I had a husband tonight and then gave birth to sons— [13] would you wait until they grew up? Would you remain unmarried for them? No, my daughters. It is more bitter for me than for you, because the LORD's hand has turned against me!" [14] At this they wept aloud again. Then Orpah kissed her mother-in-law goodbye, but Ruth clung to her. [15] "Look," said Naomi, "your sister-in-law is going back to her people and her gods. Go back with her." [16] But Ruth replied, "Don't urge me to leave you or to turn back from you. Where you go I will go, and where you stay I will stay. Your people will be my people and your God my God. [17] Where you die I will die, and there I will be buried. May the LORD deal with me, be it ever so severely, if even death separates you and me." [18] When Naomi realized that Ruth was determined to go with her, she stopped urging her. [19] So the two women went on until they came to Bethlehem. When they arrived in Bethlehem, the whole town was stirred because of them, and the women exclaimed, "Can this be Naomi?" [20] "Don't call me Naomi," she told them. "Call me Mara, because the Almighty has made my life very bitter. [21] I went away full, but the LORD has brought me back empty. Why call me Naomi? The LORD has afflicted me; the Almighty has brought misfortune upon me." [22] So Naomi returned from Moab accompanied by Ruth the Moabite, her daughter-in-law, arriving in Bethlehem as the barley harvest was beginning.

SESSION QUESTIONS

—

WEEK TWO

DAY 01   Read and think about the definition of love. Go through the passage in Ruth looking for evidence of this type of love. How is it visibly demonstrated?

DAY 02   Realizing that love isn't solely a feeling, read 1 John 4:7-12. What does this tell us about God's love? About our response?

DAY 03   Return to 1 John 4. Start in verse 7 and continue to the end of the chapter, concentrating on verses 15-21. Journal about how this passage says God's love should change our interaction with others.

DAY 04   First Corinthians 13 outlines the character of love. Read verses 4-7. Thinking about your relationships, go back and substitute your name at the beginning of each of the phrases about love. (For example: Jennifer is patient; Jennifer is kind, etc.) Are these statements accurate about you? If not, what needs to change?

DAY 05   Reread the entire passage. How do you see the virtue of love more clearly in Ruth's declaration in verses 16-17? Repeat yesterday's exercise, but this time insert "Jesus" into the text. (For example: Jesus is patient; Jesus is kind, etc.) Pray for Christ to make up for what you lack in your love toward others, since it is only in surrender to His Spirit that we are able to love the way we were created to love. What was most impactful to you in the Scripture passage this week?

▶ **ENGAGE WITH THE WORD: SEE YOUR STORY IN HIS STORY**

Read Mark 2:15-22. Why do you think so many people (then and now) have buried hatred toward Jesus? Pray for someone in your life to have his or her heart softened when it comes to God and following Jesus.

RUTH 2

"Pistis"

(Greek) meaning: trustworthy, reliable, steadfast, constant; a strong conviction
and belief in the truth of God.

V V . 1 - 7

[1] Now Naomi had a relative on her husband's side, a man of standing from the clan of Elimelek, whose name was Boaz. [2] And Ruth the Moabite said to Naomi, "Let me go to the fields and pick up the leftover grain behind anyone in whose eyes I find favor." Naomi said to her, "Go ahead, my daughter." [3] So she went out, entered a field and began to glean behind the harvesters. As it turned out, she was working in a field belonging to Boaz, who was from the clan of Elimelek. [4] Just then Boaz arrived from Bethlehem and greeted the harvesters, "The LORD be with you!"

"The LORD bless you!" they answered. [5] Boaz asked the overseer of his harvesters, "Who does that young woman belong to?" [6] The overseer replied, "She is the Moabite who came back from Moab with Naomi. [7] She said, 'Please let me glean and gather among the sheaves behind the harvesters.' She came into the field and has remained here from morning till now, except for a short rest in the shelter."

SESSION QUESTIONS

—

WEEK THREE

DAY 01 Read the definition of faithfulness, then go through the passage in Ruth. Look for this characteristic in the actions of Ruth. How does Ruth's faithfulness encourage you today?

DAY 02 Hebrews 11 gives a clearer understanding of faith. Meditate on verse 1, and then read through the rest of the chapter to see how faith was expressed in the lives of God's servants. Make a list of the actions that demonstrated their faith.

DAY 03 Reread the passage from Ruth. Do you notice anything different in the text that you didn't see in your first reading? Write down a verse that seems to stand out, and journal what you learn.

DAY 04 Look up Psalm 86. What do verses 11-15 tell you about God's faithfulness? How might a better understanding of His attributes impact your relationships? Memorize verse 11, and meditate on it. Pray for this truth to reach all the way down to your heart and soul and that God would give you an undivided heart for Him.

DAY 05 Read Matthew 23:13-23. Why was Jesus upset with the Pharisees and teachers of the law? How might justice, mercy, and faithfulness be connected (see v. 23)? Write your thoughts in your journal.

▶ **ENGAGE WITH THE WORD: SEE YOUR STORY IN HIS STORY**

Read John 3:1-16, and summarize what it means to be "born again." How can you explain it to others in an easy to understand way? Consider reading the passage in a new translation for expanded understanding.

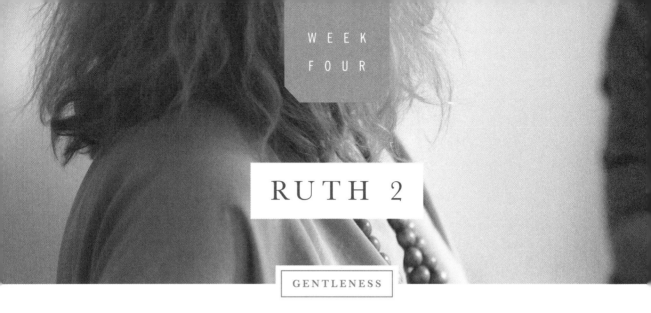

FOUR

RUTH 2

GENTLENESS

"Praotes"

(Greek) meaning: meek, humble, compassionate,
strength under control.

VV. 8-23

⁸ So Boaz said to Ruth, "My daughter, listen to me. Don't go and glean in another field and don't go away from here. Stay here with the women who work for me. ⁹ Watch the field where the men are harvesting, and follow along after the women. I have told the men not to lay a hand on you. And whenever you are thirsty, go and get a drink from the water jars the men have filled."¹⁰ At this, she bowed down with her face to the ground. She asked him, "Why have I found such favor in your eyes that you notice me— a foreigner?" ¹¹ Boaz replied, "I've been told all about what you have done for your mother-in-law since the death of your husband—

how you left your father and mother and your homeland and came to live with a people you did not know before. ¹² May the LORD repay you for what you have done. May you be richly rewarded by the LORD, the God of Israel, under whose wings you have come to take refuge." ¹³ "May I continue to find favor in your eyes, my lord," she said. "You have put me at ease by speaking kindly to your servant— though I do not have the standing of one of your servants." ¹⁴ At mealtime Boaz said to her, "Come over here. Have some bread and dip it in the wine vinegar." When she sat down with the harvesters, he offered her some roasted grain.

She ate all she wanted and had some left over. [15] As she got up to glean, Boaz gave orders to his men, "Let her gather among the sheaves and don't reprimand her. [16] Even pull out some stalks for her from the bundles and leave them for her to pick up, and don't rebuke her." [17] So Ruth gleaned in the field until evening. Then she threshed the barley she had gathered, and it amounted to about an ephah. [18] She carried it back to town, and her mother-in-law saw how much she had gathered. Ruth also brought out and gave her what she had left over after she had eaten enough. [19] Her mother-in-law asked her, "Where did you glean today? Where did you work? Blessed be the man who took notice of you!" Then Ruth told her mother-in-law about the one at whose place she had been working.

"The name of the man I worked with today is Boaz," she said. [20] "The LORD bless him!" Naomi said to her daughter-in-law. "He has not stopped showing his kindness to the living and the dead." She added, "That man is our close relative; he is one of our guardian-redeemers." [21] Then Ruth the Moabite said, "He even said to me, 'Stay with my workers until they finish harvesting all my grain.'" [22] Naomi said to Ruth her daughter-in-law, "It will be good for you, my daughter, to go with the women who work for him, because in someone else's field you might be harmed." [23] So Ruth stayed close to the women of Boaz to glean until the barley and wheat harvests were finished. And she lived with her mother-in-law.

SESSION QUESTIONS

—

DAY 01   Concentrate on the different aspects of gentleness listed in the definition. Is gentleness different than what you thought it was? In what way? Look for these aspects as you read the passage from Ruth.

DAY 02   Think more about gentleness as being "strength under control." How is that a description of Jesus? Look for evidence of Christ's power in Matthew 28:18; John 1:1; 13:3; and Colossians 1:16. What do you learn about His attitude from John 8:28; 12:49-50; 14:10?

DAY 03   Reread the section from Ruth. Write "Boaz" and "Ruth" at the top of two columns. In each column, list the ways in which each expressed gentleness.

DAY 04   Go to Philippians 2:1-8, and reflect on Christ's attitude. What are Paul's instructions to you in light of Jesus' example (reread vv. 3-4)? Write down some tangible ways that you can "value others above yourselves."

DAY 05   Read Galatians 6:1-10. What do you learn about your role as a believer toward others? How does gentleness play into that role? How could these verses impact the more difficult relationships in your life? Contemplate this topic and all you've learned in Ruth this week. Text or email your thoughts to your mentee.

▶   ENGAGE WITH THE WORD: SEE YOUR STORY IN HIS STORY

Move on to read Matthew 13. Concentrate on one of the parables that Jesus told and think about tangible ways you can apply it to your life.

RUTH 3

"Eirene"

(Greek) meaning: tranquility, harmony, rest, quietness,
contentedness, freedom from fear.

V V . 1 - 6

[1] One day Ruth's mother-in-law Naomi said to her, "My daughter, I must find a home for you, where you will be well provided for. [2] Now Boaz, with whose women you have worked, is a relative of ours. Tonight he will be winnowing barley on the threshing floor. [3] Wash, put on perfume, and get dressed in your best clothes. Then go down to the threshing floor, but don't let him know you are there until he has finished eating and drinking. [4] When he lies down, note the place where he is lying. Then go and uncover his feet and lie down. He will tell you what to do." [5] "I will do whatever you say," Ruth answered. [6] So she went down to the threshing floor and did everything her mother-in-law told her to do.

SESSION QUESTIONS

—

WEEK FIVE

DAY 01 Look up Ruth 3:1-6 in a commentary or Bible dictionary to find out more about Ruth's actions and the cultural context in this section (the *Asbury Bible Commentary* at BibleGateway.com provides great insight). Then, think through the definition of peace. Where do you see evidence of an attitude of peace in this section of Ruth?

DAY 02 Turn to Isaiah 26 and read. Meditate on verse 3. How does the prophet tell us we can possess (and maintain) peace? Memorize this verse this week.

DAY 03 Reread the passage from Ruth. Think about how Naomi may have instilled peace in Ruth. How can your words give peace in tense situations at home or work? Be intentional about being a peacemaker this week.

DAY 04 James 4 speaks directly to the cause of discord in relationships. Read this chapter, and take notes in your journal about what you learn. Thank God for a good relationship you have, and pray for one that may be struggling.

DAY 05 Read Romans 12:9-21. Make a list of what this passage says to do and not to do in order to avoid discord and live at peace. End by reading the entire Ruth passage again, reflecting on any recurring themes that continually come up in your heart.

▶ **ENGAGE WITH THE WORD: SEE YOUR STORY IN HIS STORY**

Read Matthew 6:25-34. Jesus calmed the fears of His disciples. How can His words do the same for you when you are filled with anxiety and panic?

WEEK
SIX

RUTH 3

"Egkrateia"

(Greek) meaning: the ability to regulate and govern one's desires
and passions, temperance.

VV. 7-15

[7] When Boaz had finished eating and drinking and was in good spirits, he went over to lie down at the far end of the grain pile. Ruth approached quietly, uncovered his feet and lay down. [8] In the middle of the night something startled the man; he turned—and there was a woman lying at his feet! [9] "Who are you?" he asked. "I am your servant Ruth," she said. "Spread the corner of your garment over me, since you are a guardian-redeemer of our family." [10] "The LORD bless you, my daughter," he replied. "This kindness is greater than that which you showed earlier: You have not run after the younger men, whether rich or poor. [11] And now, my daughter, don't be afraid. I will do for you all you ask. All the people of my town know that you are a woman of noble character. [12] Although it is true that I am a guardian-redeemer of our family, there is another who is more closely related than I. [13] Stay here for the night, and in the morning if he wants to do his duty as your guardian-redeemer, good; let him redeem you. But if he is not willing, as surely as the LORD lives I will do it. Lie here until morning." [14] So she lay at his feet until morning, but got up before anyone could be recognized; and he said, "No one must know that a woman came to the threshing floor." [15] He also said, "Bring me the shawl you are wearing and hold it out." When she did so, he poured into it six measures of barley and placed the bundle on her. Then he went back to town.

SESSION QUESTIONS

—

W E E K   S I X

DAY 01 Read over the definition of self-control. Then, read through the Scripture passage and look for evidence of this virtue in this portion of Ruth.

DAY 02 Read 2 Peter 1:3-10. In the middle of these verses, there is a list of qualities followers of Jesus should "make every effort" to cultivate. Think about how self-control relates to the other virtues. What does Peter say the effect of possessing these qualities will be?

DAY 03 Look up Proverbs 25:28. Think about the value of walls in the time these verses were written. Write what you think Solomon was telling us. Include how you've seen this proverb to be true in others' lives as well as in your own. Where do you think your "walls" may be "broken" due to lack of self-control?

DAY 04 Emotions often confuse the struggle with self-control, but Romans 12 makes it clear the battle is won or lost in the mind. Meditate on verses 1-8, and memorize verses 1-2. What does this passage say about how you are changed and how you can know God's will?

DAY 05 Read Proverbs 31:10-31 and consider that the word "noble" is the same word Boaz used to describe Ruth in Ruth 3:11. Think back to the Ruth introduction: Remember in the original Jewish Scriptures these books (Proverbs and Ruth) were literally back to back, illustrating Ruth as an example of a real-life "noble" woman. How do you think being a woman of "noble character" could be tied to your Spirit-given self-control?

▶ **ENGAGE WITH THE WORD: SEE YOUR STORY IN HIS STORY**

As you read Luke 18:18-30, give intentional thought to the character qualities you see Jesus express. Which is most significant to you at this specific time in your life?

RUTH 3

GOODNESS

"Agathosune"

(Greek) meaning: upright in heart and life, honorable, selfless.

VV.16-18

[16] When Ruth came to her mother-in-law, Naomi asked, "How did it go, my daughter?" Then she told her everything Boaz had done for her [17] and added, "He gave me these six measures of barley, saying, 'Don't go back to your mother-in-law empty-handed.'" [18] Then Naomi said, "Wait, my daughter, until you find out what happens. For the man will not rest until the matter is settled today."

SESSION QUESTIONS

—

WEEK SEVEN

DAY 01 Think about the definition of goodness. Then, read the passage from Ruth. Where do you see this virtue being expressed? By whom and for whom?

DAY 02 Turn to Exodus 33:12-23. Look for the use of the word "goodness" in this passage. Think about what this experience must have been like for Moses. Write down what these verses tell you about God and how His goodness is tied to His glory.

DAY 03 Read James 1:17 and 2 Thessalonians 1:11-12. Consider the source of all that is good, including your efforts to show goodness to others. What stood out to you from these passages?

DAY 04 Read James 3:13-18. Make a list of the things this passage says are at odds with a "good life." Is there one in particular that you struggle with? Ask God to give you His wisdom. Be available to pray over this topic with your mentee.

DAY 05 Turn to Romans 15:1-6, and journal about how goodness should be shown to others.

▶ **ENGAGE WITH THE WORD: SEE YOUR STORY IN HIS STORY**

As you read John 7:37-44, consider how Jesus unquestionably demonstrated He was God.

RUTH 4

PATIENCE

"Makrothumia"

(Greek) meaning: steadfastness, endurance, perseverance,
long-suffering.

[1] Meanwhile Boaz went up to the town gate and sat down there just as the guardian-redeemer he had mentioned came along. Boaz said, "Come over here, my friend, and sit down." So he went over and sat down. [2] Boaz took ten of the elders of the town and said, "Sit here," and they did so. [3] Then he said to the guardian-redeemer, "Naomi, who has come back from Moab, is selling the piece of land that belonged to our relative Elimelek. [4] I thought I should bring the matter to your attention and suggest that you buy it in the presence of these seated here and in the presence of the elders of my people. If you will redeem it, do so. But if you will not, tell me, so I will know. For no one has the right to do it except you, and I am next in line." "I will redeem it," he said. [5] Then Boaz said, "On the day you buy the land from Naomi, you also acquire Ruth the Moabite, the dead man's widow, in order to maintain the name of the dead with his property." [6] At this, the guardian-redeemer said, "Then I cannot redeem it because I might endanger my own estate. You redeem it yourself. I cannot do it."

[7] (Now in earlier times in Israel, for the redemption and transfer of property to become final, one party took off his sandal and gave it to the other. This was the method of legalizing transactions in Israel.) [8] So the guardian-redeemer said to Boaz, "Buy it yourself." And he removed his sandal. [9] Then Boaz announced to the elders and all the people, "Today you are witnesses that I have bought from Naomi all the property of Elimelek, Kilion and Mahlon. [10] I have also acquired Ruth the Moabite, Mahlon's widow, as my wife, in order to maintain the name of the dead with his property, so that his name will not disappear from among his family or from his hometown. Today you are witnesses!" [11] Then the elders and all the people at the gate said, "We are witnesses. May the LORD make the woman who is coming into your home like Rachel and Leah, who together built up the family of Israel. May you have standing in Ephrathah and be famous in Bethlehem. [12] Through the offspring the LORD gives you by this young woman, may your family be like that of Perez, whom Tamar bore to Judah."

SESSION QUESTIONS

—

DAY 01 Consider the various aspects of the definition of patience. In this section of Ruth, how does Boaz exemplify this quality?

DAY 02 Look up Psalm 37. Notice the references to patience and waiting. Why does the psalmist encourage us to "not fret"? How could you apply this to a specific situation today?

DAY 03 Go intentionally through Colossians 1:9-14. Make a list of the results believers have when we are filled with "the knowledge of his will."

DAY 04 Read through Philippians 2:12-16. Think about how patience plays a part in living the way Paul instructs. Make notes about why grumbling and arguing are so detrimental (reflect back on the last session when you went a day without it). How can patience remedy many of the complaints and arguments we may have, specifically in relationships, on a daily basis?

DAY 05 Hebrews 6:10-12 encourages us to help others, which involves patience and faith. How do these relate to each other and, when connected, what impact might they have on your relationships? Think upon all you have learned this week, and text any significant insights to your mentee.

▶ **ENGAGE WITH THE WORD: SEE YOUR STORY IN HIS STORY**

Matthew 26 chronicles the last days of Jesus' life on earth. Why did He have to die? What did His death accomplish?

RUTH 4

JOY

"Chara"

(Greek) meaning: gladness, delight, contentment derived
from confidence and assurance.

¹³ So Boaz took Ruth and she became his wife. When he made love to her, the LORD enabled her to conceive, and she gave birth to a son. ¹⁴ The women said to Naomi: "Praise be to the LORD, who this day has not left you without a guardian-redeemer. May he become famous throughout Israel! ¹⁵ He will renew your life and sustain you in your old age. For your daughter-in-law, who loves you and who is better to you than seven sons, has given him birth." ¹⁶ Then Naomi took the child in her arms and cared for him. ¹⁷ The women living there said, "Naomi has a son!" And they named him Obed. He was the father of Jesse, the father of David. ¹⁸ This, then, is the family line of Perez: Perez was the father of Hezron, ¹⁹ Hezron the father of Ram, Ram the father of Amminadab, ²⁰ Amminadab the father of Nahshon, Nahshon the father of Salmon, ²¹ Salmon the father of Boaz, Boaz the father of Obed, ²² Obed the father of Jesse, and Jesse the father of David.

SESSION QUESTIONS

—

DAY 01   Begin by focusing on the definition of joy. Think about how this quality is different from happiness. Read the last section of the Book of Ruth with this in mind.

DAY 02   Joy is most often associated with good things. Go over James 1:1-4. What do these verses say about joy in difficult times? Does this bring you comfort? In what ways? If it doesn't bring you comfort, why not?

DAY 03   Read 2 Corinthians 8:1-9. What stood out most to you? How is joy associated with giving rather than receiving? How might you begin or deepen your experience of this aspect of joy?

DAY 04   Read through John 15:1-17. Look for the source of joy. Write in your journal about what Jesus says about relationships in this passage, including thoughts about your relationship to Him and to others.

DAY 05   Read through the passage in Ruth again. Observe how Ruth's commitment to Naomi and her faithfulness to God bring joy. How can you strengthen your commitment to God and to others, so that you can spread joy? How is the end of this story an example of the joy found through the redemption of Christ?

▶   **ENGAGE WITH THE WORD:** SEE YOUR STORY IN HIS STORY

Read Matthew 27. What do you learn about God's love in this section? Think about the difference between knowing about God's love and truly experiencing it. How has what you've read affected the way you live every day?

KINSHIP

—

▲ To lean into Jesus and His heart for our relationships and to identify how He instructs us to conduct ourselves in relationship with others.

▲ To gain deeper understanding of these relational truths so that our lives reflect His heart in all our relationships and how it can change our day-to-day interactions with all people in our lives.

————— S E S S I O N   Q U E S T I O N S —————

1. How would you gauge the health of your relationships currently? With your friends? In your marriage or relationship with your significant other (if applicable)? With family? At work?

2. How do you see Jesus and His Word changing your heart for the relationships you currently find yourself in?

3. How can having a heart like Jesus transform some of your more difficult relationships?

4. What's the biggest challenge and change you know God is asking you to pursue in your current relationships?

GRATITUDE

SESSION SIX

As our time together for the year is quickly coming to an end, the word we all want to come around is *gratitude*. We are so incredibly grateful for this journey called FLOURISH! What can you thank God for doing in your life through this time in Scripture and with your mentee? Beyond that, we want to delve into the very essence of gratitude and wrap it around us like a garment. We want to be women who see life through a sharply focused lens of gratitude to Jesus that defines and shapes how we live, constantly striving to see life as He sees it, to truly look at the faces of people, and to see the beauty of life around us. That doesn't mean life is perfect, or even close to perfect. It doesn't mean we won't struggle or face hardship; the opposite is often true. This year many of us have faced difficult circumstances, grief, death, cancer, divorce, broken relationships, and more. Our feelings have been a roller-coaster of emotions: the whole gamut from elation to bitterness to joy to unthinkable pain. Being rooted in gratitude doesn't mean we downplay or disregard these very real realities. It means that in every single circumstance, the highest of highs, the lowest of lows, and every moment in between, we cling to Jesus. And we remember God's promises to us in and through Him. In the remembering, we speak the truth of who God is and who we are as a result, and it causes us to look up. We are personally reminded of God's faithfulness, not just to the world, but to you and to me. The psalmist writes: "I will give thanks to the LORD with my whole heart; I will recount all of your wonderful deeds" (Ps. 9:1, ESV). This practice of remembering builds a life of gratitude. When we remember that we have been given everything we need for life and godliness in Christ (see 2 Pet. 1:3), that His peace transcends our very understanding (see Phil. 4:7), that He is near to the brokenhearted (see Ps. 34:18), that He comforts us in all our troubles (see 2 Cor. 1:4), and we begin recounting His wonderful deeds (see Ps. 9:1) in our own lives, we are ever reminded that it truly is "Christ in [us], the hope of glory" (Col. 1:27, ESV). He is worthy of all of our praise, worship, and thankfulness both now and forever!

GRATITUDE JOURNAL

We will be keeping a gratitude journal throughout our last session. Each day we will write one entry about something for which we are grateful. It can be a good cup of coffee, a moment to be alone, or a prayer answered. We may be grateful to God for something huge or seemingly mundane, because surely Jesus is in every moment!

THE GOSPEL OF JOHN

The Book of John was written to describe events that took place between AD 27 and AD 36, although it was actually physically written by John when he was believed to be an old man, around AD 85. This gospel account, more than any other, clearly explains who Jesus is as the unique Son of God. The Word, the Way, the Truth, the Life, fully God yet fully man, fully in communion with His Father since the very beginning of time. It highlights Jesus' unique relationship with the Father, and His authoritative claim of being God in the flesh. Jesus declares in John 8:58, "Before Abraham was born, I am!" making the distinct assertion that He is in very nature God, the "I AM" of the Old Testament in a human body. And there is not, perhaps, a more succinct yet moving picture of the gospel than can be found in John 3:16. Our prayer is that we would have hearts welling up with gratitude at the thought of God sending His own Son that "whoever believes in him shall not perish but have eternal life." This is the promise we have in Jesus from the very second we trust Him and every single day moving forward. Each day, His promise is new and His mercy and love for us are renewed, giving us a brand new reason to be thankful.

JOHN 1

Grateful for ... THE WORD

VV. 1 - 18

[1] In the beginning was the Word, and the Word was with God, and the Word was God. [2] He was with God in the beginning. [3] Through him all things were made; without him nothing was made that has been made. [4] In him was life, and that life was the light of all mankind. [5] The light shines in the darkness, and the darkness has not overcome it. [6] There was a man sent from God whose name was John. [7] He came as a witness to testify concerning that light, so that through him all might believe. [8] He himself was not the light; he came only as a witness to the light. [9] The true light that gives light to everyone was coming into the world. [10] He was in the world, and though the world was made through him, the world did not recognize him. [11] He came to that which was his own, but his own did not receive him. [12] Yet to all who did receive him, to those who believed in his name, he gave the right to become children of God— [13] children born not of natural descent, nor of human decision or a husband's will, but born of God. [14] The Word became flesh and made his dwelling among us. We have seen his glory, the glory of the one and only Son, who came from the Father, full of grace and truth. [15] (John testified concerning him. He cried out, saying, "This is the one I spoke about when I said, 'He who comes after me has surpassed me because he was before me.'") [16] Out of his fullness we have all received grace in place of grace already given. [17] For the law was given through Moses; grace and truth came through Jesus Christ. [18] No one has ever seen God, but the one and only Son, who is himself God and is in closest relationship with the Father, has made him known.

SESSION QUESTIONS

—

WEEK ONE

In addition to each day's reading, make one entry in your gratitude journal per day.

DAY 01   Read the passage from John 1. Identify the truths that are evident about Jesus from these verses, and list them in your journal. What does John reveal about the relationship between the Father and the Son, and about Christ's relationship to humanity?

DAY 02   Look up Hebrews 1:1-4. How does this passage relate to John 1:1-18? What added insights regarding Jesus does the writer of Hebrews give you? Which one of these truths stands out to you? Meditate on it as you go throughout your day.

DAY 03   Compare the passage (especially vv. 1-4) to Genesis 1:1-27. Journal a few thoughts on what you can learn about the nature of Christ from these two passages.

DAY 04   Read through the Scripture in John 1:1-18 again, concentrating on verses 16-17. Cross-reference with Hebrews 3:1-6. What new insights do the passages bring to each other?

DAY 05   Grab your Scripture, and read the entirety of John 1. Considering what you have learned this week, what would you say to someone who asks, "Who is Jesus?" Take a few minutes to write about it in your gratitude journal. Pray specifically for an opportunity to encourage someone with what you've learned.

This weekend, read John 2.

▶   ENGAGE WITH THE WORD: **SEE YOUR STORY IN HIS STORY**

As you read Matthew 28:1-10, think about the difference Christ's resurrection makes in your everyday life.

WEEK

TWO

JOHN 3

Grateful for ... LIFE

V V . 1 - 2 1

[1] Now there was a Pharisee, a man named Nicodemus who was a member of the Jewish ruling council. [2] He came to Jesus at night and said, "Rabbi, we know that you are a teacher who has come from God. For no one could perform the signs you are doing if God were not with him." [3] Jesus replied, "Very truly I tell you, no one can see the kingdom of God unless they are born again."

[4] "How can someone be born when they are old?" Nicodemus asked. "Surely they cannot enter a second time into their mother's womb to be born!" [5] Jesus answered, "Very truly I tell you, no one can enter the kingdom of God unless they are born of water and the Spirit. [6] Flesh gives birth to flesh, but the Spirit gives birth to spirit. [7] You should not be surprised at my saying, 'You must be born again.' [8] The wind blows wherever it pleases. You hear its sound, but you cannot tell where it comes from or where it is going. So it is with everyone born of the Spirit." [9] "How can this be?" Nicodemus asked. [10] "You are Israel's teacher," said Jesus, "and do you not understand these things? [11] Very truly I tell you, we speak of what we know, and we testify to what we have seen, but still you people do not accept our testimony. [12] I have spoken to you of earthly things and you do not believe; how then will you believe if I speak of heavenly things? [13] No one has ever gone into heaven except the one who came from heaven—the Son of Man. [14] Just as Moses lifted up the snake in the wilderness, so the Son of Man must be lifted up, [15] that everyone who believes may have eternal life in him." [16] For God so loved the world that he gave his one and only Son, that whoever believes in him shall not perish but have eternal life. [17] For God did not send his Son into the world to condemn the world, but to save the world through him. [18] Whoever believes in him is not condemned, but whoever does not believe stands condemned already because they have not believed in the name of God's one and only Son. [19] This is the verdict: Light has come into the world, but people loved darkness instead of light because their deeds were evil. [20] Everyone who does evil hates the light, and will not come into the light for fear that their deeds will be exposed. [21] But whoever lives by the truth comes into the light, so that it may be seen plainly that what they have done has been done in the sight of God.

SESSION QUESTIONS

—

In addition to each day's reading, make one entry in your gratitude journal per day.

DAY 01 Begin by reading through John 3:1-21. Why do you think Jesus compared a relationship with Him to being "born again"? What does that tell you about this relationship's permanence?

DAY 02 Read the passage again, making note of the context of verse 16. Circle key words in this well-known verse. What do they tell you about the source, motivation, and avenue of salvation? Write what you learn in your journal.

DAY 03 In verse 16, Jesus says salvation comes to those who believe. Look for the specifics of what Scripture says about believing in Jesus as you turn to Romans 10:9-10; Ephesians 2:8-10; Hebrews 11:6; and James 1:6. Would you agree that faith is a gift we receive, while belief is a choice we make? How do the two go hand in hand? Write any thoughts you have in your journal. Your mentee may reach out to you with questions. Answer them as you can and feel free to share any additional insights you may have.

DAY 04 Scan through the passage in John again. The story of the snake Jesus was referring to (v. 14) is in Numbers 21:4-9. It is a story about the Israelites, one Nicodemus would have been very familiar with. In this passage, what was Jesus trying to tell Nicodemus? (For more discussion, reference John Piper's sermon entitled: "The Son of Man Must Be Lifted Up—Like the Serpent.")

DAY 05 Grab your Scripture, and read all of John 3. Write in your gratitude journal about anything in this passage that has made an impact on you. Text or email your mentee any new insights or meaningful verses from what you learned in your study this week.

This weekend, read John 4:1–5:47.

▶ ENGAGE WITH THE WORD: **SEE YOUR STORY IN HIS STORY**

Read Acts 9:1-22, looking for the drastic change that occurred in Paul's life. What difference has Jesus made in your life?

JOHN 6

Grateful for ... PROVISION

VV. 1 - 1 5

[1] Some time after this, Jesus crossed to the far shore of the Sea of Galilee (that is, the Sea of Tiberias), [2] and a great crowd of people followed him because they saw the signs he had performed by healing the sick. [3] Then Jesus went up on a mountainside and sat down with his disciples. [4] The Jewish Passover Festival was near. [5] When Jesus looked up and saw a great crowd coming toward him, he said to Philip, "Where shall we buy bread for these people to eat?" [6] He asked this only to test him, for he already had in mind what he was going to do. [7] Philip answered him, "It would take more than half a year's wages to buy enough bread for each one to have a bite!" [8] Another of his disciples, Andrew, Simon Peter's brother, spoke up, [9] "Here is a boy with five small barley loaves and two small fish, but how far will they go among so many?" [10] Jesus said, "Have the people sit down." There was plenty of grass in that place, and they sat down (about five thousand men were there). [11] Jesus then took the loaves, gave thanks, and distributed to those who were seated as much as they wanted. He did the same with the fish. [12] When they had all had enough to eat, he said to his disciples, "Gather the pieces that are left over. Let nothing be wasted." [13] So they gathered them and filled twelve baskets with the pieces of the five barley loaves left over by those who had eaten. [14] After the people saw the sign Jesus performed, they began to say, "Surely this is the Prophet who is to come into the world." [15] Jesus, knowing that they intended to come and make him king by force, withdrew again to a mountain by himself.

SESSION QUESTIONS

—

WEEK THREE

In addition to each day's reading, make one entry in your gratitude journal per day.

DAY 01 Read the passage. Notice the responses of Philip and Andrew to the problem of feeding the crowd of people. These two men had been with Jesus since the events recorded in John 1:35-42. How would you expect the disciples to reply based on all they had seen and experienced with Jesus? Even so, could you relate to their actual response? Based on the truth of who Jesus is, not on your shortcomings, how might you change your response to any seemingly impossible circumstances you encounter?

DAY 02 Go back through this story, this time imagining yourself as the young boy. Consider situations of real need that exist in your own life or the lives of others. What could be your role? And what is Christ's role? What in your life could you offer to Jesus and trust that He will do the miraculous work?

DAY 03 Continue reading John 6:16-47 in your own copy of the Scripture. In your journal, contrast what the people wanted with what Jesus came to give. Include how you see this disparity, this expectation gap, continuing in the world today and in your own life.

DAY 04 Resume your reading of John 6 at verses 48-59, thinking more about Jesus' self-identification as the Bread of life. Check out Exodus 16:4 (and surrounding context) for more insight on manna "from heaven." What does it mean when Jesus says, "Your ancestors ate manna and died, but whoever feeds on this bread will live forever" (6:58)? Also reference: Luke 22:17-20; 1 Corinthians 10:16-17; 11:23-24.

DAY 05 Read through all of John 6 in your own Bible with the metaphor of bread in your mind. List some practical ways that Christ sustains and satisfies you. Read the Lord's Prayer in Matthew 6:9-13 with Jesus as your "daily bread" in mind. Write appropriate thoughts in your gratitude journal.

This weekend, read John 7.

▶ ENGAGE WITH THE WORD: **SEE YOUR STORY IN HIS STORY**

Read Acts 13:44-52. Identify Paul's passion and purpose in life. Identify yours as well.

JOHN 8

Grateful for ... COMPASSION

VV. 1-11

¹ But Jesus went to the Mount of Olives. ² At dawn he appeared again in the temple courts, where all the people gathered around him, and he sat down to teach them. ³ The teachers of the law and the Pharisees brought in a woman caught in adultery. They made her stand before the group ⁴ and said to Jesus, "Teacher, this woman was caught in the act of adultery. ⁵ In the Law Moses commanded us to stone such women. Now what do you say?" ⁶ They were using this question as a trap, in order to have a basis for accusing him. But Jesus bent down and started to write on the ground with his finger.

⁷ When they kept on questioning him, he straightened up and said to them, "Let any one of you who is without sin be the first to throw a stone at her." ⁸ Again he stooped down and wrote on the ground. ⁹ At this, those who heard began to go away one at a time, the older ones first, until only Jesus was left, with the woman still standing there. ¹⁰ Jesus straightened up and asked her, "Woman, where are they? Has no one condemned you?" ¹¹ "No one, sir," she said. "Then neither do I condemn you," Jesus declared. "Go now and leave your life of sin."

SESSION QUESTIONS

—

In addition to each day's reading, make one entry in your gratitude journal per day.

DAY 01 Read through the passage from John 8. Underline key words and phrases that display the compassion expressed by Jesus toward the woman in this story.

DAY 02 Go through the passage again, focusing on the end of the story. Cross-reference what Jesus said to this woman with Romans 5:1-11; 8:1-4, 31-39; Psalm 34:21-22; and Isaiah 55:6-8. How were these passages of Scripture relevant to your past? Did this Scripture speak to your heart in a new way? How so?

DAY 03 Review this passage in your own Bible and continue reading through verse 30. Consider how Jesus' declaration to be the "light of the world" (v. 12) relates to the story of the woman caught in adultery. What does it mean for your life that whoever follows Jesus "will never walk in darkness"?

DAY 04 Pick up your reading of John 8 at verse 31 and continue through verse 41. Cross-reference Galatians 5:1; note the context of the passage—Jesus followers were falling back into a belief that they were justified by works not faith. Journal about what Jesus says is truth and how it connects to freedom.

DAY 05 Read back through John 8:1-11. Do the tenderness and compassion of Jesus surprise you? Incorporating what you learned in our earlier readings in John, what might Jesus say to you about your sin and disobedience? Write any thoughts in your gratitude journal.

This weekend, read John 8:42–10:42.

▶ ENGAGE WITH THE WORD: **SEE YOUR STORY IN HIS STORY**

Read a chapter from one of Paul's letters. Choose from options such as Romans, Galatians, or 1 & 2 Corinthians, among others. What one thing can you take away from Paul's letters?

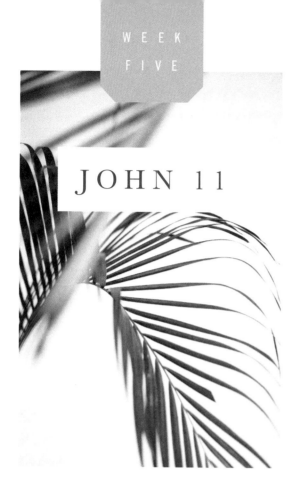

JOHN 11

Grateful for ...
RESURRECTION

VV. 1-44

[1] Now a man named Lazarus was sick. He was from Bethany, the village of Mary and her sister Martha. [2] (This Mary, whose brother Lazarus now lay sick, was the same one who poured perfume on the Lord and wiped his feet with her hair.) [3] So the sisters sent word to Jesus, "Lord, the one you love is sick." [4] When he heard this, Jesus said, "This sickness will not end in death. No, it is for God's glory so that God's Son may be glorified through it." [5] Now Jesus loved Martha and her sister and Lazarus. [6] So when he heard that Lazarus was sick, he stayed where he was two more days, [7] and then he said to his disciples, "Let us go back to Judea." [8] "But Rabbi," they said, "a short while ago the Jews there tried to stone you, and yet you are going back?" [9] Jesus answered, "Are there not twelve hours of daylight? Anyone who walks in the daytime will not stumble, for they see by this world's light. [10] It is when a person walks at night that they stumble, for they have no light." [11] After he had said this, he went on to tell them, "Our friend Lazarus has fallen asleep; but I am going there to wake him up." [12] His disciples replied, "Lord, if he sleeps, he will get better." [13] Jesus had been speaking of his death, but his disciples thought he meant natural sleep. [14] So then he told them plainly, "Lazarus is dead, [15] and for your sake I am glad I was not there, so that you may believe. But let us go to him." [16] Then Thomas (also known as Didymus) said to the rest of the disciples, "Let us also go, that we may die with him." [17] On his arrival, Jesus found that Lazarus had already been in the tomb for four days. [18] Now Bethany was less than two miles from Jerusalem, [19] and many Jews had come to Martha and Mary to comfort them in the loss of their brother. [20] When Martha heard that Jesus was coming, she went out to meet him,

but Mary stayed at home. [21] "Lord," Martha said to Jesus, "if you had been here, my brother would not have died. [22] But I know that even now God will give you whatever you ask." [23] Jesus said to her, "Your brother will rise again." [24] Martha answered, "I know he will rise again in the resurrection at the last day." [25] Jesus said to her, "I am the resurrection and the life. The one who believes in me will live, even though they die; [26] and whoever lives by believing in me will never die. Do you believe this?" [27] "Yes, Lord," she replied, "I believe that you are the Messiah, the Son of God, who is to come into the world." [28] After she had said this, she went back and called her sister Mary aside. "The Teacher is here," she said, "and is asking for you." [29] When Mary heard this, she got up quickly and went to him. [30] Now Jesus had not yet entered the village, but was still at the place where Martha had met him. [31] When the Jews who had been with Mary in the house, comforting her, noticed how quickly she got up and went out, they followed her, supposing she was going to the tomb to mourn there. [32] When Mary reached the place where Jesus was and saw him, she fell at his feet and said, "Lord, if you had been here, my brother would not have died." [33] When Jesus saw her weeping, and the Jews who had come along with her also weeping, he was deeply moved in spirit and troubled. [34] "Where have you laid him?" he asked. "Come and see, Lord," they replied. [35] Jesus wept. [36] Then the Jews said, "See how he loved him!" [37] But some of them said, "Could not he who opened the eyes of the blind man have kept this man from dying?" [38] Jesus, once more deeply moved, came to the tomb. It was a cave with a stone laid across the entrance. [39] "Take away the stone," he said. "But, Lord," said Martha, the sister of the dead man, "by this time there is a bad odor, for he has been there four days." [40] Then Jesus said, "Did I not tell you that if you believe, you will see the glory of God?" [41] So they took away the stone. Then Jesus looked up and said, "Father, I thank you that you have heard me. [42] I knew that you always hear me, but I said this for the benefit of the people standing here, that they may believe that you sent me." [43] When he had said this, Jesus called in a loud voice, "Lazarus, come out!" [44] The dead man came out, his hands and feet wrapped with strips of linen, and a cloth around his face. Jesus said to them, "Take off the grave clothes and let him go."

SESSION QUESTIONS

—

WEEK FIVE

In addition to each day's reading, make one entry in your gratitude journal per day.

DAY 01   Read through John 11:1-44. Look up 1 Thessalonians 4:13-18 and make notes on the connection to verses 23-27. How are you thankful today that you don't grieve as the rest of the world who has no hope?

DAY 02   Imagine yourself to be Martha as you read through the passage today. Make a list of the emotions you might be feeling. Do the same as you think about yourself as Mary. How did Jesus address their needs? What promises are there for you in His words?

DAY 03   Mary and Martha likely thought Jesus was late, but the story reminds us that He is always on time. Read Psalm 37. How can we lean into God during seasons of waiting?

DAY 04   Read through the passage again, focusing on the significance of Jesus' instructions in verse 44. How might this be connected to Paul's teachings in Colossians 3:1-17?

DAY 05   If you believe in Jesus, the story of Lazarus is also your story. Reread the passage thinking about the time when Jesus brought you from death to life. Write your thoughts in your gratitude journal.

This weekend, read John 11:45–13:38.

▶   ENGAGE WITH THE WORD: **SEE YOUR STORY IN HIS STORY**

As you read 2 Timothy 3:10-17, consider what you can learn from Paul's example that will help you endure trials that come your way.

JOHN 14

Grateful for ... TRUTH

V V . 1 - 3 1

[1] "Do not let your hearts be troubled. You believe in God; believe also in me. [2] My Father's house has many rooms; if that were not so, would I have told you that I am going there to prepare a place for you? [3] And if I go and prepare a place for you, I will come back and take you to be with me that you also may be where I am. [4] You know the way to the place where I am going." [5] Thomas said to him, "Lord, we don't know where you are going, so how can we know the way?" [6] Jesus answered, "I am the way and the truth and the life. No one comes to the Father except through me. [7] If you really know me, you will know my Father as well. From now on, you do know him and have seen him." [8] Philip said, "Lord, show us the Father and that will be enough for us." [9] Jesus answered: "Don't you know me, Philip, even after I have been among you such a long time? Anyone who has seen me has seen the Father. How can you say, 'Show us the Father'? [10] Don't you believe that I am in the Father, and that the Father is in me? The words I say to you I do not speak on my own authority. Rather, it is the Father, living in me, who is doing his work. [11] Believe me when I say that I am in the Father and the Father is in me; or at least believe on the evidence of the

works themselves. [12] Very truly I tell you, whoever believes in me will do the works I have been doing, and they will do even greater things than these, because I am going to the Father. [13] And I will do whatever you ask in my name, so that the Father may be glorified in the Son. [14] You may ask me for anything in my name, and I will do it. [15] If you love me, keep my commands. [16] And I will ask the Father, and he will give you another advocate to help you and be with you forever— [17] the Spirit of truth. The world cannot accept him, because it neither sees him nor knows him. But you know him, for he lives with you and will be in you. [18] I will not leave you as orphans; I will come to you. [19] Before long, the world will not see me anymore, but you will see me. Because I live, you also will live. [20] On that day you will realize that I am in my Father, and you are in me, and I am in you. [21] Whoever has my commands and keeps them is the one who loves me. The one who loves me will be loved by my Father, and I too will love them and show myself to them." [22] Then Judas (not Judas Iscariot) said, "But, Lord, why do you intend to show yourself to us and not to the world?"

[23] Jesus replied, "Anyone who loves me will obey my teaching. My Father will love them, and we will come to them and make our home with them. [24] Anyone who does not love me will not obey my teaching. These words you hear are not my own; they belong to the Father who sent me. [25] All this I have spoken while still with you. [26] But the Advocate, the Holy Spirit, whom the Father will send in my name, will teach you all things and will remind you of everything I have said to you. [27] Peace I leave with you; my peace I give you. I do not give to you as the world gives. Do not let your hearts be troubled and do not be afraid. [28] You heard me say, 'I am going away and I am coming back to you.' If you loved me, you would be glad that I am going to the Father, for the Father is greater than I. [29] I have told you now before it happens, so that when it does happen you will believe. [30] I will not say much more to you, for the prince of this world is coming. He has no hold over me, [31] but he comes so that the world may learn that I love the Father and do exactly what my Father has commanded me. Come now; let us leave."

SESSION QUESTIONS

—

WEEK SIX

In addition to each day's reading, make one entry in your gratitude journal per day.

DAY 01   Read John 14:1-31. Circle the word *believe* every time it appears in the first fourteen verses. What can you conclude from the emphasis on this term?

DAY 02   Turn to Psalm 25. Compare what the psalmist wrote to what Jesus said to His disciples in John 14. What verses or themes stand out to you?

DAY 03   Review the passage again, meditating on God's promise of the Holy Spirit detailed in verses 15-31. Cross-reference this section with Ephesians 1:13-14. Jot down any words or phrases that impact you.

DAY 04   In John 14:27, Jesus promises us His peace. Look up Psalm 119:165; Matthew 11:28-30; Philippians 4:6-7; and 1 Peter 5:5-7. How can you position yourself to experience God's peace? Which of these verses spoke to you the most and why? Write it on a card, and place it somewhere you will see it for the rest of this session.

DAY 05   Go back through the Scripture in John 14, thinking mainly about what Jesus said in verse 6. How is what He stated different from other so-called "truths" of today? Write any thoughts in your gratitude journal.

This weekend, read John 15–19:27.

▶ ENGAGE WITH THE WORD: **SEE YOUR STORY IN HIS STORY**

Read 2 Timothy 2:1-13, and summarize Paul's main point.

JOHN 19

Grateful for ... VICTORY

V V . 2 8 - 4 2

²⁸ Later, knowing that everything had now been finished, and so that Scripture would be fulfilled, Jesus said, "I am thirsty." ²⁹ A jar of wine vinegar was there, so they soaked a sponge in it, put the sponge on a stalk of the hyssop plant, and lifted it to Jesus' lips. ³⁰ When he had received the drink, Jesus said, "It is finished." With that, he bowed his head and gave up his spirit. ³¹ Now it was the day of Preparation, and the next day was to be a special Sabbath. Because the Jewish leaders did not want the bodies left on the crosses during the Sabbath, they asked Pilate to have the legs broken and the bodies taken down. ³² The soldiers therefore came and broke the legs of the first man who had been crucified with Jesus, and then those of the other. ³³ But when they came to Jesus and found that he was already dead, they did not break his legs. ³⁴ Instead, one of the soldiers pierced Jesus' side with a spear, bringing a sudden flow of blood and water. ³⁵ The man who saw it has given testimony, and his testimony is true. He knows that he tells the truth, and he testifies so that you also may believe.

³⁶ These things happened so that the scripture would be fulfilled: "Not one of his bones will be broken," ³⁷ and, as another scripture says, "They will look on the one they have pierced." ³⁸ Later, Joseph of Arimathea asked Pilate for the body of Jesus. Now Joseph was a disciple of Jesus, but secretly because he feared the Jewish leaders. With Pilate's permission, he came and took the body away. ³⁹ He was accompanied by Nicodemus, the man who earlier had visited Jesus at night. Nicodemus brought a mixture of myrrh and aloes, about seventy-five pounds. ⁴⁰ Taking Jesus' body, the two of them wrapped it, with the spices, in strips of linen. This was in accordance with Jewish burial customs. ⁴¹ At the place where Jesus was crucified, there was a garden, and in the garden a new tomb, in which no one had ever been laid. ⁴² Because it was the Jewish day of Preparation and since the tomb was nearby, they laid Jesus there.

SESSION QUESTIONS

—

In addition to each day's reading, make one entry in your gratitude journal per day.

DAY 01   Read through John 19:28-42. Compare what you read about the crucifixion with Exodus 12:21-23 and John 1:29-31.

DAY 02   Write out Psalm 22, and read it alongside the passage from John on the previous page. Underline or highlight the verses in the Psalm that relate to the crucifixion and resurrection of Jesus.

DAY 03   Go through Matthew 27:32-66; Mark 15:21-47; and Luke 23:44-56, looking for any new insights the other gospel writers bring to the death of Jesus. What emotions are evoked while reading these passages?

DAY 04   Read the resurrection story in John 20:1-8. In light of Christ's triumph, what should our response be according to Romans 6:5-14; 12:1-2?

DAY 05   Open your Scripture, and read through John 20:1-18, followed by 1 Corinthians 15:56-57. Write your personal thoughts in your gratitude journal. Text or email your mentee about something you learned this week.

This weekend, read John 20:19–21:14.

▶   ENGAGE WITH THE WORD: **SEE YOUR STORY IN HIS STORY**

Read Revelation 1–3. In what way do the warnings to the Churches in Revelation apply to your life today?

JOHN 21

Grateful for ... RESTORATION

V V . 1 5 - 2 5

[15] When they had finished eating, Jesus said to Simon Peter, "Simon son of John, do you love me more than these?" "Yes, Lord," he said, "you know that I love you." Jesus said, "Feed my lambs." [16] Again Jesus said, "Simon son of John, do you love me?" He answered, "Yes, Lord, you know that I love you." Jesus said, "Take care of my sheep." [17] The third time he said to him, "Simon son of John, do you love me?" Peter was hurt because Jesus asked him the third time, "Do you love me?" He said, "Lord, you know all things; you know that I love you." Jesus said, "Feed my sheep. [18] Very truly I tell you, when you were younger you dressed yourself and went where you wanted; but when you are old you will stretch out your hands, and someone else will dress you and lead you where you do not want to go." [19] Jesus said this to indicate the kind of death by which Peter would glorify God. Then he said to him, "Follow me!"

[20] Peter turned and saw that the disciple whom Jesus loved was following them. (This was the one who had leaned back against Jesus at the supper and had said, "Lord, who is going to betray you?") [21] When Peter saw him, he asked, "Lord, what about him?" [22] Jesus answered, "If I want him to remain alive until I return, what is that to you? You must follow me." [23] Because of this, the rumor spread among the believers that this disciple would not die. But Jesus did not say that he would not die; he only said, "If I want him to remain alive until I return, what is that to you?" [24] This is the disciple who testifies to these things and who wrote them down. We know that his testimony is true. [25] Jesus did many other things as well. If every one of them were written down, I suppose that even the whole world would not have room for the books that would be written.

SESSION QUESTIONS

—

In addition to each day's reading, make one entry in your gratitude journal per day.

DAY 01 The Gospel of John ends with the restoration of Peter. For more on the background of his story, read Luke 22:31-34,54-62. Then, read John 21:15-25. How might Peter have felt when he saw Jesus in John 21? How did Jesus respond to Peter? What does this say about the character of God?

DAY 02 Like Peter, our past mistakes often lead us to believe God is angry or disappointed in our failures. Is there a specific situation, failure, or struggle of yours that comes to mind? Journal what you learn from this passage that can help you accept the love and affirmation of God even when you fail. Write a prayer using the truth of this passage to combat any lies you may still believe about your past. Refer back to John 6:37-40. Also, see Romans 8:1-2,37-39.

DAY 03 If you are a believer in Jesus, He has restored you! On a separate piece of paper, take some time to write out the details of your restoration story. Share these beautiful reminders with your mentee and rejoice with her in hers.

DAY 04 Reread the passage. The story in John isn't just about Peter's restoration; it is also about Jesus sending him out on mission. In light of what Jesus has done in your life, spend some time in prayer asking God what He might want you to do now. Journal about what He says and any steps you can take to follow through.

DAY 05 Look up Isaiah 55:10-13, focusing on verse 11. Reflecting on this session and the entire year you have spent in the Scriptures, what purpose or purposes has God accomplished in your life through His Word? Write these thoughts in your gratitude journal.

▶ ENGAGE WITH THE WORD: **SEE YOUR STORY IN HIS STORY**

Read Revelation 22. What determination does the final few pages of Scripture give you to live for God today?

GRATITUDE

—

GOALS

▲ To develop a heart that is continually expressing thanks by focusing first on Jesus—who He is and what He's done for us. In Jesus, we find more than enough reasons to give thanks.

▲ To see the impact on our everyday lives when we choose to cultivate an intentional heart of thanksgiving, not dependent on circumstances but rather grounded in truth.

SESSION QUESTIONS

1. How often do you find yourself turning first to thanksgiving and being intentional about cultivating a life of thanks and gratitude?

2. Which do you find yourself focusing on more frequently in your everyday life—the positives or negatives of the circumstances you find yourself in?

3. How have you seen a commitment to living a life of thanks impacting your heart over time? If you've not committed to a life of thankfulness, how do you imagine your life could change if you cultivated a thankful heart?

4. Are you willing to begin making a list of things you are grateful for right now?

The Jesus Bible

NIV ✠™ &SV

sixty-six books. one story. all about one name.

theJesusBible.com

THE GROVE
PODCAST

subscribe and listen on iTunes and Spotify

ABOUT THE TEAM

The FLOURISH team at Passion City Church is passionate about pointing women to Jesus through the power of His Word. A labor of love, this ministry has been shepherded by Daniele Flickinger, Susan Marks, and Shelley Giglio.

THE GROVE

The Grove is a monthly gathering of worship, teaching, and prayer for the women of Atlanta, Georgia. Hosted by Shelley Giglio and The Grove Team, these gatherings are an extension of what Jesus is doing in and through Passion City Church.

We believe every woman (person!) is God-designed, purpose-intended, significant, and lavishly loved by the King of the universe. No matter your age, your status, your style, or whether you think you have it all together or not, you are welcome at The Grove. If you live in Atlanta or are visiting the area, you are invited to come, rest, worship, learn, and be as we celebrate the power and greatness of Jesus. You can also follow along on The Grove Podcast. The heartbeat of The Grove is to encourage women to be rooted in the unfailing Word of God, to learn to flourish where we're planted, to walk in freedom in Christ and truly live, and to give our lives as shade to the people in our paths. This is The Grove.

PASSION CITY CHURCH

Rooted in the confession of Isaiah 26:8, Passion exists to glorify God by uniting students in worship, prayer, and justice for spiritual awakening in this generation. From its start in 1995, the Passion movement has had a singular mission—calling students from campuses across the nation and around the world to live for what matters most. For us, what matters most is the name and renown of Jesus. We believe in this generation and are watching God use them to change the climate of faith around the globe. Born out of the Passion Movement, Passion City Church exists to glorify God, to proclaim the name of Jesus to people in the city and the world. Passion City Church is located in Atlanta, Georgia, and Washington, DC, and is led by Senior Pastor Louie Giglio and his wife, Shelley.

Cyril Van Der Haegen
see page 184

Stephan Martiniere
see page 38

The Best
in Contemporary
Fantastic Art

EDITED BY

Cathy Fenner &
Arnie Fenner

Underwood Books
NEVADA CITY, CA

Trade Softcover Edition ISBN 1-59929-034-0   ISBN-13: 978-159929034
Hardcover Edition ISBN 1-59929-035-9   ISBN-13: 978-1599290355

10 9 8 7 6 5 4 3 2 1

Artists, art directors, and publishers interested in receiving entry information for the next Spectrum competition should send their name and address to:
Spectrum Fantastic Art, LLC, P.O. Box 4422, Overland Park, KS 66204
Or visit the official website for information & printable
PDF entry forms: **www.spectrumfantasticart.com**
Call For Entries posters (which contain complete rules, list of fees, and forms
for participation) are mailed out in October each year.

Contents page art by **Jenna Smith**. *See page 186.*

Published by
UNDERWOOD BOOKS
P.O. BOX 1919
NEVADA CITY, CA 95959
www.underwoodbooks.com
TIM UNDERWOOD/*Publisher*

C

cONTENTS

Chairman's

Cathy steps out with Ash Wood's robot. *Photograph by Arnie Fenner*

It feels like such a long time since writing the last chairman's message for *Spectrum 15*; the whole world has seemingly changed in the months following my last attempt to put down my thoughts regarding the field of fantastic art and our book in particular.

I think the word that keeps coming to mind for me is *perseverance*. A lot of what has gone on and continues to go on in the world around us relates to this one word.

Day after unrelenting day we were inundated with bad news—about Wall Street and the housing market and airlines and unemployment and home foreclosures and manufacturing and the auto industry and retailing and publishing. About the only two businesses that seemed to be doing well were fast food restaurants and gun shops, as if people were ordering a side of .44 caliber paranoia with their Big Macs.

We're hardly immune from the turmoil: Arnie and I know people that have lost jobs. We start each day wondering if the companies we work for will be able to staunch the flow of red ink and stay in business until things turn around. If not...we could find ourselves in the same boat as many of our friends.

What has struck me most has been people's reactions to this "new world": some want to pull the covers over their heads and basically give up."It's the New Great Depression! We're all doomed!" Some are convinced of left *or* right wing conspiracies to foul everything up. But others are seeing hard times as an opportunity to reinvent themselves and explore new territory.

I feel like Arnie and I belong to the second group. We choose to look at this as a chance to reinvigorate ourselves and *Spectrum* and to find the opportunities that the future has to offer as long as we have the determination not to give up. We're going to do *more* than hang on: we're going to push *forward*. We *know* it's going to get better—for us, for you, for everyone.

The *Spectrum* jury convened on the weekend of Friday, February 28th in Kansas City. All the judges' flights were on time or a little early and we hosted a dinner the first evening so that everyone could get acquainted. On Saturday morning we were surprised by a heavy, wet snowstorm which made our normal 25 minute drive into downtown quite interesting, to say the least. Nevertheless, the judging began on time at 8:30 AM. We broke for lunch briefly at noon and went back at it, alternating between two room set-ups, until 3:30 PM. Discussions for the awards followed and lasted until almost 6:00. The awards debates are always fascinating because you never know until the last minute which piece is going to walk away with the Gold or Silver. We were able to post a video of Donato—this year's jury chairman—announcing the winners on our website almost immediately after the final vote was cast. Arnie and I had time to run home and change (the snow had miraculously all melted by then) and returned for our traditional jury dinner in a private dining room at Pierpont's in Union Station.

As in years past we were assisted by a group of dedicated individuals who generously give up their Saturday to help keep the *Spectrum* judging moving along in an organized, efficient manner: we could never pull off this event without their help. The crew this year consisted of Arlo Burnett, Lucy Moreno, Lazarus Potter, Gillian Titus, Angela Wheeler, Tracy Crawford, and Armen Davis.

The folks that helped make the weekend run smoothly, left to right: Lazarus Potter, Tracy Crawford, Armen Davis, Lucy Moreno, Gillian Titus, Angela Wheeler, and Arlo Burnett.

Spectrum is only made possible by the participation of the artists, art directors, and publishers—whether selected for inclusion in the annual or not—and to the readers that continue to purchase each volume. We might act as the ringmasters or hucksters, but this book—this ongoing project—belongs to *all* of you. To everyone we again sincerely extend our warmest thanks for allowing us to be a part of this community and to share our love of fantastic art.

—Cathy Fenner/Show Co-Chairman

KEVIN BRIMMER
artist/art director: Muller Bressler Brown

DAVID DORMAN
artist

DONATO GIANCOLA
artist/Jury Chairman

STEVEN SANDERS
artist

BOB SELF
publisher Baby Tattoo Books

KEVIN BRIMMER, DONATO GIANCOLA, BOB SELF, STEVEN SANDERS, DAVID DORMAN

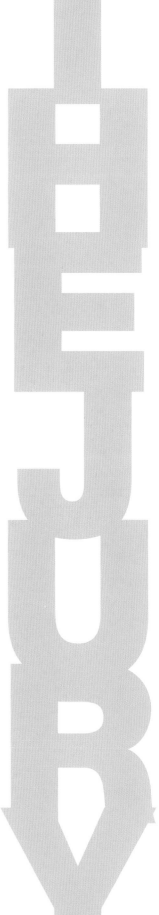

Spectrum
16

Richard V. Corben

born 1940, Anderson, MO

Richard Corben's work is singular in its humanity. He works with towering technical skill ... the wondrous thing of it all is that underneath all that technical tour-de-force is the sound of a beating heart.

Will Eisner

ARTIST, WRITER, CREATOR OF *The Spirit*

Comic artist, illustrator, film-maker, sculptor, gallery artist, photographer, writer, innovator, risk-taker, free-thinker—Richard Corben isn't easily summarized nor can he be readily categorized. He has never been satisfied with the status quo or with pat solutions; his natural curiosity has led to experimentation and innovation. In the course of his creative journey he not only became a singularly unique and influential artist, but also was responsible for an evolution of the comics industry.

Richard Vance Corben was born in Anderson, Missouri on October 1, 1940, and grew up in Sunflower (now Desoto), Kansas, a town built for workers at the government's Sunflower Ordinance Works during World War II. Thrilled by Sunday newspaper strips and *Superman* comic books, he began writing and drawing his own stories almost as soon as he could pick up a pencil and never stopped; at the age of ten he created a series of comics about the adventures of Trail, the family dog, followed quickly by copies of Jesse Marsh's *Tarzan* and imitations of *Brothers of the Spear* (a long-running backup feature in the *Tarzan* comics).

Richard also showed a deep and abiding interest in cartoons and created stacks of animated flip-books out of notepads and tablets. Following high school he was encouraged to pursue art by his parents and enrolled in the Kansas City Art Institute to study painting. The Institute's emphasis was primarily on Fine Art and didn't offer courses in film, but Corben nevertheless bucked tradition and produced an animated short based on "The Labors of Hercules" as his senior project. After graduating with a BFA he served six months in the Army Reserves and worked construction before landing a job in 1963 as an artist/animator/cameraman at Calvin Productions, a company that produced training films for corporations.

It was during his nine-year-tenure at Calvin that Richard married his wife Dona and also began to flex his artistic muscles and express his independence. His first professional sale was a cover painting for the September 1967 issue of *The Magazine of Fantasy and Science Fiction*; he also started to submit illustrations and comics to a host of fanzines like *Weirdom*, *Photon*, and *Voice of Comicdom*. For fun he spent the better part of 1968 creating a short film, *Neverwhere*. The movie's live-action opening quickly transitions into animation and tells the story of an Everyman that stumbles into another dimension and is transformed into a nude warrior-hero. Stark, moody, inventive, and effective, *Neverwhere* received a C.I.N.E. Golden Eagle Award and the President of Japan Cultural Society trophy—and also introduced audiences to what would become Corben's most famous character, Den.

The appearance of "underground comix" (a term coined by writer Bhob Stewart) featuring the often-scatological work of Robert Crumb, Dan O'Neill, and Gilbert Shelton in the late '60s opened a door of creativity for Richard and he began drawing science fiction and horror stories for such titles as *Skull*, *Slow Death*, and his own *Fantagor*. He had originally published *Fantagor* himself in 1970 as an ambitious fanzine-style showcase for his and friend Herb Arnold's work but found selling the 1000-copy press-run (at the princely sum of $1.50) almost impossible; when he allowed San Francisco publisher Last Gasp to reprint it in

the comix-format he found he not only had a hit on his hands, but a growing reputation as well. Corben's experience at storyboarding training films helped him create comix with a distinctly cinematic quality while his education, eye for detail, and overall sense of humor allowed him to create characters that were individuals, who moved in their environments and reacted to the situations he placed them in as real people might. His depictions of violence were intense and graphic but never glorified the act; his scenes featuring nudity and sex, while erotic, were not exploitative or crude. And his humor was both sly and subversive and—perhaps above all—honest. He never went for the cheap shock or laugh. It all combined to make Corben (who sometimes playfully hid behind pseudonyms like "Gore") into something of an artistic enigma whose work was often misunderstood by fans and critics alike.

Success in the underground market (which rapidly went from boom to bust) served as a springboard into mainstream publishing and Richard left Calvin to embark on a freelance career in 1972. Always experimenting with various styles he became well known for his airbrush illustrations and for his startling use of color. In the pre-digital days color separations were an expensive process beyond the means of all but the largest companies: Harvey Kurtzman's and Will Elder's "Little Annie Fanny" for *Playboy* was virtually the only comic that had been painted—and subsequently printed—in full process color. Corben devised a unique method to simulate pricey separations by "painting" the colors as four black and white halftone acetate overlays: the results were stunningly vibrant. Artists and publishers sat up and took notice—and the look of comics changed forever.

He became a regular contributor to the horror magazines *Creepy*, *Eerie*, and *Vampirella* and eventually provided color inserts to their otherwise black and white interiors. European publishers began reprinting his underground work in hardcover albums and he quickly found himself with an international audience. A story featuring *Neverwhere's* Den first appeared with little fanfare in the underground comix, *Grim Wit*; the story was translated into French for *Metal Hurlant* (and became a sensation), then came back to the U.S. for publication in *Heavy Metal* (where it was greeted with acclaim). The ensuing series of lush, erotic, and action-filled installments in what turned out to be a multi-part adventure made him a legend. And yet that is only a *small* part of the Corben legacy.

Richard co-created what is arguably the first graphic novel (1979's *Bloodstar*), published some of the first fantasy art posters and signed prints, produced one of the first collectible statues for the F&SF/comics field, painted numerous book covers for every major publisher, and created movie posters and award-winning album covers (like Meatloaf's *Bat Out of Hell*). He makes films for his own pleasure. He produces Fine Art paintings and bronzes. And he continues to do comics (*The Hulk*, *Bigfoot*, *Hellboy*) and take life-drawing classes and experiment with computer art. Richard's list of accomplishments is lengthy—and continues to grow daily.

Though the designation of "Grand Master" is well deserved, it's nothing that will surprise those familiar with his career ...

Because Richard Corben has been a Grand Master for a long time already. This award merely acknowledges the obvious.   †

GRAND MASTER HONOREES

FRANK FRAZETTA   DON IVAN PUNCHATZ   LEO & DIANE DILLON   JAMES E. BAMA   JOHN BERKEY   ALAN LEE   JEAN GIRAUD   KINUKO Y. CRAFT
MICHAEL WILLIAM KALUTA   MICHAEL WHELAN   H.R. GIGER   JEFFREY JONES   SYD MEAD   JOHN JUDE PALENCAR   RICHARD V. CORBEN

THE YEAR IN REVIEW
by Arnie Fenner

2008

It's a recession when your neighbor loses his job; it's a depression when you lose yours.
—*Harry S Truman*

If you ever start to feel too good about yourself, they have this thing called the Internet.
You can find a lot of people who don't like you.
—*Tina Fey*

Where were you when the Blitt hit the fan?
—*Mark Summers referring to a controversial* New Yorker *cover by Barry Blitt featuring Barack and Michelle Obama*

2008, to put it mildly, was a year for the history books.

Politics, war, the environment, the global economy—all took their turns dominating the public psyche through the year.

The presidential campaigns that culminated in the election of Barack Obama as the first African American President of the United States were as exciting as they were polarizing, replete with high drama, good guys and villains (who was which depended on your point of view), rhetoric, accusations, promises, symbols, hopes, fears, and dreams. The election of Obama—whose fondness for *X-Men* and *Conan* comics, as Heidi MacDonald pointed out in her blog, made him "one of us"—was a rare bright spot (unless you were a supporter of the McCain/Palin ticket...in which case, not so much) in a year that had more than its fair share of challenges.

The controversial surge of fresh American troops into Iraq proved to be effective in quelling sectarian violence and made a conclusion to the war finally seem possible; news wasn't quite as good in Afghanistan, however, as the Taliban and Islamic militants stepped up their attacks on NATO troops and had effectively seized control of portions of Pakistan. Russia briefly pummeled Georgia in the breakaway province of South Ossetia, Israel and Hamas continued to poke at each other, there was violence in India, Tibet, Kashmir, Nigeria, Somalia (*arrr! pirates!*), and Zimbabwe. Iran and North Korea continued to respond to criticism of their nuclear programs by conducting more missile tests—though Iran "increased" the number of rockets it claimed to have launched by adding several via Photoshop to pictures released to the foreign press.

Natural disasters added to the globe's miseries in 2008, includ-

Above: *Art Star Andrew Jones played his over-sized Wacom like a guitar while teaching at the "Revelations" seminar in January.* **Opposite:** *Sanjulian's stunning painting—inspired by the Conan story, "Black Colossus"—was sold by Heritage Auctions for a tidy $6572 in November.*

ing a 7.9-magnitude earthquake in China's Sichuan province that killed an estimated 70,000, a monster cyclone that killed 130,000 in Burma, the worst flooding India had experienced in 50 years, and Hurricane Ike, which smashed into Galveston Island in the U.S. and left $12 billion in damages.

Oh, and there seemed to be a little something going on with the economy. Never having been in a position to live beyond my means, I've always sat on the sidelines and watched as others bought things they couldn't afford and borrowed money they could never repay, all while Federal, state, and municipal government agencies spent money like drunken sailors on shore leave. I wondered how such an arrangement could possibly last and 2008 gave me the answer:

It couldn't.

The first "official" signs of trouble began in 2007 as problems with investment bank Bear Stearns caused a broader implosion of the subprime mortgage market as a whole (a crooked industry from the outset no matter how you spin it), which lead to a credit crisis. A bubble economy based on debt-denial and readily-available loans popped last year and created a mess for everyone. Spiraling fuel costs (prices topped out at over $4 for a gallon of Regular in the U.S.) resulted in higher prices for goods and services and contributed to declines in spending on entertainment and in overall retail sales. The auto industry suffered significant losses as unsold inventory swelled, banks began to fail, home foreclosures jumped, and the stock market took a nose-dive—$6.5 trillion in global losses were racked up in two days alone (October 6 and 7). Retirement funds disappeared ($50 *billion* worth thanks to Ponzi-scheme master Bernie Madoff), 401K

accounts dried up, and unemployment figures began to climb as businesses scrambled to keep their doors open anyway they could. Cathy and I sadly watched friends laid off at the companies we work for, well aware that it could have just as easily been either—or both—of us. Bad economic news beget bad news—the "adverse reaction loop," as Federal Reserve Chairman Ben Bernanke called it—and governments around the globe began to take actions to stabilize the markets and stimulate their economies with a variety of incentives and spending packages. How well any of it will work is anyone's guess; though there's been plenty of gloom, I don't think we're doomed. Things *will* improve. Society

Above: *This was one of a pair of AIDS-awareness posters for Europe created by the—heh— obscenely talented James Jean—which subsequently won a Bronze Lion Award at Cannes.*

learned a few lessons from the Great Depression, a few more from the Dot.Com bust; hopefully we'll learn something from the meltdown of '08 as well.

And, yes, of *course*, there were many positive events last year.

Setting aside, oh, any number of interesting topics that might be raised regarding actions and policies of the Chinese government, the Olympics in Beijing *were* spectacularly mounted with amazing venues, thrilling events (Michael Phelps' quest for eight Gold Medals for swimming kept audiences riveted), stunning architecture, and astonishing opening and closing ceremonies (staged by director Zhang Yimou).

In the wonderful world of science the Phoenix probe landed on Mars and not only discovered minerals that suggests that the planet's surface once held liquid seas, but also detected snowfall. The Large Hadron Collider in Geneva, Switzerland finally fired up in September after twenty-five years of construction (costing $6 billion

and involving over 9000 scientists) with the idea of smashing protons together at almost the speed of light in the hopes of unlocking some of the secrets of the universe. Critics feared that the LHC particle collisions might produce doomsday phenomena, involving the production of stable microscopic black holes or the creation of hypothetical particles called strangelets (sort of a mini-quark star)—great ideas, but it didn't happen. In fact, the Collider suffered something of a meltdown less than two weeks after they flipped the on switch and repairs were estimated to take a year.

Several news stories seemed to be straight out of SF (artists take note): doctors examined the theory that water might have a "memory"; Japanese researchers said they might be able to bring mammoths back to life through genetic engineering; European egg-heads manipulated test-subjects' perceptions to make them think they had swapped bodies with another person; and still other Japanese scientists claimed to have found a way to extract images directly from the brain, suggesting that one day we might be able to watch our thoughts or dreams on TV (lots of people will be pissed off if they ever get to see mine). I think my favorite pseudo-science story of 2008 was the hoax perpetrated by two knotheads in Georgia, who claimed they had a dead Bigfoot in a freezer; of course it turned out to be a not very-convincing gorilla costume, but you've got to hand it to them for getting CNN and other TV stations to give them publicity.

Last year nine of the top ten films at the box office were fantasy-themed (ten of ten if you want to consider the latest James Bond movie, *Quantum of Solace*, a "fanta-

sy"). *The Dark Knight* was the winner (both financially and critically, thanks in no small part to the late Heath Ledger's portrayal of the Joker) followed by *Iron Man* (which helped propel Robert Downey Jr. back to the Hollywood "A" list), *Indiana Jones and the Kingdom of the Crystal Skull*, *Hancock*, *WALL-E*, and *Twilight*. Frank Miller's adaptation of Will Eisner's *Sin City 2*, uh, I mean, *The Spirit* didn't make the top ten...or the top 100 for that matter (which surprised none of the people who were sitting in the audience laughing at clips previewed at the San Diego Comic-Con).

In the Fine Art world, "street artist" Shepard Fairey's "Hope" poster promoting the Obama campaign became wildly popular before prompting an infringement complaint from the Associated Press, who wanted credit and compensation for Fairey's use of a copyright-protected photo shot for the A.P. by Manny Garcia. Sotheby's in London auctioned 223 works by Damien Hirst over a two-day span. realizing over $200 million in sales. (Shoot. That adult zebra preserved in formaldehyde would have looked *so good* sitting next to our TV.) Closer to our area of interests, All Star Auctions sold Frank Frazetta's painting for the 1979 paperback of *Escape On Venus* for $251,000 (a new record for a Fritz painting); All Star also pulled in an equally unbelievable $115,000 for a comics page from *Green Lantern* #84 by Neal Adams. Heritage Auctions was similarly successful in enticing buyers: "Wanderers of Wonderlands," an oil painting by Carl Barks, brought $119,500, Wally Wood's pen and ink cover for *Weird Science* #16 fetched a whopping $200,000 in a private sale brokered by the company, and a series of new Conan paintings by Manuel Pérez Clemente aka Sanjulian realized healthy prices and electrified fans. Nobody—and I mean *nobody*—does deep, rich color like Sanjulian.

Given the curve balls thrown our way in '08 it's hard to predict what 2009 will bring. We'll get some bad news, I'm sure, along with some good news as well: let's hope it all evens out in the end.

ADVERTISING

The advertising industry has had its share of challenges in recent years as the audiences (meaning consumers) have changed their habits and become a more elusive target. Traditional media—newspapers, magazines, television, and radio—that has relied on advertising revenues to achieve and maintain profitability has suffered tremendously during the recession; as clients tightened their belts, ad dollars dried up and we began to see an alarming number of staff cuts across the board. An A.C. Nielsen survey found that advertising spending dropped 2.6% in '08. The print media category was hardest hit with local newspapers' ad revenues down 10.2% and the local Sunday supplements down 11%. Ad spending in national newspapers tumbled by 7.6%. Internet advertising was off 6.4% and network TV ad support was down 3.5%.

At the same time many online ad sources—including paid product searches primarily dominated by Google—remained optimistic. Zenith Optimedia predicted that online advertising worldwide would be up 18% in 2009 even as overall U.S. advertising is predicted to drop 6.2%. However, Internet startups modeled to depend on advertising alone were having an extremely difficult time securing funding (like every other company looking for credit).

Twitter, Facebook, YouTube, Flickr, and MySpace (though its day appears to be done) via computers and smartphones (IPhone, BlackBerry, etc.) were increasingly used for advertising and promotion. (When politicians are Tweeting, I worry.) In exchange for watching a few ads customers could watch TV for "free" on their PCs through Hulu...which made me wonder what the real difference was between Hulu and regular TV with a DVR. Gadgets!

This morphing of the marketplace, the transitioning from one method of ad "delivery" to another, raised more questions than it offered answers. How do you reach *real* customers...and how will you know *when* you actually do?

Of course there will *always* be print advertising and artists will always be called upon to create it (either with paint or pixels). And when they do credits will be typically hard to come by. Some of the work that caught my eye in '09 included pieces by Tara McPherson, Yuko Shimizu, Robert Rodriguez, and James Jean.

B O O K S

I wish I could say that the publishing industry had been immune to the recession last year. I wish I could, but you already know the truth.

Along with every other business that creates goods for the retail market, the book world was hit hard by the economic collapse. Book sales, which had actually been puttering along okay for most of '08, plummeted in the last part of the year and the major chains reported huge losses. Borders lost a staggering $184.7 million, prompting worries about the company's long-term health. As consumers closed

their wallets in anticipation of hard times, stores big and small felt the pinch, and publishers began to see massive returns of unsold titles as retailers tried to protect their bottom line by cutting inventory. December 3 became "Black Wednesday" as the crisis seemed to reach the breaking point and companies began to freeze salaries, lay off staff, and cut their future lines. Editors, art directors, and even a V.P. or two were let go at Random House, Simon & Schuster, McMillan, Penguin, HarperCollins, and on and on and painfully on: *no* company seemed to be untouched. I think we'll be seeing the effects for some time to come: there will be fewer books from publishers, smaller press runs, a reduced selection from brick & mortar retailers—and maybe fewer stores overall when the dust settles.

And Amazon.com, the 800 pound gorilla of the book (and DVD/Blu-Ray™, CD, electronics, vitamin, et al) world? They did just fine, thank you very much. Though they tussled with various states looking to collect sales tax, their discounts, selection, and rapid shipping gave them an edge that other sellers found difficult to compete with. Their Kindle e-book reader was so popular that they had difficulty matching production with demand—however, competitors were lurking in the wings as Sony unveiled a full-color e-reader in Japan (with an eye on the U.S.) and rumors began to circulate about Apple developing a "Kindle Killer" as a follow-up to their incredibly successful IPhone.

Me? I haven't bought an e-reader yet (though our publisher has and loves it). I'm still concerned for the same reasons I mentioned in last year's review (a widening gulf between the haves and have-nots through access to information), but I seem to be talking into the wind. E-books and the "digital delivery of content" were all the buzz last year (and this year, too) as the publishing industry looked for ways to bring back customers. There's another shift in the culture taking place, but it's a little too early to know where exactly that shift will take us. (Yeah, I'll probably buy some sort of e-reader at some point—grumbling all the way—and I *am* an Apple man...)

Good old regular books are *never* going to go away, of course—we just may see fewer of them someday. In the meantime there were some great titles published in 2008.

Easily one of the *best* books of the year was *The Prince Valiant Page* by Gary Gianni [Flesk Publications]; it not only provided excellent insight into Gary's creative process, but also served as an indispensible tutorial for other artists. *Fables Covers by*

James Jean [Vertigo/DC Comics] was a staggering collection of stunning works by an artist who simply shouldn't be as good as he is at such a tender age. The much-delayed but well-worth-the-wait *Ray Caesar* [Mark Murphy Designs] proved to be wonderfully disturbing and I was quite happy to pick up a copy of *Men and Angels: The Art of James C. Christensen* [Greenwich Workshop Press], which was jam-packed with exceptional paintings. Another welcome addition to my bookshelf was *Shadowline: The Art of Iain McCaig* [Insight], a cleverly written and designed examination of the career of an influential illustrator and concept artist (*Star Wars*, *Harry Potter*, etc.). David Saunders put

Above: *Gary Gianni's* The Prince Valiant Page *should be mandatory reading for art students.*

together the definitive book about his dad's work—featuring everything from magazine illos to *Mars Attacks!* cards—with *Norman Saunders* [Illustrated Press]. Lawrence and Judy Cutler's *J.C. Leyendecker: American Imagist* [Abrams] was similarly comprehensive, featuring 600-some color pieces. *Sparrow: Rick Berry* [IDW] was a little powerhouse of a book collecting the artist's recent gallery paintings while Ragnar's *Symptomatica* [Baby Tattoo Books] was bright and brilliant—his retro-chic people and designs are the epitome of "cool." *Archetype: The Art of Tim Bradstreet Vol 2* [Desperado] was a beefy display of incredible linework, *Benign Icons: Patrick Woodroffe's World* [Fantasmus] cast a welcome spotlight on the mixed-media art of a true visionary, and *Modern Masters: Mike Ploog* [TwoMorrows] was a fine celebration of the art of an influential comics and concept artist. *Grand Master of Fantasy: The Paintings of J. Allen St. John* by Stephen D. Korshak and J. David Spurlock [Vanguard] provided a solid selection of pulp-era art by one of the greats. *As I See: Boris Artzybasheff* [Titan] was a fitting tribute to a mid-century master of irony and biting political commentary, *Igor Grechanyk: L'Alchimie du Bronze* [Galerie Princesse de Kiev] was a satisfying collection of the sculptor's recent figures, while *Elixer 1: In Silence* by Mélanie Delon [Heavy Metal] was a lovely compilation of emotive, sometimes erotic digital paintings. *The Art of Alex Niño* edited by Manuel Auad [Auad Publishing] included a significant number of energetic drawings and color works, *Counterweight: The Art and Concepts of Rick O'Brien* [Design Studio Press] nicely showcased an award-winning painter, *The Tree Show* by Mark Ryden [Porterhouse] chronicled an event at L.A.'s Michael Kohn Gallery and was engagingly creepy, and *The Daily Zoo: Keeping the Doctor Away With A Drawing a Day* by Chris Ayers [Design Studio Press] was an inspirational, often hilarious chronicle of defiance as Chris battled leukemia by drawing a new creature everyday for a year. Mentioned without comment (other than to say we were proud to have been a part of it) was our *Brush With Passion: The Life and Art of Dave Stevens* [Underwood Books].

There was another memorable out-pouring of single artist booklets created for summer convention appearances in '08. I was *really* impressed by a pair produced by Big Wow!: *Space Girl* by Travis Charest (I can never get enough of Travis' fine work) and the self-titled *Sanjulian* (ditto!). *Arthur Adams Sketchbook 7* was overflowing with tasty line drawings (and Arthur doesn't wholesale his books so you either buy one in person or pay ten times the cover price on ebay), *Neal Adams 2008 Sketchbook* included a special Buck Rogers strip, *The Illustration of David Palumbo* was a pocket-sized keepsake, while *Battle Milk Volume 1* was a first-class collection by Kilian Plunkett, Thang Le, Wayne Lo, and Jackson Sze. And did I miss snagging copies of *More Drawings* by Mike Mignola and *Hissy Fit* by Adam Hughes? You know better.

Multiple artist "anthology" books that put me on American Express' "we like *this* guy" list included the requisite *Illustrators 49* edited by Jill Bossert [CollinsDesign]—if you're an artist or art director, you'll not only want this book, you'll *need* it. The granddaddy of the art annuals has been around for five decades for good reason. *Juxtapoz: Illustration* included some outstanding samples by James Jean, Tomer

Hanuka, Amy Sol, and the always amazing Barron Storey; *Swallow #5,* edited by Ashley Wood [IDW], featured memorable folios by Sam Weber, Jim Mahfood, Camile d'Errico, and John Watkiss; and *Erotic Fantasy Art*, edited by Aly Fell and Duddlebug [Collins Design], boasted a nice mix of sexy work by Brom, Julie Bell, and Matt Busch. *Metamorphosis 2: 50 Contemporary Surreal, Fantastic and Visionary Artists,* edited by Jon Beinart [beinArt Publishing], featured exceptional paintings by Heidi Taillefer, Shawn Barber, Scott G. Brooks, and Michael Hussar among many other notables; *Imaginaire 1: Magic Realism 2008-2009*, edited by Claus Brusen [Fantasmus], starred striking pieces

Above: *Trick or...treat? The very cheeky 10th Anniversary Naked Pumpkin Run in Boulder, Colorado turned more than a few heads.*

by David Bowers, Steven Kenny, and Kinuko Craft; *Device Volume 1: Fantastic Contraption* [IDW] boasted a diverse selection of mechanically-themed works (2D and 3D); *Beasts 2*, edited by Jacob Covey [Fantgraphics], starred pieces by Travis Louie, Yuko Shimizu, and Jaime Hernandez; and the latest installment in the *Exposé* series (#6), edited by Daniel Wade and Paul Hellard [Ballistic], featured a colorful mix of marvelous CG art by the likes of Linda Bergkvist and Cory Strader. But the *real* attention-grabber in 2008 was *A Lovecraft Retrospective: Artists Inspired by H.P. Lovecraft* [Centipede Press]: not only was it physically imposing at 12"x16" and 400 color pages, not only was the $395 price-etag sobering, but...it was pretty damn definitive with only a few omissions (I'm thinking of Jack Jackson's and Richard Corben's comix adaptations). Giger, Wrightson, Palencar, Whelan, Potter—they're all here and *much more*. Voters must be vacationing in Innsmouth if it doesn't win some kind of award.

Looking at the "Illustrated Books" shelf, I loved *Beowulf: Grendel the Ghastly* by Michelle L. Szobody with splendid illustrations by Justin Gerard [Portland Studios], *Tales From Outer Suburbia* by Shaun Tan

[Allen & Unwin], *Fairies and Dragons: Art is Magic* by Ciruelo [DAC Editions], and the definitive new edition of Mary Shelly's *Frankenstein* with illustrations by the incomparable Bernie Wrightson [Dark Horse]. Greg Broadmore produced a whimsical wonderment with *Doctor Grordbort's Contrapulatronic Dingus Directory* [Weta/Dark Horse], and *Spectrum* regular Petar Meseldzija at last completed his *Legend of Steel Bashaw* book [Zmaj], which was produced in a lovely over-sized edition in Serbia: let's hope a savvy American publisher snaps it up. *Tales from the Perilous Realm* by J.R.R. Tolkien [Houghton Mifflin Harcourt] included another batch of wondrous watercolors by Alan Lee, Del Rey released *The Horror Stories of Robert E. Howard*, edited by Jim and Ruth Keegan and powerfully illustrated by Greg Staples, while Subterranean Press published a deluxe edition of *Kull: Exile of Atlantis* that featured Justin Sweet's authoritative color work. Mentioned without comment (since I designed it and wrote the intro) was the BlackBart/Underwood Books edition of Conan stories *"...and their memory was a bitter tree..."* that included new color art by Brom and classic paintings by Frank Frazetta as illustrations.

A handful of the covers that caught my eye included those by Rick Berry (*Bring Down the Sun* by Judith Tarr [Tor]), Kinuko Y. Craft (*The Bell At Sealey Head* by Patricia A. McKillip [Ace]), Justin Sweet (*The Breath of God* by Harry Turtledove [Tor]), Dave McKean (*Prince of Stories: The Many Worlds of Neil Gaiman* edited by Hank Wagner [St. Martins]), and Dan Dos Santos (*Iron Kissed* by Patricia Biggs [Ace]). When you consider memorable covers by Donato Giancola, Cliff Nielsen, Jon Foster, Stephan Martiniere, and too many others to credit properly here, it's easy to see why, regardless of challenges, I still think we're experiencing a Golden Age for F&SF cover art.

C O M I C S

The box office success of both *The Dark Knight* and *Iron Man* was the tail that wagged the comic book dog last year: the movie buzz made comics characters hot media properties without actually translating into an influx of new readers for the DC and Marvel originals. With the exception of *Watchmen*, that is (much to the chagrin of crusty author Alan Moore): the advance fan excitement for the 2009 film release shot the original graphic novel to the top of the bestseller lists where it remained—duking it out with *Diary of a Wimpy Kid* and *Naruto* for #1—for the better part of the year.

There were numerous strategies (i.e. gimmicks) to capture people's attention throughout '08, including teaming up Stephen Colbert and President Obama (in separate issues, natch) with Spider-man. All of the companies began to package and market their backlist titles more aggressively and even began to acquire defunct publishers' comics and release them in "archive" editions. And, of course, there were the typical number of variant covers, movie adaptations and spin-offs, character cross-overs, and "earth-shattering" events. While some of the hoopla paid off, much didn't and the industry began to worry that the glum economy was going to hit them as hard as it had every other part of the country. By year's end the manga express train (one of the most profitable areas of comics for the last few years) had hit a wall, several imprints had closed down (Virgin was probably the one with the highest profile), and both the mass and direct markets began to show price resistance to books they had cheerfully stocked in better times. Diamond, the major distributor of all-things-comics-related, began to implement policies to minimize stocking less-than-profitable merchandise—which had many smaller publishers protesting that they were being frozen out of the market.

Until employment figures turn around it is almost inevitable that discretionary spending will decrease proportionally. How that will ultimately affect the overall health of the comics field remained to be seen by the end of 2008.

I always tend to talk about DC first in these reviews simply because I cut my teeth on their comics growing up (when they were called National and cost 12¢). And I *still* like DC and what they do—they can still surprise me. Pleasantly. (Yes, I know the mob history and the Siegel & Schuster saga and the fussing about this that and the other: find me another entertainment company in the world that *doesn't* have a storied past. I won't hold my breath.) I wasn't that excited by their main event specials like *Final Crisis* or *Trinity,* but did enjoy *Tor* by the masterful Joe Kubert, *Justice Society of America* (written by Geoff Johns and Alex Ross, art by Dale Eaglesham and Prentis Rollins, and covers by Alex Ross), *Simon Dark* (written by Steve Niles and Scott Hampton with art by Hampton), a reinvisioned *House of Mystery* (written by Matthew Sturges and Bill Willingham with art by Lucca Rossi and Jill Thompson with excellent covers by Sam Weber), and *The War That Time Forgot* (written by Bruce Jones with art by Al Barrionuevo and Jimmy

Palmiotti) in no small part because of the covers by Neal Adams, Mark Schultz, Russ Heath, Mike Kaluta, and Brian Bolland. I thoroughly enjoyed miscellaneous covers and stories throughout '08 by Mark Chiarello, James Jean, Joshua Middleton, Tomer Hanuka, Dustin Nguyen, Kelley Jones, and especially the brilliant work for *Catwoman* by the amazing Adam Hughes.

Robert Downey Jr.'s bravura performance in *Iron Man* had Marvel sitting comfortably atop the industry heap early in the year until *The Dark Knight's* half billion dollars in box office receipts brought them back to earth. Still, with another hugely profitable franchise in the offing (let's not mention *The Hulk 2* or *The Punisher*—would this make 3?), Marvel had a *lot* to be happy about. Their traditional bestsellers—*Spider-man, X-Men, Thor,* and *The Avengers* in all their variations—remained extremely popular while their adaptation of Stephen King's *Dark Tower: The Long Road Home* (scripted by Robin Furth and Peter David with art by Jae Lee and Richard Isanove) received positive attention in the mainstream press. Marvel's center ring event for the year was *Secret Invasion,* written by Brian Michael Bendis with art by Leinil Francis Yu ("*Skrulls!!!*") and proved to be pretty popular with readers. I was impressed by the variety of artists and styles that were on display throughout their line and made special note of works by Aleksi Briclot, Claire Wendling, Cary Nord, Marko Djurdjevic, Frank Cho, Arthur Adams, Brandon Peterson, and Kaare Andrews. To say that it was a very good year both financially and artistically for Marvel is an understatement.

Dark Horse Comics continued to diversify their product lines with books, statues, toys, and stationary products—and they had their connections with popular Hollywood productions as well, with their adaptation of *Indiana Jones and the Kingdom of the Crystal Skull,* their plethora of *Star Wars* titles, and *Hellboy*—though

Above: *Neal Adams' thrilling cover to* The War That Time Forgot #1

there was no comics tie-in to '08's film *Hellboy II: The Golden Army,* there was *Abe Sapien, B.P.R.D., Lobster Johnson, Hellboy: The Crooked Man* (written by Mike Mignola and powerfully illustrated by Richard Corben), and *Hellboy: In the Chapel of Moloch* (script and art by creator Mignola). Jon Foster provided a series of outstanding covers for *Buffy the Vampire Slayer,* Frank Cho did likewise for *Conan the Cimmerian,* Nathan Fox eerily illustrated Joe Lansdale's interpretation of Robert E. Howard's *Pigeons From Hell,* and James Jean added his magic to the covers of *The Umbrella Academy.* Naturally I couldn't resist their first two archive editions of Warren's classic *Creepy* magazines (with more on the way). Greg Ruth, Jason Shawn Alexander, Jo Chen, and Eric Powell all produced excellent work for DH throughout the year.

Ambling around the comics racks, I spotted nice work by Greg Capullo, Jim Mahfood, Steve Pugh, David Hartman, and Peter Bergting at Image, while over at IDW the contributions by Ashley Wood, Ben Templesmith, Bill Sienkiewicz, and Rebecca Wrigley caught my eye. Underwood Books released a fat and colorful collection of Frank Frazetta's 1950s classic comics, *Telling Stories* edited by Edward Mason, Andrews McMeel collected three years of *Prince Valiant: Far From Camelot* by Gary Gianni (art) and Mark Schultz (scripts), and HarperCollins produced P. Craig

Above: *Barry Blitt's funny but controversial cover for* The New Yorker.

Russell's pensive graphic novel adaptation of Neil Gaiman's *Coraline.* Radical Publishing lassoed Jim Steranko to do a cover for their *Hercules* series, Penny Farthing Press boasted a nice painting by Glen Orbik for *The Victorian,* and I noted some great work for a variety of publishers by Frank Cho, Jeff Smith (anyone want to

My feelings about Dave Stevens through the years were always divided almost equally between delight and frustration. Delight in that he was enormously talented, an artist whose *Rocketeer* series reminded everyone how good comics could be, a creator whose work literally sparkled with personality. Delight, too, because Dave was genuinely a pleasure to be around: smart, funny, charming, and incredibly knowledgeable about a wide variety of subjects. People have tossed around the term "obsessed" when describing Dave's interests (particularly about his friend and muse, Bettie Page), but I never thought that was accurate: I would say a better description might be that he was passionate about the things—and people—he loved. In our many talks through the years he always displayed a mature and well-balanced perspective of whatever or whomever he was enthusiastic about.

But the frustration aspect kicks in simply because Dave only rarely (if ever) capitalized on his talent, popularity, and gifts. Doing art precisely the way he wanted—and drawing or painting only those subjects that he really wanted to—meant that he lost out on many lucrative oppor-

Rasl?), Stuart Immonen, Gabriele Dell'otto, Joe Jusko, and J.G. Jones among others..

I had slightly mixed feelings about Tom Roberts' *Alex Raymond: His Life and Art* [Adventure House]; it was quite thorough, but the landscape format was a bit uncomfortable to read and I wished *Flash Gordon* had been better represented. *Scorchy Smith and the Art of Noel Sickles* [IDW] was similarly unwieldy at 11"x11" and 392 pages, but nevertheless was an extremely valuable resource (as was the Raymond book). *Strange & Stranger: The World of Steve Ditko* by Blake Bell [Fantagraphics] was an unflinching bio of one of the most significant yet contentious creators of sequential art while *Kirby: King of Comics* by Mark Evanier [Abrams] was an affectionate celebration of, well, *the king of the comics*. Finally, I was suitably impressed by all the research that went into *The Ten-Cent Plague: The Great Comic Book Scare and How It Changed America* by David Hajdu [St. Martins]. It served as a cautionary warning of what can happen when pop culture and government butts heads.

DIMENSIONAL

Even before the economic poo hit the fan last year (and I hate to keep mentioning it, but its effects were and are far-reaching), the creators of 3D collectibles had been squeezed as various channels for their lines dried up and disappeared. Bankruptcies of SunCoast Video, K.B. Toys, and Sam Goody effectively eliminated outlets for all manner

of figurines and toys; concerns over budgets negatively impacted the gallery market. Instead of speculating on possible sales many comics shops began to place orders for statues and props only at customer requests. Which didn't mean there wasn't some great dimensional work created in 2008—there definitely was—but only that it could be more difficult to encounter some of this marvelous stuff by accident than it had been when times were flush. 2009 will undoubtedly offer more challenges.

DC Direct was busy, busy, busy last year with any number of cool items. I really liked Jack Matthews' "Batman: Black & White/Bob Kane" statue and Alterton Bizarre's multi-figure "JLA Build-A-Scene" (a really clever concept). The "Superman Vs. Darkseid" statue (sculpted by Ray Villafane) was dramatic and I was nostalgically tempted by the "1966 Batmobile Replica" (also sculpted by Jack Matthews). There were incredibly detailed toys devoted to various story arcs and mini series, "Ame-Comi" interpretations of several female characters, dandy busts, large dolls, and hip props (the Superman cape would've been great to have instead of the bath towel I used to tie around my neck when I was 5 pretending to be George Reeves).

Marvel produced 3D versions of their characters themselves and through multiple licensors the the quality was generally top-notch. Randy Bowen sculpted figures of "Luke Cage," "Odin," and "Wolverine." Kotobukiya produced an excellent "Iron

Man" (sculptor unknown) and Diamond Select produced—thanks to sculptor Gabriel Marquez—a spot on interpretation of "Captain America" from the cover of Avengers #4...the only problem being that, as with their previous Steranko "Nick Fury" statue, they failed to credit Jack Kirby—the artist whose work made the statue a possibility in the first place—anywhere in their ads or on their packaging. Come on, boys: it ain't that hard to include a line of type.

Todd MacFarlane added even more highly detailed dragons to their line, Tim Bruckner created an amazing "Vampire Hunter D" bust for Dark Horse, and Mindstyle finally released the second pair of creepy figures based on characters from Brom's novel, *The Plucker*.

And, yes, I *still* want one of the steampunk rayguns that Weta produces—they've even created a Blunderbuss in '08, for goodness' sakes! Arlo, our webmaster, has a Manmelter 3600ZX Sub-Atomic Disintegrator Pistol and I'm green with envy. (Weta also created some outstanding statues in their Hellgate London series, including "The Female Templar" and "The Hunter.") On the other hand, I was *not* tempted by ReelArt's "Egyptian Queen" statue based on Frazetta's painting: despite a sincere effort, I think it missed the mark.

I'm not exaggerating when I say that there were literally tons of statues, busts, and toys based on *Star Wars, Harry Potter, Halo, The Dark Knight,* "tooned-up" *Lord of the Ring*s maquettes, naughty Japanese gals with gigantic, uh, *attributes*, miscella-

tunities and we in turn lost out on seeing much more of his superlative work. His very private battle with leukemia (which lasted for the better part of a decade and about which at his request we had deflected queries from the concerned or curious through the years) had very little to do with his decisions: he'd simply say "no" to projects far more often than he'd ever say "yes," regardless of his health. For the last three years Cathy and I had worked closely with Dave on his autobiographical art book, *Brush With Passion*. The sad part is that, after so much planning and labor, Dave isn't here to see the finished volume—but, of course, time was never an issue with Dave Stevens, especially when it came to doing something the way he thought it should be done. The day before he died, despite a bleak prognosis, his thoughts were on the tasks still ahead: he told a

friend from his hospital bed, "I'll be on my feet in a few days and finish those last paintings for the book." Typical Dave.

Harlan Ellison (one of his many friends) has said that the hardest thing about getting older is having to bury your pals.

I never really knew how true that was until Dave died.

My friendship with Dave Stevens spanned over 20 years; he served on the first *Spectrum* jury and was an advisor and frequent participant. I don't think I ever knew him quite as well as he probably knew me (and I believe many of his friends would say the same thing), but I *do* know that I miss him.

Requiescat in pace, Rocketeer.

JOHN BERKEY 1932-2008

"Being fearful of failure or having little confidence just becomes something to climb over."

—*John Berkey*

Science fiction is supposed to be the

domain of the adventurous, of the forward thinkers, of people who are open to the unique and the new. Yet when it comes to science fiction *art*, aficionados too often tend to gravitate to the safe and familiar, to works and styles and artists that remind us of our first encounter with a genre that we come to love rather than to those that challenge our perceptions and engage or intellect. Our nostalgia has a way of blinding us to the accomplishments and import of contemporaries.

John Berkey was, unfortunately, often taken for granted by the majority of readers in our field. His spacecraft didn't look like modified V2s, his people weren't well-groomed models, his landscapes owed more to Monet than to the pulps. He was an artist that did a lot of high-profile work yet escaped the radar of many. Forget about winning a Hugo for Best artist: regardless of assertions otherwise, he was never even nominated...

But that was probably perfectly fine with John. A relatively shy and

neous characters from comics, tv shows, and movies—as well as all sorts of gallery pieces and Fine Art and designer toys (which are too goddamn cool for words) and one-of-a-kind dolls. If you want to find out where at least some of these great works might be lurking I suggest picking up a wide variety of magazines for starters, including *Amazing Figure Modeler*, *Toyfare*, *Hi Fructose*, *Giant Robot*, *Sculpture Review*, *ARTnews*, and *World Sculpture News*.

EDITORIAL

The single word that best summed up the newspaper business in 2008 was "dire." Every morning I'd check favorite websites (which, I admit shamefacedly was probably contributing to the problem) and there would be a headline titled "Newspaper Armageddon Watch" that would detail who was laying off staff and what papers were being sold and who was closing their doors for good. The magazine business didn't fare much better as an estimated 545 titles went belly-up in the U.S. last year (around 400 new ones started). But even though '08 was bad for magazine failures, 2007 was actually *worse*: Mediafinder counted 591 magazines that had ceased publication that year. The problem, of course, was linked to the drop in advertising spending (the life blood of a mass-market title) and disinterest from young consumers: the cover price, even when it's stiff, contributes relatively little to the bottom line. It takes from three to ten

copies sitting on the magazine rack to sell one—the rest are returned for credit as the next issue comes out—so subscriptions and ad revenues are what generates real profits. When both decline it is just a matter of time before the grim reaper knocks.

The genre's short-fiction magazines continued to struggle with dropping circulations and rising production costs. *Realms of Fantasy*—the field's only magazine with color art—abruptly folded (even though *their* circulation had actually *increased*) only to be purchased by Warren Lapine with the promise of resurrection by mid-'09. *Weird Tales* became more comfortable with their outré design direction and ran some attention-grabbing covers (including those by Viktor Koen and Jason Levesque), *The Magazine of F&SF* included some nice work by Vincent Di Fate, Maurizio Manzieri, Cory and Catska Ench, and Mark Evans while *Isaac Asimov's SF* and *Analog* featured some some excellent covers by David Hardy, George Krauter, Donato Giancola, Bob Eggleton, Mark Garlick, and Scott Grimando. *Interzone*, the U.K.'s premiere SF title, included some good paintings by Paul Drummond and Christopher Nurse.

As the year progressed, magazines as a whole tended to get thinner and thinner and original art began to disappear in an alarming degree. Perennial illustration favorites *Playboy* and *The New Yorker* continued to hold the line and featured new paintings (Olivia and Donato Giancola in the former, Peter de Sève and Barry Blitt in the latter) and cartoons—but both report-

ed struggles in this hard economy. And then, despite all the market worries, here came *Esquire* in October with the first *battery-powered* cover. Talk about *balls*! Cool!

My list of favorite artist-friendly publications was virtually unchanged from last year's and included Dan Zimmer's superlative *Illustration* (I encourage everyone to subscribe), *Communication Arts*, *Juxtapoz*, *Hi-Fructose*, *Print*, *Art Scene International*, *Airbrush Digest*, *Cinefex*, *SciFi* (soon to by *SyFy*?) and *ImagineFX: Fantasy & Sci-Fi Digital Art* (the pages are literally packed with tips for artists).

INSTITUTIONAL

"Institutional" has always been *Spectrum's* catch-all category, featuring works that were created for exhibit announcements, self-promotion, package design, prints, corporate reports, and any any number of other venues or uses that don't easily fit within our other categories.

Disaster struck Richard Solomon/Artists Representative on March 15th in New York City when a crane collapsed on their building, demolishing it. Fortunately no one was in the office at the time, but a number of paintings were destroyed, including works by John Jude Palencar, Brad Holland, Greg Manchess, and C.F. Payne.

It was interesting to watch as hands-on how-to workshops for artists—taught by *other* artists and not looking to sell attendees books or supplies or computer software—began to increase in popularity.

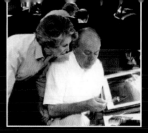

soft-spoken man, John Berkey didn't paint for accolades or recognition or honors, he painted because...he just loved to paint.

Born in 1932 in Edgley, North Dakota, Berkey knew that he was going to be an artist by age 15. He apprenticed at a variety of small advertising agencies to learn the ropes before taking a staff position with St. Paul's Brown & Bigelow calendar company in 1955. Eight years and 500 paintings later, John decided to become a freelancer and new clients greeted him with open arms: designers and art directors from Paramount Pictures and *Time* and Ballantine Books *all* vied for his remarkable talent. Utilizing an Impressionist's approach to his subjects, Berkey's histori-

car paintings had a sense of immediacy which placed the viewer in the middle of unfolding events, his portraits were both thoughtful and thought-provoking, his nudes eschewed the prurient and instead epitomized intimacy and grace, while his unconventional and majestic spacecraft influenced artists of all sensibilities.

Though the SF community didn't recognize Berkey's achievements with any honors, other organizations were more than happy to address the oversight. John was presented with the Spectrum Grand Master Award in 1999, was inducted into the Society of Illustrators Hall of Fame in 2004, and was selected as the *Exposé 5* Grand Master in 2007; a

pair of exceptional books featuring his art were published in his lifetime (*Painted Space* edited by Michael Friedlander in 1991 and *The Art of John Berkey* edited by Jane Frank in 2003), but it's not the awards and not the collections that John will be remembered for. Rather it's the cumulative impact of his *imagination*, of a unique vision, that will resonate in the years to come; John's influence will continue to be powerfully felt within the field and without. There is a timelessness to Berkey's work, a freshness and vibrancy that will continue to speak to new audiences for many years to come. John may no longer be with us, but his art will live on—not as artifacts of nostalgia, but as compelling celebrations of an unmatchable imagination. No artist could ask for a better memorial. †

Massive Black's "Revelations" seminar took place in Seattle in January and drew a mass of enthusiastic students; Rebecca Guay's Illustration Master Class was held in Amherst in June and was such a success that it looked like it would become an annual teaching opportunity; and we joined with Tor.com to sponsor painting demonstrations by Jon Foster, Greg Manchess, Rick Berry, and Stephan Martiniere at the San Diego Comic-Con and the resulting crowds caused neighboring exhibitors to give us the stink eye.

Bob Self hosted the second annual Baby Tattooville, in which 50 attendees got to hob-nob with a select group of guest artists, including Shag, Glenn Barr, and Michael Whelan. A number of illustrators attended Patrick and Jeanne Wilshire's IlluxCon (a small collector-focused confab in Altoona, PA) to sell originals and prints.

A few of the art calendars I saw and liked in '08 included *Pirates* by Don Maitz, *Dragons* by Ciruelo, *The Art of Luis Royo*, *Juxtapoz* (which featured the art of Robert Williams), and *Women of Enchantment* by Kinuko Y. Craft, and *Boris Vallejo's & Julie Bell's Fantasy Calendar*. We brokered a *Spectrum 2009* calendar for Andrews McMeel and divided all of the proceeds equally between the twleve artists.

Most artists sell prints of one sort themselves these days; Flesk Publications was one of the few publishers that offered a new print in '08, an action-filled Xenozoic scene by the gifted Mark Schultz.

If you live in any fair-sized city it's a safe bet that there were a host of group and single artist gallery shows spread throughout the year. "First Friday" is the monthly event in K.C. that attracts people to the city's Freight House Arts District, where scores of galleries welcome visitors (and dispense free booze!). A mere handful of the shows in other cities that attracted patrons included "Illuminate," featuring Mia Araujo, Robert Bellm, and Angelique Houtkamp at the Corey Helford Gallery in Culver City; Skot Olsen's "Architeuthis" at The Shooting Gallery in San Francisco; "Retinal Delights: The Juxtapoz Factor" group show at the Laguna Art Museum; and "Royals & Crocodiles" spotlighting Erik Siador and "Emroca" Flores at the L.A.'s ThinkSpace.

R E Q U I E M

In 2008 we noted the passing of these friends and talented creators:
Fuji Akatsuka [b 1935] manga artist
Wes Alexander [b 1966] cartoonist
Sergio Angeletti [b 1952] artist
Ed Arno [b 1916] cartoonist
Gus Arriola [b 1917] cartoonist
Jack Barrett [b 1929] artist
Pauline Paynes [b 1922] illustrator
James Bearcloud [1949] photographer
John Berkey [b 1932] illustrator
Bob Bierman [b 1921] cartoonist
Barbara Bradley [b 1927] illustrator
Donald Brautigan [b 1946] illustrator

Edd Cartier [b 1914] illustrator
José Casanovas Sr [b 1934] comics artist
Mel Casson [b 1920] cartoonist
Jim Cawthorn [b 1930] illustrator
Anne Cleveland [b 1916] cartoonist
Mario DeMarco [b 1921] illustrator
Boris E. Fimovich [b 1900] cartoonist
Will Elder [b 1925] comic artist
William Ellis Green [b 1925] cartoonist
Brian Hara [b 1945] cartoonist
Hawley Harris [b 1931] cartoonist
Walt Howarth [b 1928] illustrator
Carolyn Jagodits [b ?] cartoonist
Jack Kamen [b 1920] comic artist
Charles E. Kavenagh [b 1925] artist
Alton Kelley [b 1931] artist
Ted Key [b 1912] cartoonist
John James Knudsen [b 1922] cartoonist
Gérard Lauzier [b 1932] artist
Ray Lowry [b 1944] cartoonist
Maurice Marechal [b 1922] cartoonist
Carlos Meglia [b 1957] illustrator
Phil Meigh [b 1926] cartoonist
Bill Melendez [b 1917] animator
Ardeshir Mohassess [b 1938] artist
Jim Mooney [b 1919] comic artist
Bettie Page [b 1923] model
Franco Paludetti [b 1924] comic artist
Guy Peellaert [b 1934] artist
Stéphane Peru [b 1982] comic artist
Robert Rauschenberg [b 1926] artist
Dave Stevens [b 1955] artist
Robert Testu [b 1913] cartoonist
Michael Turner [b 1971] comic artist
Mike Western [b 1925] comic artist
Steve Whitaker [b 1955] artist
Stan Winston [b 1946] SPFX creator   †

The Show

"Grand Central" — *Call For Entries poster by Peter de Sève*

artist: **Ryohei Hase**

client: **FIGHTSTAR – Raw Power Management**   *title:* **Go Forward and Forward**   *size:* **28"x10"**   *medium:* **Digital**

artist: **Yuko Shimizu**
art director: **Andrew Cook**   *client:* **Microsoft UltimatePC**   *title:* **Little Polka Dots and Other Stories**
size: **22"x30"**   *medium:* **Ink drawing with digital color**

1
artist: Matt Cavotta
client: Thanatopsis Records
title: Chaosface
medium: Digital *size:* 13"x13"

2
artist: René Milot
art director: Jonathan Nicol
client: Cirque du Soleil_Criss Angel
title: Criss Angel: screaming rabbit
medium: Digital *size:* 36"x72"

3
artist: Adam Bray
art director: Dan Kamf
client: Rival Game Studios
title: Kensei
medium: Digital *size:* 12"x15"

4
artist: Andy Park
art director: Stig Asmussen
client: Sony Computer Entertainment
title: God of War III [*Game Informer* cover]
medium: Digital *size:* 14"x17"

1

2

3

God of War™ is a registered trademark of Sony Computer Entertainment America Inc. © 2009 Sony Computer Entertainment America Inc.

artist: **Dan Dos Santos**
client: Crew Creative *title:* Hellboy II *medium:* Mixed *size:* 28"x40"

artist: **Daren Bader**

art director: Jessica Cardinale *client:* Hamagami/Carroll, Inc. *title:* Age of Reckoning *size:* 32"x32" *medium:* Digital

artist: **Stephan Martiniere**

art director: Dennis Beloff *client:* Interactive-Retail Solutions *title:* Machiavelli Luxury Boutiques *medium:* Digital

1
artist: Dan Seagrave
art director: Dan Seagrave
client: Pulverised Records
medium: Acrylic
size: 15"x15"

2
artist: Mark Ouvell
client: Copro Nason Gallery
title: Sweet As Ether
medium: Oil
size: 12"x20"

3
artist: Joe Jing
art director: John Kleber
designer: Joe Jing
client: Sierra Entertainment
title: Snow White
medium: Photoshop
size: 20"x40"

4
artist: Chris Buzelli
art director: Alexander Lagoet
client: Tropen Museum/
Satchi & Sattchi
title: Ghana Coffin for Fisherman
medium: Oil
size: 18"x24"

1

2 3

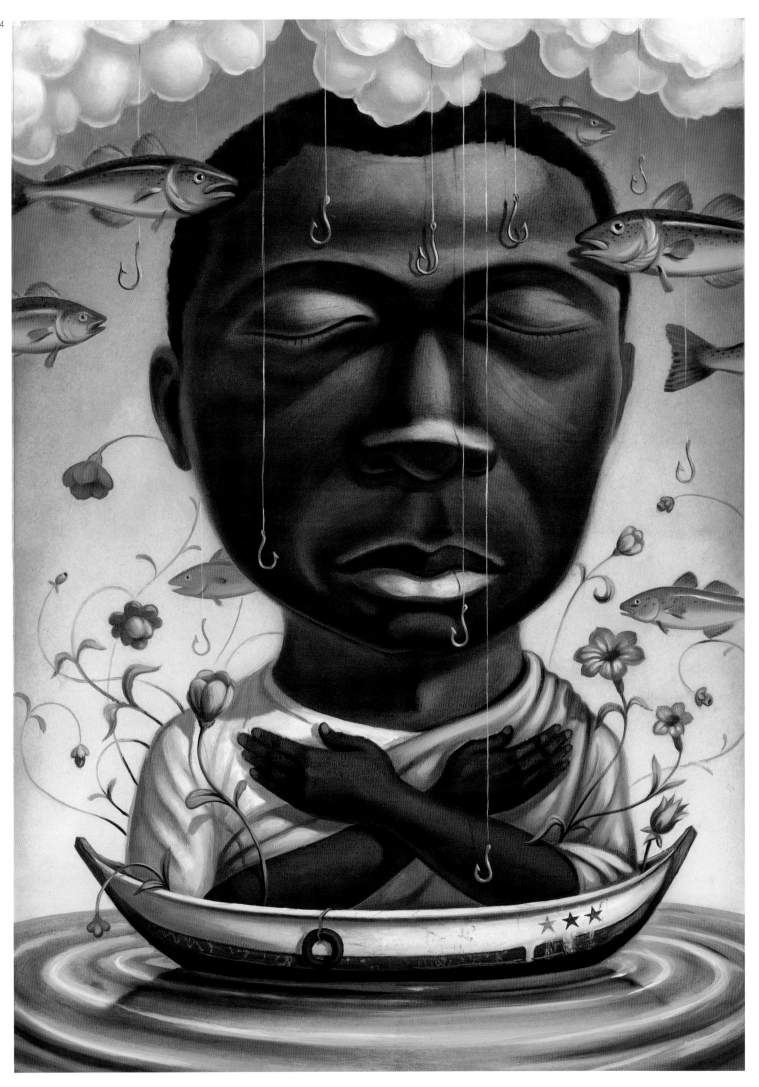

1
artist: David Dorman
art director: David Pearson
designer: David Dorman
client: Wiensien Brothers Ent
title: Arthur and the Invisibles
medium: Mixed
size: 16"x30"

2
artist: Frank Grau
art director: David Glanzer
designer: Frank Grau
client: Comic-Con International
medium: Ink/digital
size: 8 1/2"x7"

3
artist: Greg Spalenka
& Romie Shrestha
client: Project Peace On Earth
title: Peace Has Begun
medium: Mixed/digital
size: 24"x36"

4
artist: Dorian Iten
art director: Christoph Schiess
designer: Dorian Iten
client: Metzgerlehner Worldwide Partners
title: Puonak Audéo 1
medium: Photoshop/Illustrator

5
artist: Lee Moyer
art director: Sarah Jane Hardy
designer: Lee Moyer
client: Northwest Children's Theater
title: Hansel & Gretel
medium: Digital
size: 12"x16"

6
artist: Jerrell Conner
title: "Bloodlines" A
medium: Mixed
size: 4"x6"

1

2

3

4

5

6

artist: **Luis Diaz**
art director: Anais Thomassian *client:* Corel Corporation *title:* Fish Circus *medium:* Painter *size:* 28"x12½"

artist: **Yuko Shimizu**
art director: Andrew Cook *client:* Microsoft UltimatePC *title:* Little Red Polka Dots and Other Stories *medium:* Ink/digital color *size:* 30"x22"

artist: **Andrew Jones**
art director: Josie Schimke *client:* Black Rocks Art Foundation *title:* Artumnal Dancer *medium:* Painter X

artist: **Adam Hughes**

art director: Ron Boyd   *client:* Silver Snail Comics   *title:* That New Robot Smell   *medium:* Mixed/digital color   *size:* 6¹/₂"x10"

artist: **Kan Muftic**
client: NCSoft Europe *title:* Armada *medium:* Digital

artist: **Adam Hughes**
art director: Mark Chiarello *client:* DC Comics *title:* Women of DCU *medium:* Mixed/digital color *size:* 40$^{1}/_{2}$"x20$^{1}/_{2}$"

artist: **Donald Caron**
client: Les Productions En Pleine Face   *title:* Cul-de-Sac [film poster]   *medium:* Digital

artist: **Jeff Wack**

art director: Jorge Calleja, Barney Hobson designer: Weiden/Kennedy Amsterdam client: Coca-Cola title: A Little Lift... medium: Digital size: 24"x35"

artist: **Petar Meseldžija**
client: Zmaj, Novi Sad   *title:* The Legend of Steel Bashaw 4   *size:* 30¹/₄"x27¹/₂"   *medium:* Oil

artist: **Jean-Baptiste Monge**

art director: **Jean-Baptiste Monge** *client:* **Au Bord des Continents...** *title:* **Dunlee Darnan** *medium:* **Watercolor** *size:* **11⁷/₁₆"x 17⁵/₈"**

1 *artist:* **Stephan Martiniere**
art director: Lou Anders
client: Pyr *title:* Desolation Road
medium: Digital

2 *artist:* **Jim Burns**
art director: Claire Ward
client: Transworld Publishers *title:* The Third God
medium: Digital

3 *artist:* **Stephan Martiniere**
art director: Irene Gallo
client: Tor Books *title:* The Price of Spring
medium: Digital

4 *artist:* **Stephan Martiniere**
art director: Nick May
client: Orion Books *title:* Ace of Skulls
medium: Digital

artist: **Petar Meseldžija**
client: Zmaj, Novi Sad *title:* The Legend of Steel Bashaw 15 *medium:* Oil *size:* 30¼"x27½"

artist: **Ritche Sacilioc**
title: Playground *medium:* Digital

artist: **Matt Stewart**
art director: Irene Gallo *client:* Tor Books *title:* Valley of Shadows *medium:* Oil on paper on masonite *size:* 44¹/₂"x20"

artist: **Lars Grant-West**
art director: *Mari Kolkowsky* *client:* Wizards of the Coast *title:* Iron Dragon *medium:* Oil on canvas *size:* 16"x12"

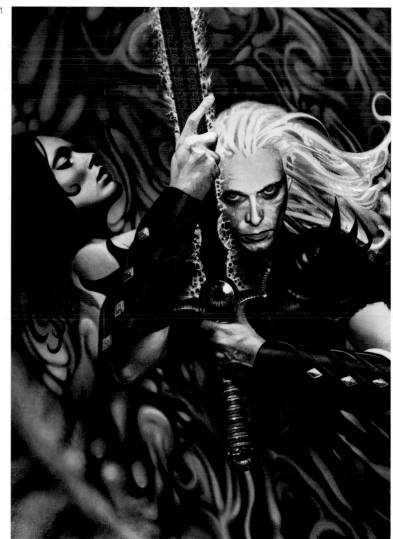

1 *artist:* John Picacio
art director: David Stevenson
client: Ballantino/Dol Roy
title: Elric: The Sleeping Sorceress
medium: Mixed/digital
size: 12"x17"

2 *artist:* Brom
art director: Brom
client: Eos
title: Lady Modron
medium: Oil

3 *artist:* Joe Jusko
art director: Joe Jusko
client: Hermes Press
title: Conan the Barbarian
medium: Acrylic
size: 15"x21"

4 *artist:* Brom
art director: Arnie Fenner
client: Underwood Books
title: Amra
medium: Oil

1 *artist:* Iain McCaig
client: Palace Press/Insight Editions
title: Shadowline [back cover]
medium: Traditional/digital

2 *artist:* Omar Rayyan
art director: Tim Szczesuil
client: NESFA Press
title: Magic Mirrors
medium: Watercolor *size:* 11"x14"

3 *artist:* Woodrow J. Hinton III
art director: Craig S. Grant
client: White Wolf Publishing
title: Toys in the Attic
medium: Mixed/digital *size:* 11"x15"

4 *artist:* Iain McCaig
client: Palace Press/Insight Editions
title: Shadowline [front cover]
medium: Traditional/digital

artist: **John Jude Palencar**
art director: Irene Gallo *client:* Tor Books *title:* Hidden World *medium:* Acrylic *size:* 27"x23"

artist: **Ritche Sacilioc**
art director: Mike Jolley *title:* The Messenger *medium:* Digital

artist: **Scott M. Fischer**
designer: Irene Gallo client: Tor Books title: An Evil Guest medium: Digital

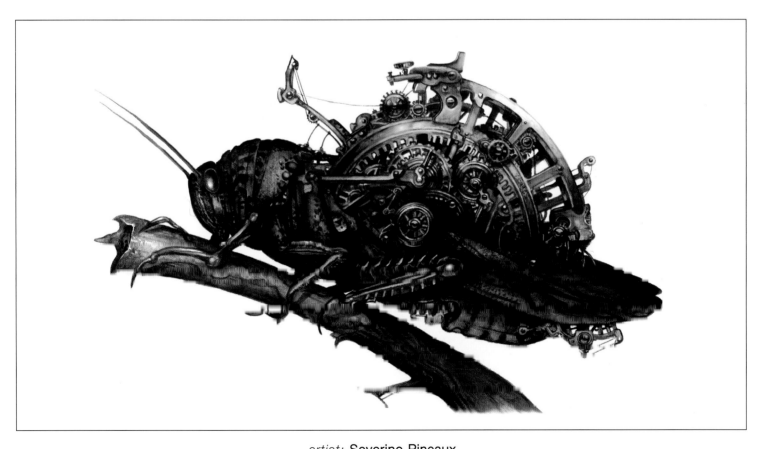

artist: **Severine Pineaux**
art director: Severine Pineaux client: Tournon Ed title: Tinie Cricket – Ysambre medium: Watercolor size: 15³/4"x12/4"

b

o
o
k

1 *artist:* **Agata Kawa**
art director: Chun-Liang Yeh
client: HougFei Editions
title: The Sleep
medium: Digital *size:* 7 3/4 x9 3/4

2 *artist:* **Lisa L. Cyr**
art director: Lisa L. Cyr
client: North Light Books
title: The Courageous
medium: Acrylic, oil, collage & assemblage
on canvas over masonite & board
with wooden framework
size: 19"x30 3/4"x2 1/2"

3 *artist:* **Tomar Hanuka**
art director: Irene Gallo
client: Tor Books
title: The Darker Mask
medium: Digital

4 *artist:* **Sam Weber**
art director: Irene Gallo
client: Tor Books
title: Nine Gates
medium: Acrylic

1

2

3

1 *artist:* **Jon Foster**
art director: Irene Gallo
client: Tor Books
title: Dragon and Savior
medium: Digital *size:* 19"x23"

2 *artist:* **Chris McGrath**
art director: Seth Lerner
client: Tor Books
title: Red
medium: Digital

3 *artist:* **Jin Hyung Kim**
art director: Jin Hyung Kim
client: Sungandang
title: Steam Giant
medium: Digital

4 *artist:* **Vance Kovacs**
art director: Dave Stevenson
client: Dabel Bothers/Del Rey
title: The Hard Call
medium: Digital

1

2

3

4

1 *artist:* **Travis A. Louie**
art director: Dice Tsutsumi
client: Totoro Forest Project *title:* Uncle Walter of Forest
medium: Acrylic on board *size:* 8"x10"

2 *artist:* **Adam Rex**
client: Harcourt *title:* Garlic Bread? Bluh!
medium: Digital *size:* 4"x7"

3 *artist:* **Bobby Chiu**
art director: www.IMAGINISMSTUDIOS.com
client: Totoro Forest Project *title:* Twins
medium: Digital

4 *artist:* **Kei Acedera**
art director: www.imaginismstudios.com
client: Totoro Forest Project *title:* Enoki, Forest Song
medium: Gouache *size:* 11"x14"

b
o
o
k

artist: **Todd Lockwood**

art director: Matt Adelsperger   *client:* Wizards of the Coast   *title:* The Ghost King   *medium:* Digital   *size:* 21"x15"

artist: **Alex Alice**

art director: Olivier Souillé   *client:* Galerie Daniel Mazhen   *title:* Jörmungand   *medium:* Oil on canvas

artist: **Todd Lockwood**
art director: Matt Adelsperger   client: Wizards of the Coast   title: The Pirate King   medium: Digital   size: 21"x15"

artist: **Raymond Swanland**
art director: Matt Adelsperger   client: Wizards of the Coast   title: Dragon War   medium: Digital

1 *artist:* Eric Orchard
client: Totorro Forest Project
title: Guardian of Autumn
medium: Pencil *size:* 18"x20"

2 *artist:* Ciruelo
client: DAC Editions
title: Bolt
medium: Oil *size:* 20"x27"

3 *artist:* Chris McGrath
art director: Lou Anders
client: Pyre Books *title:* Midwinter
medium: Digital

4 *artist:* Donato Giancola
art director: Irene Gallo
client: Tor Books *title:* Archer of the Rose
medium: Oil on panel

1 *artist:* E.M. Gist
art director: Kevin Siembieda
client: Palladium Books
title: Dead Reign
medium: Oil on hard board
size: 24"x36"

2 *artist:* David Palumbo
art director: Matthew Kalamidas
client: Science Fiction Book Club
title: Prey for Mercy
medium: Oil and liquid acrylic
size: 12"x18"

3 *artist:* Dan Dos Santos
art director: Irene Gallo
client: Tor Books
title: Green
medium: Oil
size: 16"x20"

4 *artist:* Dan Dos Santos
art director: Judith Murello
client: Ace Books
title: Bone Crossed
medium: Oil
size: 16"x26"

1

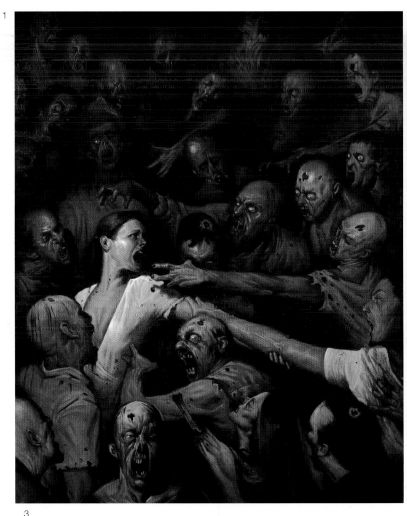

2

3

4

1 *artist:* **Gene Mollica**
art director: Dave Stevenson
client: Ballantine/Del Rey
title: A Woman Worth Ten Coppers
medium: Digital
size: 11"x14"

2 *artist:* **Raymond Swanland**
art director: Irene Gallo
client: Tor Books
title: Books of Glittering Stone
medium: Digital

3 *artist:* **Howard Lyon**
art director: Jon Schindehette
client: Wizards of the Coast
title: Ancestral Path
medium: Digital
size: 9⁷/₈"x14"

4 *artist:* **Scott Altmann**
art director: Christina Quintero
client: Penguin Group USA/Grosset & Dunlap
title: The Mysterious Mr. Spines; Flight
medium: Oil/digital
size: 30"x40"

4

artist: **Andrew Jones**
designer: Matt Adelsperger *client:* Wizards of the Coast *title:* Heaven's Bones *medium:* Digital

artist: **John Jude Palencar**

art director: Irene Gallo *client:* Tor Books *title:* The Mystery of Grace *medium:* Acrylic *size:* 29³/₄"x27¹/₄"

1 *artist:* **Chris Ayers**
client: Design Studio Press
title: Stuck
medium: Pen, marker, colored pencil
size: 5"x5"

2 *artist:* **Chris Ayers**
client: Design Studio Press
title: Steamed
medium: Digital
size: 6½"x8"

3 *artist:* **Robh Ruppel**
client: Design Studio Press
title: Otto
medium: Digital
size: 9"x12"

4 *artist:* **Craig Phillips**
art director: Elizabeth Phillips
client: Penguin Books
title: The Missing Link
medium: Pencil/digital
size: 8"x11"

1

2

3

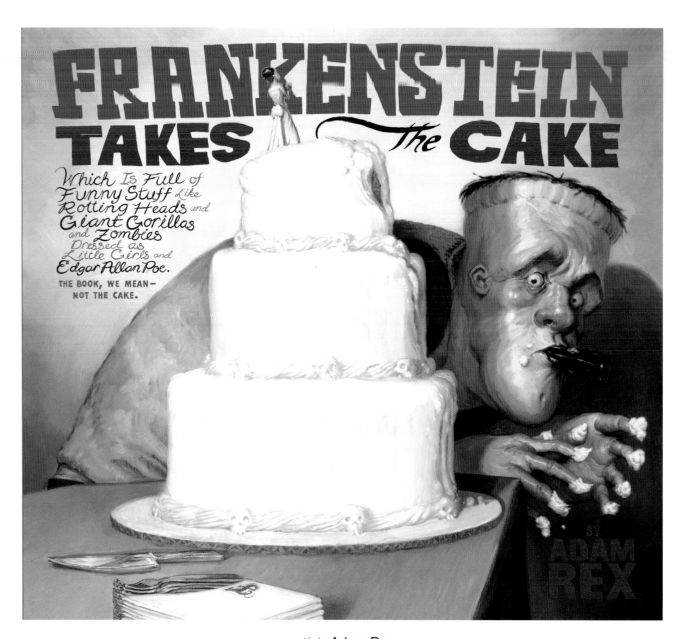

artist: **Adam Rex**
client: Harcourt *title:* Frankenstein Takes the Cake *medium:* Oil/digital *size:* 22"x20"

artist: **Jonny Duddle**
art director: Mike Jolley *client:* Templar Publishing *title:* Treasure Hunting!! *medium:* Digital

artist: **Francis Vallejo**
art director: Dice Tsutsumi client: Totoro Forest Project title: Super Load medium: Ink, gouache, zip-a-tone size: 22"x18"

artist: **José Emroca Flores**
client: I am 8-Bit title: I Thought I Came to Plumb medium: Oil on wood size: 40"x25"

1 *artist:* **Cory & Catska Ench**
art director: Linda McCarthy
client: Penguin Books
title: Chalice
medium: Oil on canvas
size: 20"x20"

2 *artist:* **Jody A. Lee**
art director: Sheila Gilbert
designer: George Long
client: DAW Books
title: The Hidden City
medium: Oil
size: 19"x23"

3 *artist:* **Raven Mimura**
art director: Stacy Longstreet
client: Wizards of the Coast
title: Lich Beholder
medium: Digital

4 *artist:* **Tom Kidd**
art director: Bill Schafer
client: Subterranean Press
title: Stonefather
medium: Oil
size: 30"x40"

1

2

3

artist: **Michael Komark**
client: Subterranean Press *title:* Gardens of the Moon *medium:* Digital

artist: **Michael Komark**
art director: Stacy Longstreet *client:* Wizards of the Coast *title:* Zithiruun *medium:* Digital

artist: **Donato Giancola**
art director: Judy Murello *client:* Berkley Publishing *title:* Fortune and Fate *medium:* Oil on panel *size:* 24"x20"

artist: **Georg Huber**
art director: Georg Huber *client:* Haus 21 Art Books *title:* Tree of Life *medium:* Acrylic on canvas *size:* 31"x23"

1 *artist:* E.M. Gist
art director: Matt Adoloporgor
client: Wizards of the Coast
title: Fangod Crown
medium: Oil on hard board
size: 22"x22"

2 *artist:* Wayne Reynolds
art director: Mari Kolkowsky
client: Wizards of the Coast
title: Dungeon Master's Guide
medium: Acrylic
size: 9"x12"

3 *artist:* Douglas Smith
art director: Richard Aquan
client: HarperCollins
title: A Lion Among Men
medium: Scratchboard

4 *artist:* Jesper Ejsing
art director: Christian Petersen
client: Fantasy Flight Games
title: Sword of Frost
medium: Acrylic
size: 15½"x19½"

1

2

3

artist: **Gregory Manchess**
art director: Gregory Manchess *designer:* Kirk Smith *client:* Lucasfilm Ltd. *title:* C3PO *medium:* Oil *size:* 20"x20"

artist: **Bob Eggleton**
designer: Desert Isle Design *client:* Subterranean Press *title:* Project Moon Base *medium:* Oil *size:* 30"x20"

artist: **Rick Berry**
art director: Alan Dingman *client:* Simon & Schuster *title:* Star Trek: Wounds *medium:* Charcoal/digital

1 *artist:* Greg Swearingen
art director: Anne Diebel
client: Egmont
title: Candle Man
medium: Mixed
size: 6"x5"

2 *artist:* William Stout
art director: William Stout
designer: William Stout
client: Comic-Con International
title: Farewell, Dave
medium: Ink & zip-a-tone on board
size: 12"x18"

3 *artist:* Petar Meseldžija
client: Zmaj, Novi Sad
title: The Legend of Steel Bashaw 16
medium: Oil
size: 19 1/2"x27 1/2"

4 *artist:* Shaun Tan
art director: Wolfgang Bylsma
designer: Skye Ogden
client: Gestalt Publishing
title: Never Leave a Red Sock
on the Line
medium: Pastel crayon/digital
size: 13 3/4"x19 1/2"

4

1 *artist:* **Vince Natale**
art director: Vince Natale
client: Bloodletting Press
title: The Nocturne
medium: Oil
size: 16"x20"

2 *artist:* **Patrick Arrasmith**
art director: William K. Schafer
client: Subterranean Press
title: Seven For a Secret
medium: Scratchboar/digital color
size: 9"x13"

3 *artist:* **Dave Seeley**
art director: Christian Dunn
client: Games Workshop
title: War Machine
medium: Oil/digital
size: 30"x45"

4 *artist:* **Dave Seeley**
art director: Matthew Kalamidas
client: Sci-Fi Book Club
title: Virga 1.2
medium: Oil/digital
size: 30"x45"

1

2

3

4

artist: **Cris Ortega**
art director: Cris Ortega   client: Norma Editorial   title: White Queen
medium: Digital   size: 20"x25"

artist: **Michael Komark**
art director: Irene Gallo   client: Tor Books   title: Busted Flush
medium: Digital

artist: **Stephen Player**
art director: Liz Laczynska   client: Random House   title: Drome Attack   medium: Watercolor   size: 16"x12"

artist: **David Dorman**
art director: Charlie Athanas, Denise Dorman *client:* The Devil's Candy Story *title:* Damali Richards: Entangled
medium: Oil/acrylic *size:* 14"x20"

1
artist: John Jude Palencar
art director: Irene Gallo
client: Tor Books
title: Not Flesh Nor Feathers
medium: Acrylic
size: 27"x23"

2
artist: Miss Mindy
art director: Robert Self
client: Baby Tattoo Books
title: Honnie
medium: Acrylic on wood
size: 10"x15"

3
artist: Michael Wm. Kaluta
art director: Irene Gallo
client: Tor Books
title: Traitor's Gate
medium: Ink & watercolor

4
artist: Gregory Manchess
art director: Lia Ribacchi
client: Dark Horse Publishing
title: The Satan Factory
medium: Oil
size: 20"x36"

1

2

3

artist: **Jon Foster**
art director: Chris Stengel *client:* Scholastic, Inc. *title:* Lyonesse *medium:* Digital

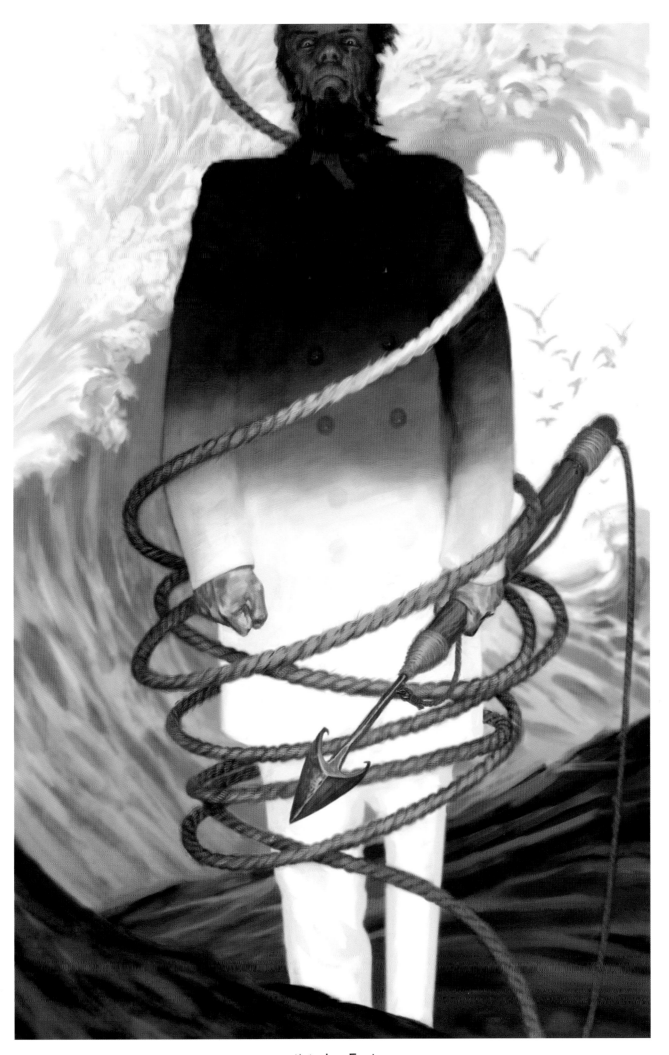

artist: **Jon Foster**
art director: William Schafer *client:* Subterranean Press *title:* Moby Dick *medium:* Digital

artist: **Vincent S. Proce**
art director: Jon Schindehette *client:* Wizards of the Coast *title:* Draconimicon Battle *medium:* Digital

artist: **Sally Wern Comport**
art director: Rebekah Sell *client:* International Bible Society *title:* Jonah and the Whale *medium:* Mixed *size:* 21"x15"

artist: **Adam Hughes**
art director: Jim Zubkavich *client:* Udon *title:* Street Fighter Tribute *medium:* Ink/digital color *size:* 9"x12"

artist: **Jon Foster**

art director: **Scott Alley**   *client:* **Dark Horse Comics**   *title:* **Buffy the Vampire Slayer #14**   *medium:* **Digital**

artist: **Aleksi Briclot**

art director: Bill Roseman   *client:* Marvel Entertainment, Inc.   *title:* Annijilation: Conquest #5   *medium:* Digital

1 *artist:* Mike Mayhew
art director: Nick Low
client: Marvel Comics
title: X-Men Origins: Jean Grey [page 19]
medium: Watercolor
size: 11"x17"

2 *artist:* Francis Tsai
client: Marvel Comics
title: Weapon X
medium: Digital
size: 11"x17"

3 *artist:* Steve Rude
designer: Steve Rude
client: Atlanta Dragon-Con
title: Valley of the Living Rocks
medium: Oil
size: 20"x30"

4 *artist:* Paolo Rivera
client: Marvel Comics
title: Mythos: Captain America [page 14]
medium: Acrylic and gouache
size: 11"x17"

1 *artist:* **Frank Cho**
art director: Frank Cho
designer: Frank Cho *Inker:* Dave Stewart
client: Dark Horse Comics *title:* Conan #1
medium: Ink/digital color *size:* 14"x21"

2 *artist:* **Dan Panosian**
client: Dynamite Entertainment/Dynamic Forces
title: Red Sonja #27
medium: Pencil, ink, Photoshop *size:* 11"x17"

3 *artist:* **Nathan Fox**
art director: Philip Simon
client: Dark Horse Comics *title:* Pigeons From Hell #1
medium: Brush & ink, digital color *size:* 9"x12"

4 *artist:* **Frank Cho**
art director: Frank Cho
designer: Frank Cho *Inker:* Dave Stewart
client: Dark Horse Comics *title:* Conan #2
medium: Ink/digital color *size:* 14"x21"

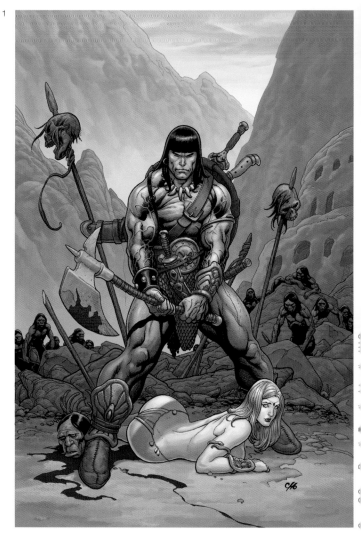

JOE R. LANSDALE | NATHAN FOX | DAVE STEWART

1 *artist:* **Steve Mannion**
art director: Frank Forte
client: Asylum Press
title: Fearless Dawn/The Bomb
medium: Brush & ink/digital color *size:* 6³/4"x10¹/2"

2 *artist:* **Jonathan Wayshak**
art director: Scott Peterson
client: Wildstorm Comics
title: Ferryman
medium: Ink *size:* 11"x17"

3 *artist:* **Arthur Adams**
client: Marvel Comics
title: Avengers Classics #12
medium: Pen & ink *size:* 15¹/2"x20¹/2"

4 *artist:* **Philip Straub**
client: Unity Entertainment/Utherworlds
title: The Clouding
medium: Digital *size:* 9"x12"

5 *artist:* **David Hartman**
client: Rob Zombie
title: Werewolf Women of the SS
medium: Mixed/digital color *size:* 10"x15"

6 *artist:* **Aleksi Briclot**
art director: Brian Haberlin, Tyler Jeffers
client: Todd MacFarlane Productions
title: Spawn: Architect of Fear
medium: Digital *size:* 8"x12"

2

3

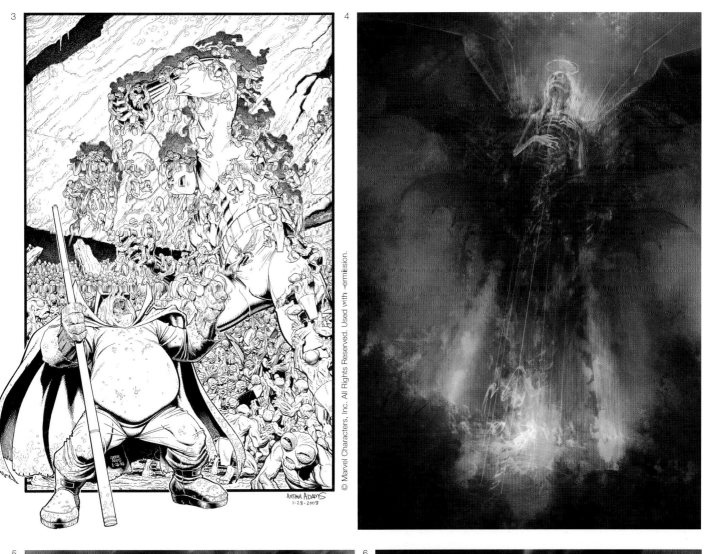

4

5

6

C
o
m
i
c
s

1 *artist:* Brandon Peterson
client: Marvel Comics   *title:* X-Men: Quilting Time #1
medium: Pen & ink/digital color   *size:* 7"x10½"

2 *artist:* Glen Orbik
art director: Charles Hancock   *designer:* Glen Orbik, Laurel Blechman
client: Penny-Farthing Press   *title:* The Victorian: Act V
medium: Oil   *size:* 15"x23"

3 *artist:* Glen Orbik
art director: Casey Heying   *designer:* Glen Orbik, Laurel Blechman
client: Buymetoys.com   *title:* The Oz/Wonderland Chronicles
medium: Oil   *size:* 17"x25"

4 *artist:* Paolo Rivera
client: Marvel Comics   *title:* Mythos: Captain America [pages 18-19]
medium: Acrylic, gouache   *size:* 22"x17"

5 *artist:* Andy Ristaino
client: Slave Labor Graphics   *title:* Tell Me a Story
medium: Pen & ink/Photoshop   *size:* 20"x15"

4

5

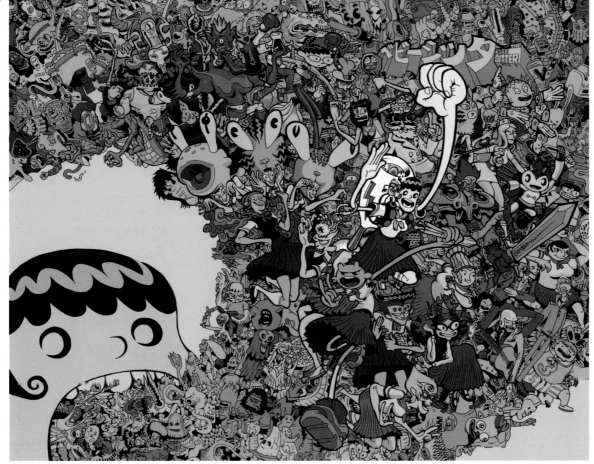

1 *artist:* Jeff Preston
art director: Shawna Gore *designer:* Jeff Preston
client: Dark Horse Comics *title:* Meet the Creepys
medium: Mixed *size:* 12"x19"

2 *artist:* Hoang Nguyen, Khari Evans, Kinsun Loh
art director: Hoang Nguyen
inker: Hoang Nguyen *colorist:* Kinsun Loh
client: Liquidbrush Productions *title:* Carbon Greys
medium: Pencil & ink/digital color *size:* 11"x17"

3 *artist:* Yuko Shimizu
art director: Karen Berger, Pornsak Pichetshots
client: DC Comics/Vertigo *title:* The Sandman: The Dream Hunters
medium: Ink/digital color *size:* 14 1/2"x22"

4 *artist:* Shelly Wan
art director: Sonny Liew
client: Image Comics *title:* Liquid City
medium: Digital *size:* 6 1/4"x10 1/2"

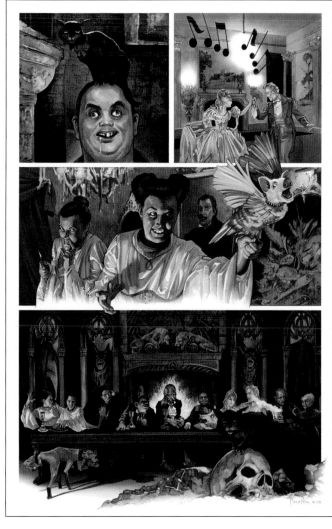

artist: **Andrew Robinson**
art director: Jeremy Jarvis client: Wizards of the Coast
title: Fuel the Fire [page 6] medium: Digital

artist: **Doug Williams**
title: Family
medium: Digital size: 13"x20"

artist: **Dice Tsutsumi**
client: Random House title: Out of Picture 3 medium: Digital

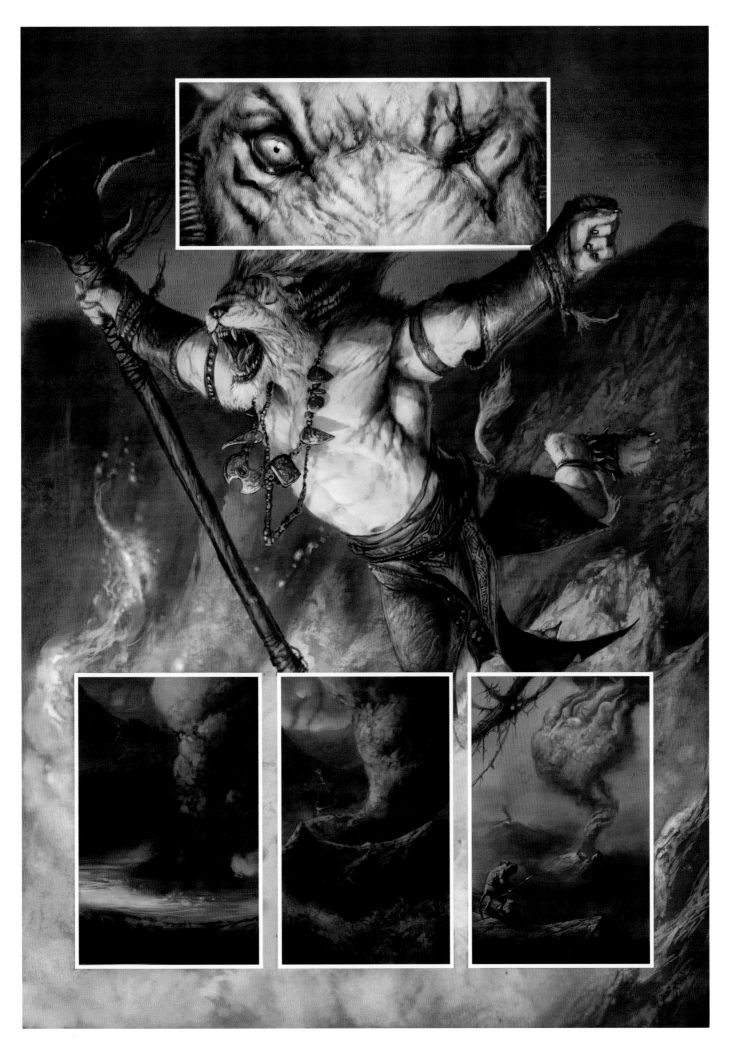

artist: **Dave Kendall**
art director: Jeremy Jarvis   *client:* Wizards of the Coast   *title:* Flight of the Cat [page 7]   *medium:* Digital

artist: **Ben Templesmith**
client: IDW Publishing title: Wormwood: Gentleman Corpse – Calamari Rising [cover] medium: Mixed size: 22"x17"

artist: **Ben Templesmith**
client: IDW Publishing title: Welcome to Hoxford #2 [cover A] medium: Mixed size: 17"x11"

artist: **Ben Templesmith**
client: IDW Publishing *title:* Wormwood: Gentleman Corpse Collection [French cover] *medium:* Mixed *size:* 17"x11"

artist: **Greg Ruth**
art director: Scott Alley *client:* Dark Horse Comics *title:* Conan: Born On a Battlefield *medium:* Mixed *size:* 14"x9"

1 *artist:* **Arthur Adams**
title: Sketchbook 7 Cover
medium: Pen & ink *size:* 11"x15"

2 *artist:* **Brian Haberlin, Geirrod Van Dyke**
art director: Brian Haberlin
client: Anomaly Productions *title:* Anomaly [page 1]
medium: Mixed *size:* 17"x11"

3 *artist:* **Adam Hughes**
art director: Mark Chiarello
client: DC Comics *title:* Catwoman #81
medium: Mixed/digital color *size:* 6⅝"x10½"

3

1 *artist:* **Dice Tsutsumi**
client: Random House
title: Dream of Kyosuke
medium: Digital
size: 9"x12"

2 *artist:* **Rolando Cicatelli**
art director: Pedro Adelante
client: Nicola Pesce Editore
title: Lische
medium: Oil on canvas
size: 25"x20"

3 *artist:* **Gary Gianni**
art director: John Fleskes
client: Flesk Publications
title: Twenty-Thousand Leagues
Under the Sea
medium: Oil

artist: **Daniel Dociu**
art director: **Daniel Dociu**   *client:* **Arena Net/GuildWars**   *title:* **Mole Tunnels**   *medium:* **Digital**

artist: **Richard Anderson**
art director: Daniel Dociu   *client:* Arena Net   *title:* Head Chop   *medium:* Photoshop   *size:* 8¹/₂"x11"

artist: **Vance Kovacs**
art director: Murphy Michaels   *client:* Midway Home Entertainment   *title:* Hydra   *medium:* Digital

artist: **Jason Chan**
art director: Jon Bailey *client:* Bioware *title:* Dragon Age: Origins (Elven Mage) medium: Digital size: 16½"x24"

c
o
n
c
e
p
t

a
r
t

1 *artist:* Devon Cady-Lee
art director: Harry Teasely
client: Turbine Games, Inc.
title: Moria Orc
medium: Digital

2 *artist:* James Paick
art director: James Paick
client: Scribble Pad Studios
title: Network System
medium: Digital *size:* 12¼"x22"

3 *artist:* Kekai Kotaki
art director: Daniel Dociu
client: Arena Net
title: Gunner
medium: Digital *size:* 7"x11"

4 *artist:* Tara Rueping
art director: Harry Teasely
client: Turbine Games, Inc.
title: Stand Off/Lord of the Rings Online
medium: Digital

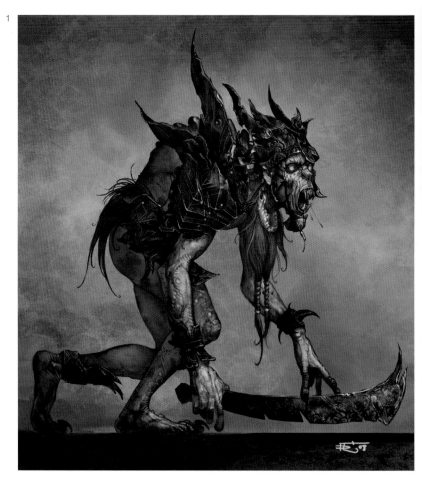

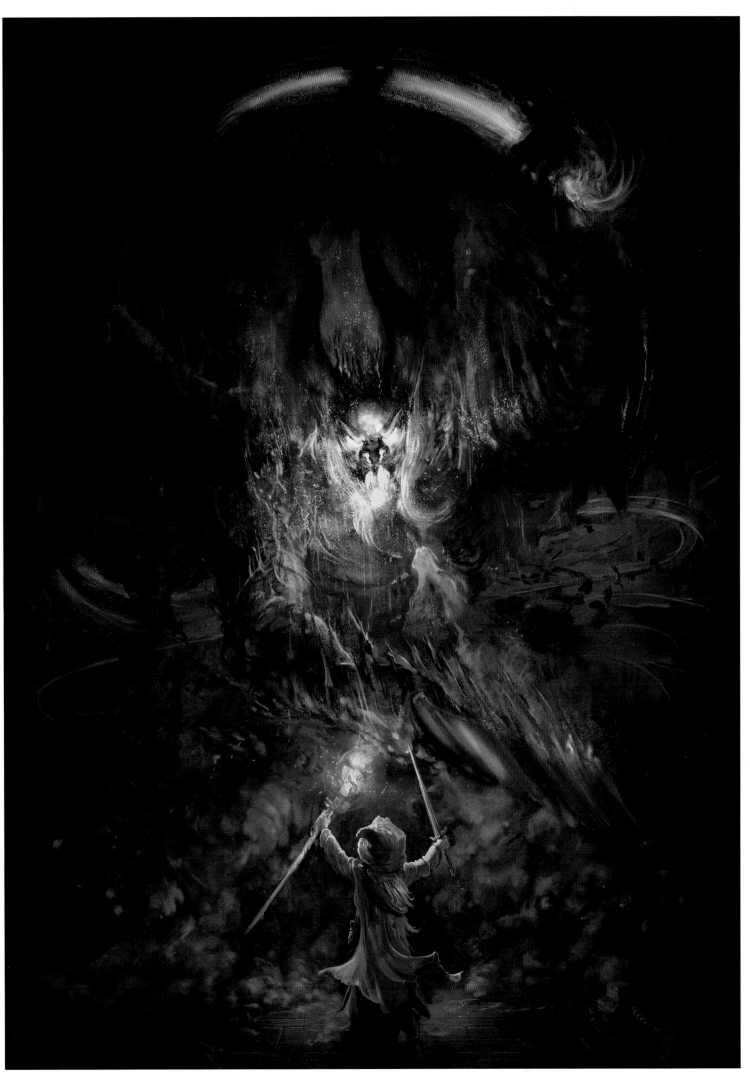

artist: **Philip Straub**
art director: Philip Straub *client:* Unity Entertainment/Utherworlds *title:* Cohabitation *medium:* Digital *size:* 15¹/₂"x8¹/₂"

artist: **Philip Straub**
art director: Philip Straub *client:* Unity Entertainment/Utherworlds *title:* Adesonaz *medium:* Digital *size:* 16"x9"

artist: **Jason Stokes**
art director: Daniel Dociu *client:* Arena Net *title:* Arch *medium:* Photoshop *size:* 10"x7¼"

artist: **Kan Muftic**
art director: Kan Muftic *client:* NCSoft Europe *title:* Snow Troll *medium:* Digital *size:* 17"x11"

1 *artist:* **Sam Brown**
art director: Coro
client: Massive Black *title:* Robots
medium: Photoshop

2 *artist:* **Doug Williams**
art director: Daniel Dociu
client: Arena Net *title:* Scarecrow
medium: Digital *size:* 36"x71"

3 *artist:* **Horia Dociu**
art director: Daniel Dociu
client: Arena Net/Guild Wars *title:* Undead
medium: Photoshop

4 *artist:* **Daniel Dociu**
art director: Daniel Dociu
client: Arena Net/Guild Wars *title:* Steam Demon
medium: Digital

1

2

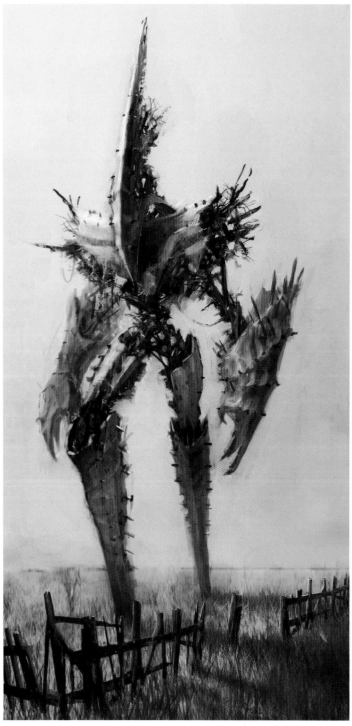

3

4

artist: **Jeff Haynie**

art director: Jeff Haynie *designer:* Adrian Woods *client:* Big Fish Games *title:* Blackpool Trolly *medium:* Digital *size:* 12"x9"

artist: **Robh Ruppel**

client: Naughty Dog *title:* Tree of Life *medium:* Photoshop *size:* 29"x17"

artist: **Brian Thompson**
art director: Brian Thompson *client:* Big Fish Games *title:* The Enchanted Forest *medium:* Photoshop *size:* 16"x9"

artist: **Shane Pierce**
art director: Chris Perna *client:* Epic Games, Inc. *title:* Landown One *medium:* Digital

1 *artist:* Daarken
art director: Greg Grimsby
client: Mythic Entertainment *title:* Liche Priest Shar'Hetef
medium: Photoshop

2 *artist:* Ted Pendergraft
art director: Carlo Arellano
client: Concept Design Academy *title:* Survival Horror Hero
medium: Digital *size:* 11"x17"

3 *artist:* Jason Chan
art director: Jon Bailey
client: Bioware *title:* Dragon Age: Origins – Morrigan and the Ogre
medium: Digital *size:* 24"x36"

4 *artist:* Horia Dociu
art director: Daniel Dociu
client: Arena Net/Guild Wars *title:* Slayer
medium: Photoshop

1

2

3

artist: **Daniel Dociu**
art director: Daniel Dociu client: Arena Net/Guild Wars title: Nucleus medium: Digital

artist: **Daniel Dociu**
art director: Daniel Dociu client: Arena Net/Guild Wars title: Broken Ring medium: Digital

artist: artist: **Kekai Kotaki**
art director: Daniel Dociu *client:* Arena Net/Guild Wars *title:* Guardian *medium:* Digital *size:* 11"x7"

artist: **Justin Sweet**
art director: Roger Ford *client:* Walden/Walt Disney Studios *title:* Raz in the Mist *medium:* Digital

1 *artist:* **Shaun Tan**
art director: Shaun Tan
client: Passion Pictures Australia
title: Proud Parents
medium: Pencil *size:* 16"x12"

2 *artist:* **Paul Sullivan**
art director: Bryan Johnston
client: Namco Bandai Games America
title: Afro/Droid Airbattle
medium: Digital

3 *artist:* **Peter de Sève**
art director: Peter de Sève
client: Totoro Forest Project
title: Bad Weather
medium: Crayon

4 *artist:* **Wesley Burt**
art director: Glenn Israel, Jason Whiteside
client: Volition, THQ
title: Character concepts:
"Red Faction–Guerrilla"
medium: Photoshop

1

2

3

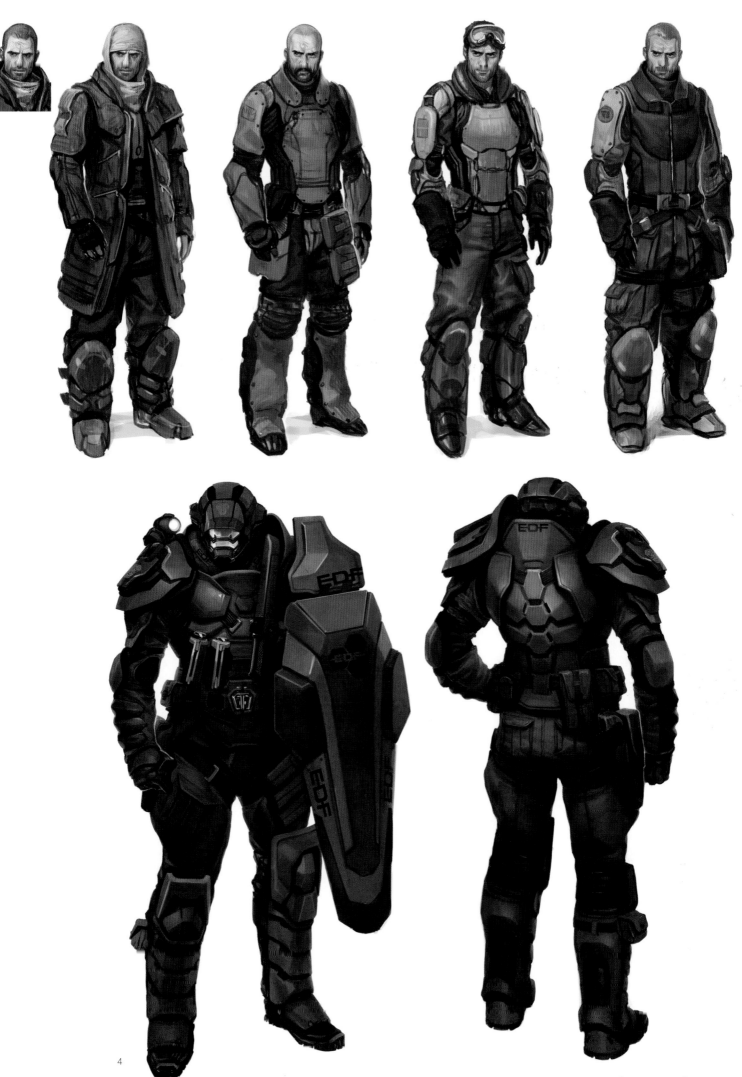

4

artist: **Wade Furlong**
colorist: Halil Ural *client:* Andrew Alexander *title:* Flippin' Birdy *medium:* Ink, graphite, digital

artist: **Ed Ko**
art director: Lana McCarthy *client:* Zynga – "Vampires" *title:* Lilith's Children *medium:* Digital

artist: **Miles Teves**
art director: Tom Duffield   *client,* Walt Disney Studios   *title:* Red Queen   *medium:* Pencil, digital   *size:* 11"x17"

artist: **Akihito Ikeda**
photographer: **Akihito Ikeda** *client:* **Kazuhiro Tuji** *title:* **Elegant Medusa** *medium:* **Resin** **size: H 18" x W 10" x D 8"**

artist: **David Meng**

photographer: **Steve Unwin**   *title:* **Satyr's Head**   *medium:* **Polymer clay**   *size:* **H 8½"**

artist: **Tim Bruckner**

art director: Georg Brewer, Tim Bruckner   *client:* DC Direct   *title:* Kinetics: Wonder Woman   *medium:* Painted resin   *size:* 11" H

artist: **Tim Bruckner**

art director: Georg Brewer, Tim Bruckner   *client:* DC Direct   *title:* Kinetics: Aquaman   *medium:* Painted resin   *size:* 10½" H

artist: **Richard A. Moore III**
photographer: Brian McClernon *title:* Octohandy *medium:* Bronze *size:* H 18" x W 24" x D 24"

artist: **Vincent Villafranca**
client: Private collection *title:* Otherworldly Procession *medium:* Bronze *size:* H 16" x L 32" x W 12"

artist: **Rachel Young**
title: Black Rabbit *medium:* Polymer clay, acrylic size: H 11"

1 *artist:* **John Mahoney**
title: Robo Girl
medium: Sculpey, plastic
size: H 15" x W 6"

2 *artist:* **Andrew Sinclair**
art director: Andrew Sinclair
client: Dennis Publishing
title: Kong Kicks Arse
medium: Bronze, copper, steel
size: H 9' x W 9'

3 *artist:* **Igor Grechanyk**
itle: Lion's Spirit: Vision In Time
medium: Bronze
size: H 22"

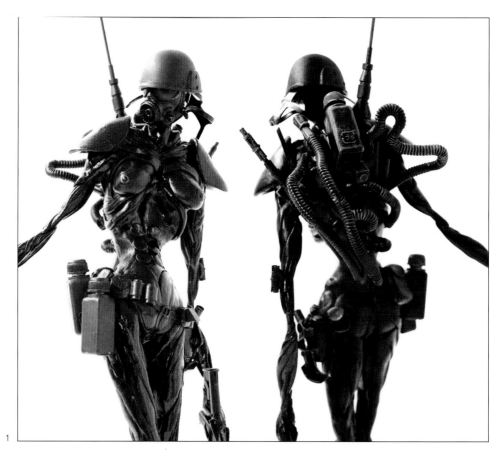

1

2 [detail]

2

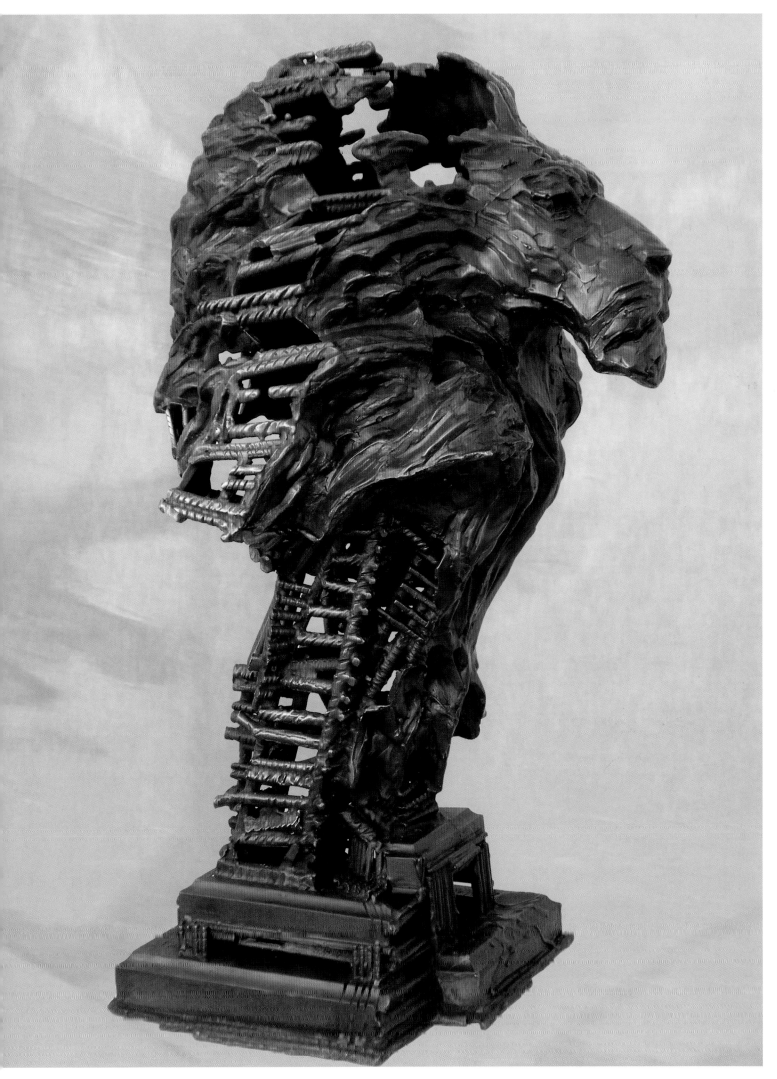

1
artist: **Mike Rivamonte**
photographer: Mike Rivamonte
title: Walt
medium: Mixed

2
artist: **Igor Grechanyk**
itle: Memories of Lost Eden
medium: Bronze
size: H 45"

3
artist: **Dave Pressler**
itle: The Early Days of the
Modern Vacuum Cleaner
medium: Super Sculpey, wood, wire
size: H 9" x L 7"

4
artist: **Mike Rivamonte**
photographer: Mike Rivamonte
title: Blade
medium: Mixed

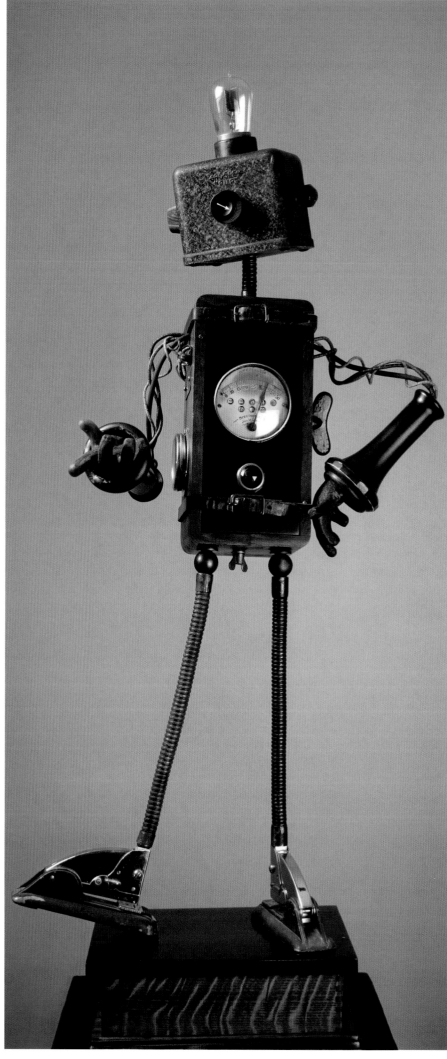

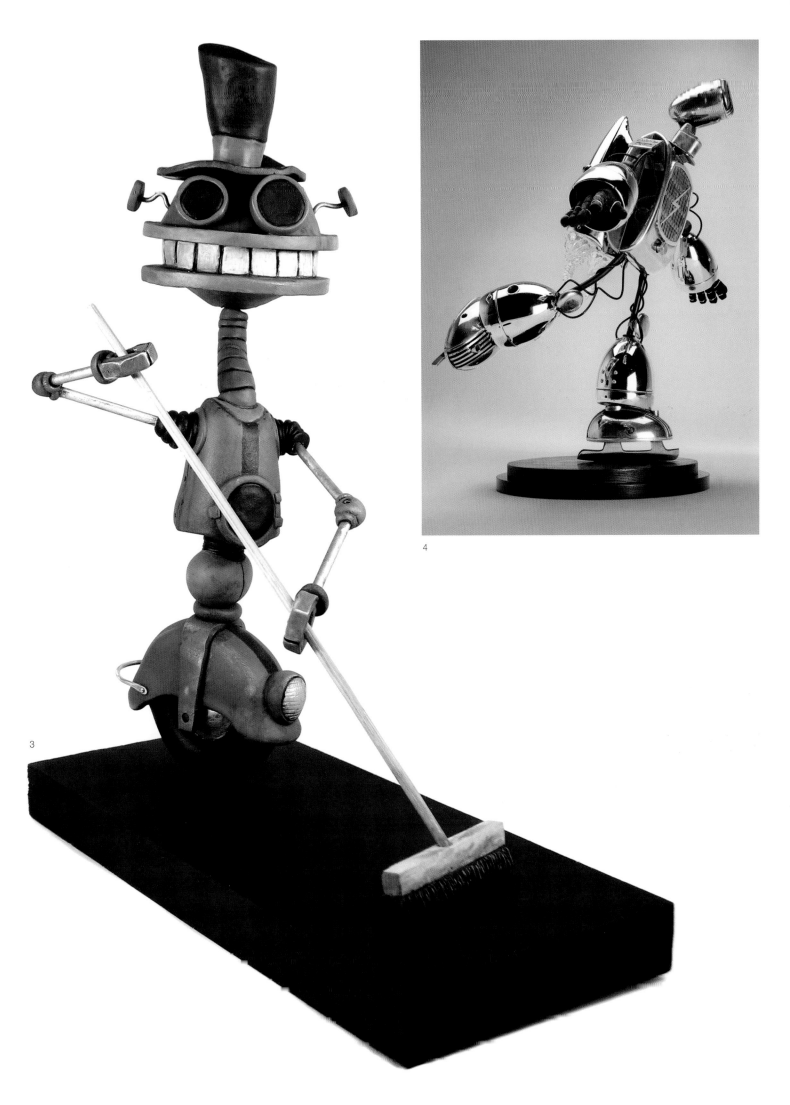

3

4

1 *artist:* **Allan Carrasco**
designer: Allan Carrasco
title: True Face
medium: Painted polymer clay
size: H 5"

2 *artist:* **Mark Nagata**
client: Max Toy Company
title: Kaiju Tripus
medium: Soft vinyl + V color paint
size: H 10½"

3 *artist:* **Irene Mátar**
photographer: Eric Balisle
client: Stargate Worlds
title: Jaffa Warrior
medium: Super Sculpey
size: H 15"

4 *artist:* **Javier Diaz**
photographer: Jose Rios
title: Akinor and His Goblins
medium: Super Sculpey, wood
size: H 11"x W 6"

1 *artist:* H.G. Yoder
photographer: Jafe Parsons
title: Crown of Poppies
medium: Bronze
size: 22" round

2 *artist:* H.G. Yoder
photographer: Jafe Parsons
title: Monarch Faerie Jar
medium: Bronze
size: H 9" x W 6"

3 *artist:* James Shoop
jewelry: Jen Ramautar
colorist: Kimberly Murphy
client: Shoop Scuptural Design, Inc.
title: Ramautar [portrait of Jen Ramautar]
medium: Bronze
size: H 18" x W 11" x D 10"

1

2

artist: **Walter O'Neal**
art director: Randy Bowen *designer:* Walter O'Neal *client:* Bowen Designs, Inc. *title:* Cloak & Dagger
medium: Super Sculpey, polymer clay *size:* H 11"

artist: Virginie Ropars
title: Grass Fairy *medium:* Mixed *size:* 20"x36" framed work

1 *artist:* **Tim Bruckner**
client: The Art Farm, Inc.
title: A Little Mischief
medium: Painted resin
size: Half life-size

2 *artist:* **Virginie Ropars**
title: Lunah 911 Dark Angel
medium: Mixed
size: H 33"

3 *artist:* **Tim Bruckner**
client: The Art Farm, Inc.
title: Lucifer's Lawyer
medium: Painted resin
size: Half life-size

4 *artist:* **Julie Mansergh**
art director: Faeries In the Attic (FITA)
client: Private Collection
title: Wish Faerie
medium: Polymer clay
size: H 8"

1

2

3

artist: Thomas S. Kuebler
title: Grandma Hoodoo and Zombie John *medium:* Silicone/mixed *size:* Life-size

artist: **Thomas S. Kuebler**
title: Schlitzie *medium:* Silicone/mixed *size:* Life-size

artist: **Craig Elliott**

director: **Charlie Athanas, Denise Dorman**   *client:* **Devil's Candy Store**   *title:* **Damali Richards**   *medium:* **Acrylic**   *size:* **8"x10'**

artist: **Nate Van Dyke**
art director: Evan Pricco   client: Juxtapoz Magazine   title: Pool Hall Brawl   medium: Ink on paper   size: 18"x24"

artist: **Yuko Shimizu**
art director: SooJin Buzelli *client:* Plansponsor Magazine
medium: Ink drawing with digital color *size:* 17"x22"

artist: **Dave Leri**
art director: Laura Cleveland *client:* Realms of Fantasy
title: All Beautiful Things *medium:* Oil *size:* 8³/₄"x11³/₄"

artist: **Malcolm McClinton**
art director: John O'Neil *client:* Black Gate Magazine #13 *title:* Gladiatrix *medium:* Digital *size:* 15¹/₂"x10¹/₂"

artist: **William Stout**
art director: Mike Fredericks *designer:* William Stout *client:* Prehistoric Times *title:* Carcharodontosaurus
medium: Ink & watercolor on board size: 14"x18"

artist: **Brad Holland**
art director: Irene Gallo *client:* Tor.com
medium: Oil

artist: **Peter de Sève**
art director: Françoise Mouly *client:* The New Yorker
title: Summer Getaway *medium:* Ink & watercolor

artist: **Adam Hughes**
art director: Scott Anderson *client:* Playboy *title:* Peep Culture *medium:* Mixed/digital *size:* 17½"x12"

artist: **Arthur Adams**
client: Comic Book Legal Defense Fund *medium:* Pen & ink *size:* 21"x16³/₄"

artist: **Oliver Meinerding**
art director: Sean Hughes *client:* City Beat *title:* Astrosquid *medium:* Ink/digital *size:* 17"x19"

artist: **Kurt Huggins, Zelda Devon**
art director: Laura Cleveland *client:* Realms of Fantasy *title:* Fragments of a Fantasy Life *medium:* Digital *size:* 9³/₄"x15"

artist: **José Emroca Flores**
title: Cashcow medium: Oil on wood size: 3'x3'

1 *artist:* Chris Rahn
art director: Derek Rainey
client: L.A. Weekly
title: The Rat Ladies
medium: Digital *size:* 9"x12"

2 *artist:* Red Nose Studio
art director: Irene Gallo
client: Tor.com
title: Things That Make Me Weak and Strange
medium: Mixed

3 *artist:* Joe Kovach
art director: Julie Fanning
client: The New Physician
title: Fighting the Depths
medium: Acrylic *size:* 16½"x20½"

4 *artist:* Sam Weber
art director: Irene Gallo
client: Tor.com
title: Eros
medium: Acrylic

1

2

3

artist: **Chris Buzelli**
art director: SooJin Buzelli *client:* Plansponsor Magazine *title:* Muddy Waters *medium:* Oil *size:* 14"x19"

artist: **Bill Carman**
client: Idaho Historical Society title: Sharlie & Bigfoot medium: Mixed size: 0"x0"

artist: **Bruno Werneck**
client: IDN Magazine *title:* Neo New York *medium:* Digital *size:* 12"x9"

artist: **Woodrow J. Hinton III**
art director: Andrew Jennings *client:* CityBeat
title: This What You Want *medium:* Mixed/digital *size:* 11"x17"

artist: **Kerry P. Talbott**
art director: Tom Bond *client:* Richmond Times-Dispatch
title: Fright Night *medium:* Digital *size:* 8x9"

artist: Jeff Preston

art director: Jeff Preston *client:* Little Shoppe of Horrors *title:* The Curse of Frankenstein *medium:* Marker, color pencil *size:* 12"x17"

artist: **James Gurney**
art director: **Patrick Gyger** *client:* **Maison D'Ailleurs/Reteur À Dinotopia** *title:* **Song In the Garden** *medium:* **Oil** *size:* **17"x18"**

artist: **Jaime Jones**
art director: Jeremy Jarvis   *client:* Wizards of the Coast   *title:* Progenitao   *medium:* Photoshop   *size:* 10¹/₂"x8"

artist: **David Delamare**
client: Bad Monkey Productions title: Rabbit Punch medium: Oil size: 36"x24"

artist: **Luis Royo**
art director: Luis Royo client: Norma Editorial title: Dead Moon [Portfolio cover] medium: Ink, watercolor size: 14"x10"

artist: **Michael Whelan**
client: IO Gallery *title:* Pipe Dream *medium:* Acrylic on canvas *size:* 30"x20"

artist: **David Delamare**
client: Bad Monkey Productions *title:* History of Lightning *medium:* Oil *size:* 48"x24"

artist: **Mark Zug**
art director: Jeremy Jarvis *client:* Wizards of the Coast *title:* Merlock *medium:* Oil on linen

artist: **Matt Stewart**
art director: Jeremy Jarvis *client:* Wizards of the Coast *title:* Knight–Paragon of Etlan *medium:* Oil on paper on masonite *size:* 15 1/4"x11 5/8"

artist: **Gregory Manchess**
art director: Gregory Manchess *client:* Massive Black *title:* Above the Timberline *medium:* Oil *size:* 40"x25"

artist: **Raoul Vitalo**
client: Private Collection *title:* Scouts *medium:* Oil on masonite *size:*36¹/₂"x24¹/₂"

1 *artist:* **Chet Phillips**
art director: Chet Phillips
client: Chet Phillips
title: The Kraken
[Series: Mysterious Coin Operations]
medium: Painter X
7"x8³/₄"

2 *artist:* **Carlos Huante**
title: Love 2 – Buron Shared
medium: Graphite/digital

3 *artist:* **Aaron Robinson**
title: Pixelfingers
medium: Oil on board/digitaldigital

4 *artist:* **Carlos Huante**
title: Weight and Measures
medium: Graphite/digital

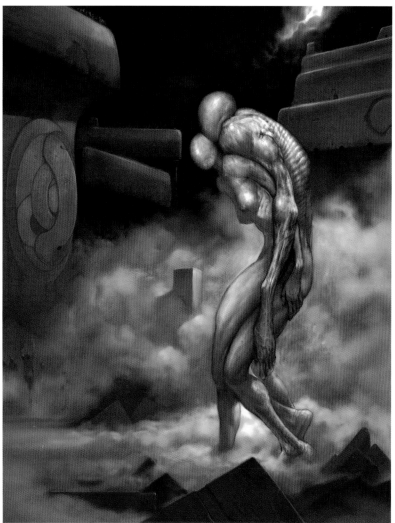

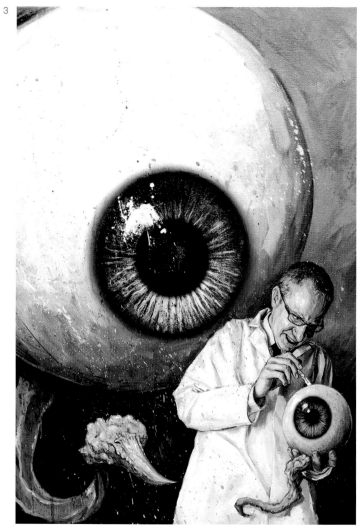

1 *artist:* **Terese Nielsen**
art director: Terese Nielsen
client: Lucasfilm Ltd./Lucas Licensing
title: Padmé Amidala
medium: Acrylic, oil gold leaf
size: 6"x16"

2 *artist:* **Terese Nielsen**
art director: Paul Hebron
client: Wizards of the Coast
title: Padmé Illum Outfit
medium: Acrylic, oil

3 *artist:* **Steve Argyle**
art director: Jeremy Jarvis
client: Wizards of the Coast
title: Bola's Grasp
medium: Digital

4 *artist:* **Randy Gallegos**
art director: Jeremy Jarvis
client: Wizards of the Coast
title: Balance
medium: Oil
size: 24"x18"

n
s
t
i
t
u
t
i
o
n
a
l

1
artist: **Cathie Bleck**
client: Mark Murphy Exhibit/
"Know" Show
title: Course of the Horse
medium: Ink & kaolin on clay board
size: 10"x10"

2
artist: **Andrew Jones**
art director: Robert Clinton
client: Random Rab
title: Arose
medium: Painter X

3
artist: **Andrew Jones**
art director: Charles Dooher
client: SoulFly
title: Conquer
medium: Painter X

1

2

3

artist: **Dave Laub**
title: He, Who Is Klaag *medium:* Digital *size:* 10"x8"

artist: **Matt Gaser**
title: Primrobb's Threshold *medium:* Digital *size:* 11"x6"

artist: **Ron Wilson**
art director: Brian K. Graham   designer: Brian K. Graham, Ron Wilson   client: Graham Tool Co., Inc.   title: The Electrician
medium: Digital   size: 10¹/₂"x8"

artist: **Jeff Miracola**
title: Run, Run, Run   medium: Digital   size: 60"x30"

artist: **Steve Argyle**
art director: Jeremy Jarvis *client:* Wizards of the Coast *title:* Sun Seeder *medium:* Digital

artist: **Justin Gerard**
art director: Tom Quantrille *designer:* Justin Gerard *client:* Advanced Composite Materials *title:* The Lady of the Forest
medium: Watercolor/digital *size:* 22"x14"

artist: **Todd Lockwood**
art director: Jeremy Cranford *client:* Upper Deck *title:* I Am Captain America, and So Can You *medium:* Digital *size:* 12"x9"

artist: **Joerg Warda**
title: The Forgotten *medium:* Digital *size:* 21^1/$_4$"x13^7/$_8$"

1 *artist:* **David Hong**
title: Descent
medium: Digital
size: 9³/₄"x11"

2 *artist:* **Toshiaki Takayama**
art director: Akira Hamada, Syuichi,
Dawn Murin, Yumiko Hayakawa
client: Wizards of the Coast
title: Gabriella, Elemental of Divine Light
medium: Digital
size: 16"x16"

3 *artist:* **Andrew Bawidamann**
client: www.bawidamann.com
title: Witch Girl
medium: Digital
size: 18"x24"

1 *artist:* **Mark A. Nelson**
client: Grazing Dinosaur Press
title: SS: Imagination
medium: Pencil
size: 10½"x13½"

2 *artist:* **David Ho**
client: Lucasfilm Ltd.
title: The Sacrifice
medium: Digital
size: 24"x12"

3 *artist:* **Mark A. Nelson**
client: Grazing Dinosaur Press
title: AH: Salomé
medium: Pencil, digital color
size: 10½"x13½"

1

2

artist: **Scott Bakal**
art director: Scott Bakal, Julia Breckenreid client: Icons: New York – Real & Imagined title: Intergalactic Neighbors #1
medium: Acrylic, ink, watercolor size: 14"x11"

artist: **Jason Chan**
title: Zombie Playground medium: Digital size: 14"x8"

artist: Dan Santat
client: Gallery 1988 *title:* Rampage *medium:* Ink, mixed *size:* 16"x20"

1 *artist:* Cyril Van Der Haegen
art director: Zoe Robinson
client: FFG
title: Innsmouth [cover]
medium: Digital

2 *artist:* Ed Binkley
client: Stark-Raving Studios
title: Scarecrow Dreams:
Sunrise
medium: Digital
size: 15"x11"

3 *artist:* William Stout
art director: Carlos Durbán Colubi
designer: William Stout
client: Diseccionando Fantasías:
Los Secretos de Guillermodel Toro
title: Guillermo del Toro's Secrets
medium: Ink & watercolor on board
size: 14"x21"

4 *artist:* Ed Binkley
client: Stark-Raving Studios
title: Scarecrow Dreams:
Ecstasy
medium: Digital
size: 15"x11"

artist: **Nigel Quarless**
art director: Nigel Quarless *client:* Mixed Bag Mythography
title: March! *medium:* Digital *size:* 8³/₄"x11¹/₄"

artist: **Jim Mahfood**
art director: Gina Bolton *colorist:* S. Steven Struble
client: SushiandRobots.com *title:* Sushi and Robots *medium:* Mixed

artist: **Jenna Smith**
title: A Monster Trail *medium:* Digital *size:* 37"x28"

artist: **Bill Carman**
title: Test Ride *medium:* Acrylic *size:* 8"x10"

artist: **Michael Komark**
art director: Jeremy Jarvis *client:* Wizards of the Coast *title:* Rafiq of the Many *medium:* Digital

artist: **Jason Chan**
art director: Jeremy Jarvis *client:* Wizards of the Coast *title:* Apocalypse Hydra *medium:* Digital

artist: **Greg Staples**
art director: Jeremy Jarvis *client:* Wizards of the Coast *title:* Empyrial Archangel *medium:* Mixed/digital

artist: **Chris Rahn**
art director: Jeremy Jarvis *client:* Wizards of the Coast *title:* Enigma Sphinx *medium:* Oil

1
artist: José Emroca Flores
title: Hungry Hammerhead
medium: Oil on wood
size: 12"x12"

2
artist: **Brian Despain**
client: Gino Joukar
title: The Haunting
medium: Oil on board
size: 7"x7"

3
artist: **Dave Cooper,
Ana Bagayan, Glenn Barr,
Bob Dob, Shag, Amy Sol,
Daniel Peacock, Joe Ledbetter,
Brandi Milne, Michael Whelan**
art director: Bob Self
client: Baby Tattoo Books
title: Baby Tattooville 10-In-1
Limited Edition
medium: Mixed
size: 17"x22"

1

2

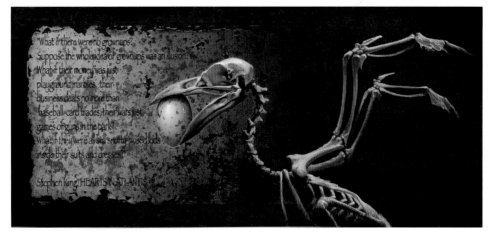

artist: **Scott Gustafson**
designer: Scott Gustafson *client:* The Greenwich Workshop *title:* The Fox Guarding the Hen House *medium:* Oil *size:* 14"x11"

artist: **Kei Acedera**
client: www.imaginismstudios.com *title:* Little Red and Wolf *medium:* Color pencils on paper *size:* 10¹/2"x7"

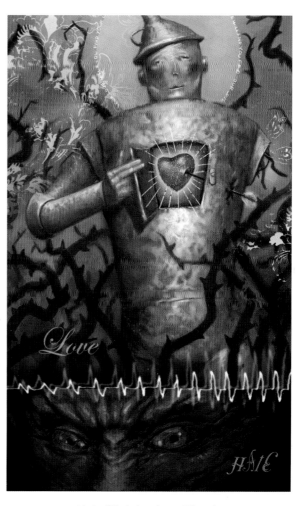

artist: **Bobby Chiu**
client: www.imaginismstudios.com *title:* Tigger
medium: Digital

artist: **Christopher Chuckry**
art director: Chris Pointon *client:* A Paw In My Face
title: Love/Hate *medium:* Digital *size:* 5"x8"

artist: **Scott Gustafson**
designer: Scott Gustafson *client:* The Greenwich Workshop *title:* A Parliament of Owls *medium:* Oil *size:* 14"x10"

artist: **Daarken**
art director: Ben Thompson *client:* Upper Deck *title:* Eye Blast *medium:* Photoshop

artist: **Chippy**
art director: Jeremy Jarvis *client:* Wizards of the Coast *title:* Master Transmuter *medium:* Digital

artist: **Adam Volker**
client: CGSociety.org *title:* The Headless Horseman *medium:* Digital *size:* 12"x13"

artist: **Paul Bonner**
art director: Theo Bergquist *title:* Drakar Och Demoner *medium:* Watercolor *size:* 28"x19"

artist: **Paul Bonner**
art director: Jeremy Jarvis *client:* Wizards of the Coast *title:* Grixis *medium:* Watercolor *size:* 15"x10"

artist: **Frank Cho**

art director: Frank Cho   *designer:* Frank Cho   *client:* Hasbro   *title:* Jungle Trinity   *medium:* Pen & ink   *size:* 28"x21"

artist: **Jim Murray**

art director: Jeremy Jarvis   *client:* Wizards of the Coast   *title:* Sphinx Ambassador   *medium:* Oil, acrylic

artist: **Jeremy Enecio**
title: Koi   *medium:* Oil, acrylic   *size:* 18"x12"

artist: **Dave Laub**
title: **She's Back**   *medium:* **Digital** *size:* **8"x10"**

1
artist: Yasmine Putri
title: Feathers & Arrows
medium: Digital
size: 11"x8¹/₂"

2
artist: Miguel "Glue" Lantigua
art director: Joe Thiel
title: The Boy Who Cried Wolf
medium: Acrylic on board
size: 24"x36"

3
artist: Mónico Chávez
art director: Craig Nelson
title: Last Train
medium: Digital

4
artist: Joe Quinones
title: Yield For Snails
medium: Pen & ink/digital color
size: 11"x12¹/₂"

1

2

3

artist: **Steven Kenny**
title: Leda and the Swan   *medium:* Oil on canvas   *size:* 48"x36"

artist: **Vladimir Outcharov**
title: Passing Through   *medium:* Oil on board   *size:* 40"x30"

artist: **Andrea Kowch**
title: No Turning Back *medium:* Acrylic on canvas *size:* 48"x24"

artist: **Eric Fortune**
title: I Want to Believe *medium:* Acrylic *size:* 20"x14"

1
artist: **Jared Moraitis**
client: Pop-Monkey Stuff
title: Gorilla Vs Octopus:
Street Fight
medium: Pen & ink/digital
size: 17"x17"

2
artist: **Scott Schomburg**
client: The Internets
title: The Bridge
medium: Digital
size: 8"x14"

3
artist: **Mia**
art director: Jan Corey
client: Corey Helford Gallery
title: Thania
medium: Acrylic on panel
size: 18"x24"

4
artist: **Jared Moraitis**
client: Pop-Monkey Stuff
title: Pac-Samurai
medium: Pen & ink/digital
size: 11"x14"

1

2

3

1 *artist:* **Bob Doucette**
title: The Sacred Heart
medium: Digital
size: 18"x24"

2 *artist:* **Jon Foster**
title: Migration
medium: Oil on skateboard

3 *artist:* **Augie Pagan**
client: Koo's Gallery
title: Frankenshy
medium: Acrylic on canvas
size: 10"x24"

4 *artist:* **Eric Joyner**
client: McCaig Welles Gallery
title: Does Not Compute
medium: Oil on wood panel
size: 31"x30"

1

2

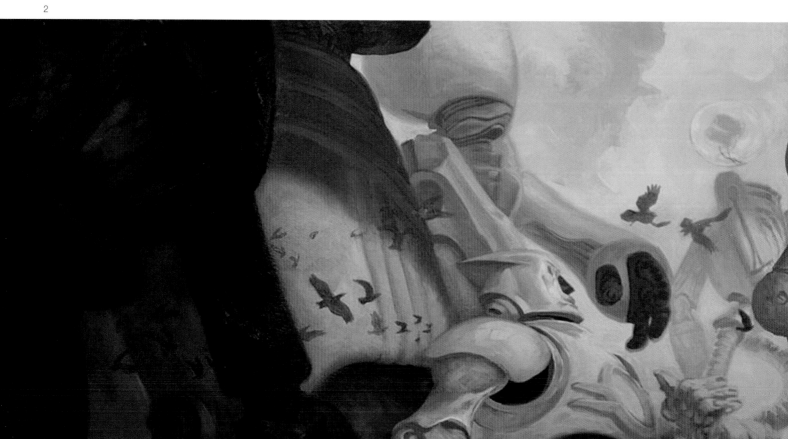

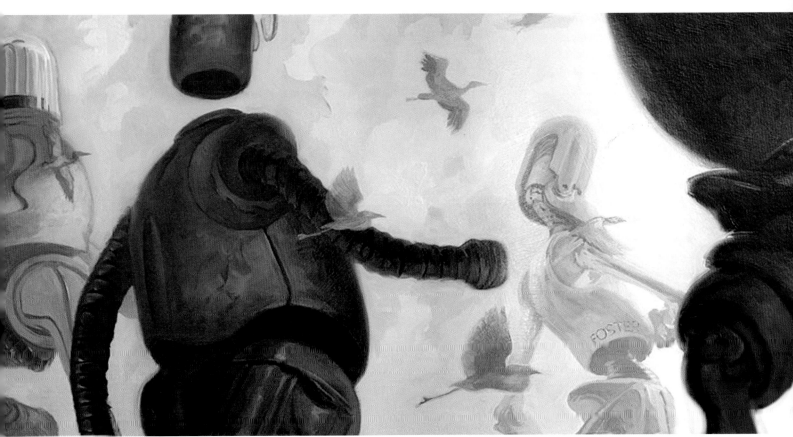

1 *artist:* **Dominique Fung**
title: Desolate Porcelain

2 *artist:* **Daniela Outcharov**
title: Flora
medium: Oil on canvas
size: 22"x46"

3 *artist:* **Aly Fell**
title: Outbreak
medium: Photoshop
size: 7"x11"

4 *artist:* **Joao Ruas**
title: Scowrers
medium: Watercolor, gouache
size: 12"x16"

1

2

3

1
artist: **Eric Fortune**
title: A Moon of My Own
medium: Acrylic
size: 11"x11"

2
artist: **John Malloy**
title: Dry Mouth
medium: Pen & Ink, oil, digital
size: 13"x19"

3
artist: **Bruce Holwerda**
title: One For the Road
medium: Acrylic/digital
size: 30"x40"

4
artist: **Eric Fortune**
title: Life's Objective
medium: Acrylic
size: 21"x29"

1

2

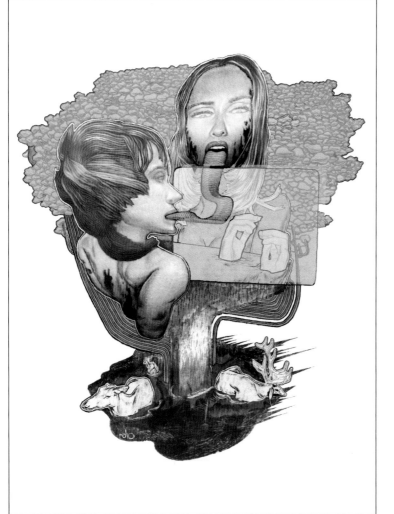

3

1 *artist:* **Brian Despain**
title: Ghosts
medium: Oil on board
size: 16"x20"

2 *artist:* **Keith Thompson**
title: Race: Saint of Parasites
medium: Mixed
size: 7"x12"

3 *artist:* **Jeff Haynie**
art director: Jeff Haynie
title: The Deep Dive
medium: Digital
size: 9"x14"

4 *artist:* **Brian Despain**
title: The Escape
medium: Oil on board
size: 16"x20"

2

3

4

artist: **Bobby Chiu**
client: www.imaginismstudios.com *title:* Babylon *medium:* Digital

artist: **Bob Pitt**
title: Zzott!! *medium:* Acrylic on canvas *size:* 60"x40"

artist: **Joe Vaux**
title: The Flood medium: Acrylic on wood panel size: 14"x10"

artist: **Joe Vaux**
title: The Flood medium: Breach of Contract size: 60"x36"

artist: **David Bowers**
client: Klaudia Marr Gallery *title:* The Gift *medium:* Oil on linen *size:* 16"x18"

artist: David Bowers
title: Paulina's Dream *medium:* Oil on panel *size:* 18"x22"

artist: **Scott Schomburg**
client: The Internets *title:* Dearly Departed
medium: Digital *size:* 5¹/2"x8³/4"

artist: **Sean "Muttonhead" Murray**
title: Witch's Pet *medium:* Acrylic

artist: **Dave Pressler**
title: The Bearer of Bad News *medium:* Acrylic on masonite *size:* 25¹/2"x17"

artist: **Bradley Parker**
designer: Honu Editions client: Tiki Shark Hawaii, Inc.
title: Bela Lugosi has a Zombie medium: Acrylic size: 24"x30"

artist: **Cathy Wilkins**
title: Schitz medium: Digital size: 8¹/₂"x11"

artist: **Shane Devries**
photographer: David Solm client: Monsterkid: Solo Exhibition title: Where Robots Come From medium: Oil size: 55"x39¹/₈"

artist: **Sam Bosma**
title: Monkey King *medium:* Acrylic *size:* 10¼"x13¾"

artist: **Bill Carman**
title: Made a Baby *medium:* Acrylic *size:* 8"x10"

artist: **Kali Ciesemier**
title: Catch of the Day *medium:* Ink, digital *size:* 17"x10⅝"

artist: **Kali Ciesemier**
title: The Naturalist *medium:* Ink, digital *size:* 7¹/₂"x12"

1 *artist:* Ho-Jun Lee
client: Wico Evergreen
title: Chrysalis No. 5
medium: Oil on canvas on wood board
size: 12"x12"

2 *artist:* Joe Jusko
title: Cuddle the Corpse/
The Women of Noir Calendar
medium: Acrylic *size:* 12"x18"

3 *artist:* Richard Anderson
title: Outbreak
medium: Photoshop *size:* 8 1/2"x11"

4 *artist:* Brom
art director: Bonnie Nakornratana
client: Bonnie Nakornratana
title: Seeing *medium:* Oil

5 *artist:* Viktor Koen
title: The Boy
medium: Digital *size:* 11"x19"

6 *artist:* Oleksandra Barsheva
title: Unchosen Destiny
medium: Watercolor, charcoal
size: 15"x22"

7 *artist:* Michael Reedy
title: Once Removed
medium: Charcoal, colored pencil, ink,
watercolor, stain
size: 32"x41"

1

2

3

5

7

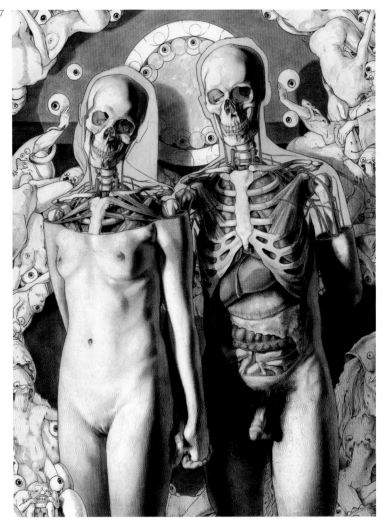

artist: **Ilich Henriquez**
title: History of the Ancestry medium: Digital size: 17"x11"

artist: **Jeremy Enecio**
title: The Watersnake medium: Watercolor, acrylic size: 19"x11"

artist: **Donato Giancola**
client: Wendt Gallery *title:* Progeny *medium:* Oil on panel *size:* 60"x36"

artist: **Bryan Beus**
title: Thieves *medium:* Painter X *size:* 17"x10"

1
artist: **Leah Palmer Preiss**
title: Freelancer
[after Bosch's "Wayfarer"]
medium: Acrylic on map on canvas
size: 10"x10"

2
artist: **Rene Zwaga**
title: Personal Strength
medium: Oil
size: 34¹/₂"x44¹/₂"

3
artist: **Ron Spears**
art director: Ron Spears
title: Sentinel Two
medium: Oil on canvas
size: 22"x35"

4
artist: **Rene Zwaga**
title: The Destination
medium: Oil
size: 34¹/₂"x48¹/₂"

1

3

4

1
artist: **Christian Alzmann**
title: There Lived a King with One Daughter
medium: Mixed, digital
size: 9"x16 1/2"

2
artist: **Antonio Javier Caparo**
title: The Dreams Machine
medium: Acrylic
size: 13"x18"

3
artist: **Patrick J. Jones**
title: Song of the Siren
medium: Oil on canvas
size: 36"x48"

4
artist: **Dennis Brown**
title: Sodium
medium: Mixed
size: 11"x14"

5
artist: **Armand Baltazar**
title: Medea
medium: Pencil, digital
size: 11"x17"

1

MEDEA

A. BALTAZAR © 2008

artist: **Jaime Jones**
title: Docked medium: Photoshop size: 10¹/₂"x7"

artist: **Matt Ray**
title: Her Majesty's Airship *Indefatigable* engages the *Nobunaga*, South China Sea, Night of Jan. 8th, 1971 medium: Oil size: 36"x24"

artist: **Jaime Jones**
title: Dooms Day medium: Photoshop size: 10¹/₂"x6"

artist: **Bruno Werneck**
client: Luis De Vega title: Mars Post Attack medium: Digital size: 17"x8"

1 *artist:* **David Ho**
title: Show Me the Honey #3
medium: Digital
size: 8"x13"

2 *artist:* **Anita Kunz**
title: Hairdo Horrors
medium: Acrylic
size: 15"x18"

3 *artist:* **Craig Davison**
title: Pet Hate
medium: Oil
size: 23"x31"

4 *artist:* **Doug Panton**
title: Private Eye
medium: Digital
size: 11"x17"

4

1 *artist:* Ken Wong
title: Mistaken Identity
medium: Digital

2 *artist:* Ruslam Hasanov
title: Grop-Brot In Pursuit
medium: Digital
size: 20"x32"

3 *artist:* William Joyce
title: Guardians of Childhood
medium: Graphite/digital color
size: 11"x17"

4 *artist:* Pascal Campion
title: Rough Landing
medium: Digital

5 *artist:* Sacha Lees
title: Madame Fox
medium: Pen & ink/digital
size: 20"x17"

1

2

Known on Earth as the Boogeyman

artist: **Mark Elliott**
client: Krueger Gallery *title:* Reappraisal *medium:* Acrylic on panel *size:* 20"x20"

artist: **David Kang**
title: Envy *medium:* Digital *size:* 11"x5¹/₂"

artist: **Doug Williams**
title: Midwest Monster medium: Digital size: 16"x10"

artist. **Jason Edmiston**
title: Cereal Monsters medium: Acrylic on panel size: 4'x2'

1
artist: Ragen Mendenhall
title: Raku
medium: Oil, gold leaf
size: 24"x24"

2
artist: Rebecca Guay
title: Gwenevere
medium: Oil
size: 24"x38"

3
artist: Herman Smorenburg
title: Dreams of Infinity
medium: Oil on Wood
size: 23"x31"

4
artist: David Bollt
title: While She Was Sleeping
medium: Acrylic on canvas
size: 44"x74"

1 *artist:* **Omar Rayyan**
title: Interlude With the Gryphon
medium: Watercolor
size: 11"x14"

2 *artist:* **Shelly Wan**
title: Underneath It All
medium: Digital
size: 17"x36"

3 *artist:* **Omar Rayyan**
title: Interlude Dog of the Hare
medium: Watercolor
size: 10"x14"

4 *artist:* **Omar Rayyan**
title: Interlude Croquet
medium: Watercolor
size: 10"x15"

artist: **Tran Nguyen**
title: Fine Line *medium:* Photoshop *size:* 9¹/2"x8"

artist: **Augie Pagan**
title: Cyclops Munchies *medium:* Digital *size:* 9"x11"

artist: **Justin Sweet**
title: Kern *medium:* Oil

1 *artist:* William Joyce
title: Guardians of Childhood
medium: Oil
size: 24"x24"

2 *artist:* Forrest Card
title: Satellite Sally
medium: Mixed, digital
size: 8 1/2"x31 1/2"

3 *artist:* William Joyce
client: Warner Bros./Oz Anniversay
title: Monkey on a Wire
medium: Oil
size: 30"x30"

4 *artist:* Justin Gerard
title: The Trouble With Trolls
medium: Watercolor, digital
size: 16"x21"

2

1

3

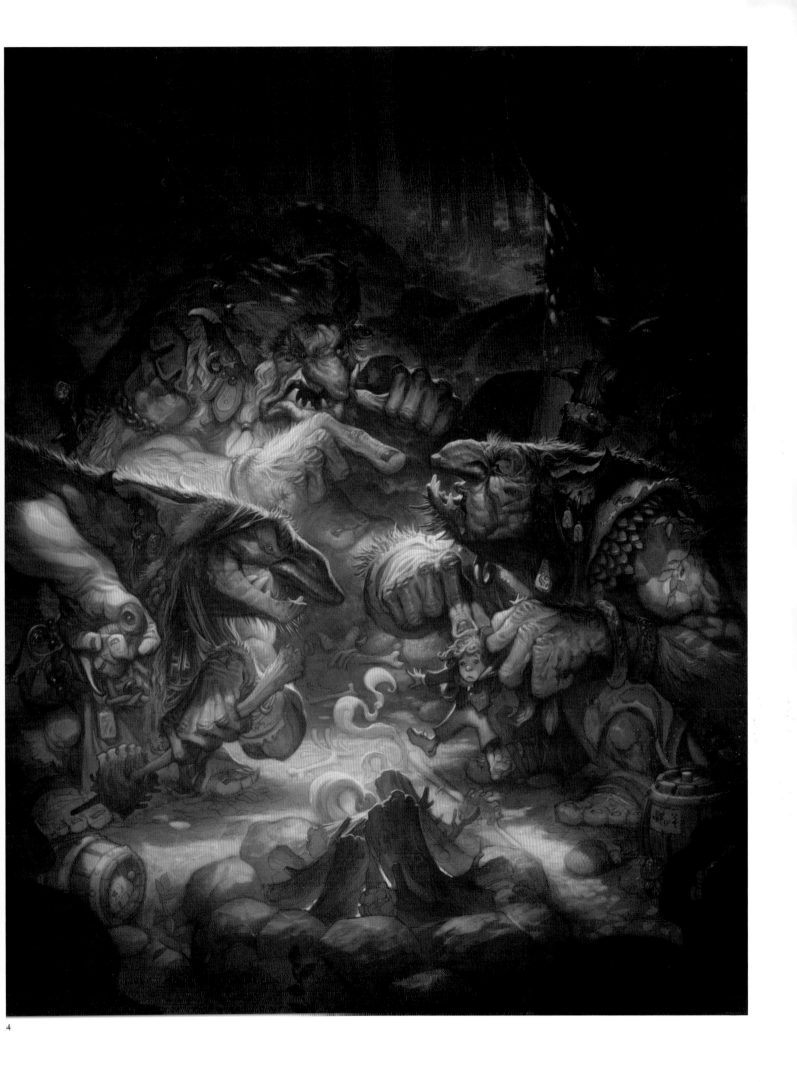

4

artist: **Yannick Germain**
title: Lancelot *medium:* Ink, oil on board *size:* 32¼"x40¼"

artist: **William Stout**
client: Gallerie Daniel Meghan *title:* Dragon of the Cliffs
medium: Ink, watercolor on board *size:* 12"x16"

artist: **Scott Gustafson**
title: The Company Makes the Feast *medium:* Oil *size:* 14"x10"

artist: **Dennis Nolan**
title: Midnight *medium:* Watercolor *size:* 22"x16"

artist: **Hethe Srodawa**
title: The Warden *medium:* Digital *size:* 13"x6 1/8"

1 *artist:* Rick Berry
title: Red Bandages [study]
medium: Oil
size: 32"x48"

2 *artist:* Tran Nguyen
title: Wraith in Disguise
medium: Mixed on board
size: 10"x20"

3 *artist:* David Bowers
title: The Cock Thief
medium: Oil on linen
size: 24"x22"

4 *artist:* Herman Smorenburg
title: The Vision of a Mortal Life
medium: Oil on wood
size: 36 1/2"x52 1/2"

1

2

3

artist: **Tyler West**
title: Final Launch medium: Photoshop

artist: **Whit Brachna**
art director: Coro title: Tank Defense medium: Digital

artist: **Lawrence A. Williams**
art director: Victoria Williams   *client:* L.A. Williams Art, Inc.   *title:* The Queen   *medium:* Digital   *size:* 18"x24"

1 *artist:* Jeremy Enecio
title: Milk
medium: Digital

2 *artist:* Eric Joyner
client: Corey Helford Gallery
title: Titanticus
medium: Oil on wood panel
size: 40"x40"

3 *artist:* Jason John
title: A Long Wait
medium: Oil on board
size: 30"x20"

4 *artist:* Diana Diriwaechter
title: Ms Jane
medium: Photography
size: 14"x10½"

1

2

4

1 *artist:* Nicholas McNally
title: The Bite
medium: Acrylic
size: 11½"x9½"

2 *artist:* Lee Moyer
title: Miss Lewis Carroll
medium: Digital
size: 12"x17"

3 *artist:* Eric Bowman
title: Switch Witch
medium: Oil
size: 10"x14½"

4 *artist:* John Mueller
title: The Butcher Vs The Strongman
medium: Digital
size: 7"x11"

2

3

u
n
n
u
b
l
i
s
h
e
d

1

3

5

1 *artist:* Tran Nguyen
medium: Mixed on board
size: 9"x11"

2 *artist:* Volkan Baga
title: One Ring to Rule Them All
medium: Oil
size: 28⁷/₈"x30⁷/₈"

3 *artist:* David Hong
title: Knights & Armors
medium: Digital
size: 12¹/₄"x17¹/₂"

4 *artist:* Volkan Baga
client: Tim Pope
title: Elric in the City of Screaming Statues
medium: Oil
size: 19¹/₃"x27¹/₂"

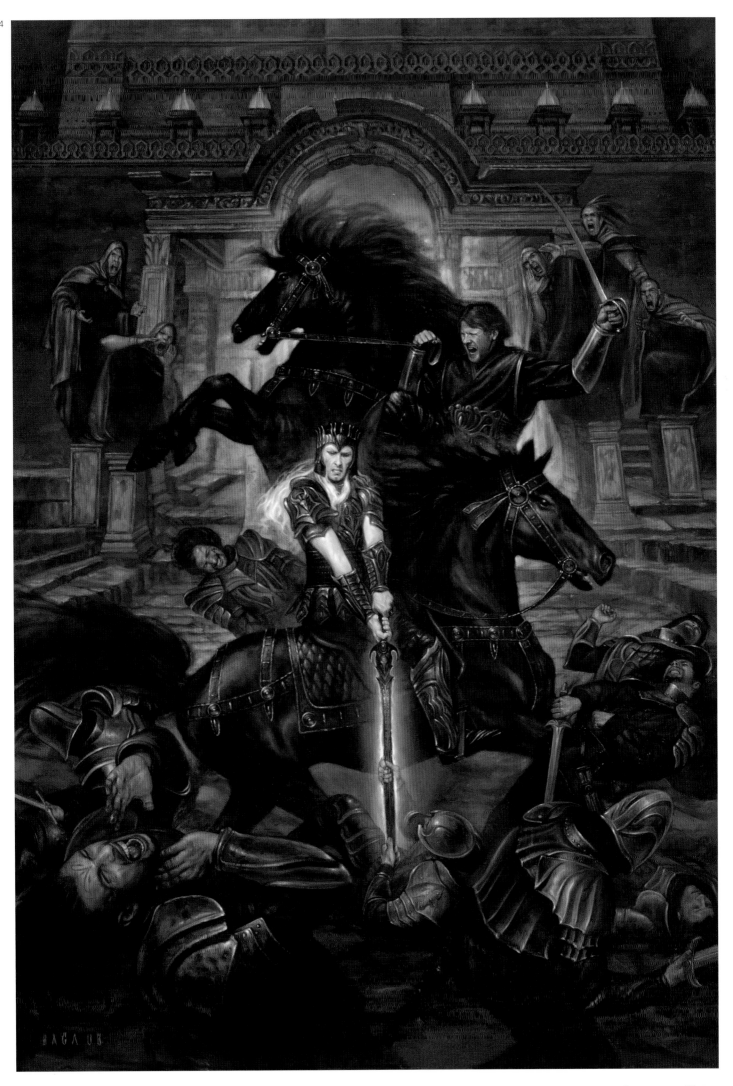

4

artist: **Martin Wittfooth**
client: *Copro Nason Gallery*   *title:* Svetogorsk   *medium:* Oil on linen   *size:* 32"x24"

artist: **Martin Wittfooth**
client: Galerie D'Art Yves Laroche   *title:* A Day Without Rain   *medium:* Oil on canvas   *size:* 36"x24"

artist: **Michael Whelan**
title: Lumen 5 *medium:* Acrylic on canvas *size:* 36"x60"

Artists, art directors, and publishers interested in receiving information for the SPECTRUM 17 competition should send their name and address to:

Spectrum Design
P.O. Box 4422, Overland Park, KS 66204
or visit our website: www.spectrumfantasticart.com